THE POWER OF 360 DEGREE FEEDBACK

SECOND EDITION

THE POWER OF 360 DEGREE FEEDBACK

The India Way for Leadership Effectiveness

SECOND EDITION

T.V. Rao
Raju Rao

www.sagepublications.com
Los Angeles • London • New Delhi • Singapore • Washington DC

Copyright © T.V. Rao and Raju Rao, 2014

All rights reserved. No part of this book may be reproduced or utilized in any form or by any means, electronic or mechanical, including photocopying, recording or by any information storage or retrieval system, without permission in writing from the publisher.

First published in 2005
This second edition published in 2014 by

SAGE Response
B1/I-1 Mohan Cooperative Industrial Area
Mathura Road, New Delhi 110 044, India

SAGE Publications Inc
2455 Teller Road
Thousand Oaks, California 91320, USA

SAGE Publications Ltd
1 Oliver's Yard, 55 City Road
London EC1Y 1SP, United Kingdom

SAGE Publications Asia-Pacific Pte Ltd
3 Church Street
#10-04 Samsung Hub
Singapore 049483

Published by Vivek Mehra for SAGE Publications India Pvt Ltd, typeset in 10.5/12.5pt Adobe Caslon by Diligent Typesetter and printed at Chaman Enterprises, New Delhi.

Library of Congress Cataloging-in-Publication Data

Venkateswara Rao, T.
 The power of 360 degree feedback : the India way for leadership effectiveness / T.V. Rao, Raju Rao.— Second edition.
  pages cm
 Includes bibliographical references and index.
  1. Personnel management. 2. Leadership. 3. Organizational behaviour. I. Rao, Raju. II. Title. III. Title: Power of three hundred sixty degree feedback.
 HF5549.V395   658.4'092—dc23   2014   2014018434

ISBN: 978-81-321-1969-2 (PB)

The SAGE Team: Sachin Sharma, Alekha Chandra Jena, Anju Saxena and Dally Verghese

In the loving memory of
Fr D. Gordon S.J.
and
Dr E.G. Parameswaran
who nurtured and influenced us
with their warmth and expectations

Thank you for choosing a SAGE product! If you have any comment, observation or feedback, I would like to personally hear from you. Please write to me at contactceo@sagepub.in

—Vivek Mehra, Managing Director and CEO,
SAGE Publications India Pvt. Ltd, New Delhi

Bulk Sales

SAGE India offers special discounts for purchase of books in bulk. We also make available special imprints and excerpts from our books on demand.

For orders and enquiries, write to us at

Marketing Department
SAGE Publications India Pvt. Ltd
B1/I-1, Mohan Cooperative Industrial Area
Mathura Road, Post Bag 7
New Delhi 110044, India
E-mail us at marketing@sagepub.in

Get to know more about SAGE, be invited to SAGE events, get on our mailing list. Write today to marketing@sagepub.in

This book is also available as an e-book.

Contents

List of Tables and Boxes ix
Preface to the Second Edition xi
Preface to the First Edition xiii
Introduction xix

PART 1. DEVELOPING MANAGERS INTO LEADERS

1. How to Be an Effective Person? 3
2. What Makes Managers Effective? 14
3. What Makes a Good Leader? 20
4. Managerial and Leadership Roles 32
5. Managerial and Leadership Styles 45

PART 2. DESIGNING AND IMPLEMENTING A 360 DEGREE FEEDBACK PROGRAMME

6. 360 Degree Feedback: The Power Tool 63
7. Competence Building through 360 Degree Feedback 83
8. Coaching in 360 Degree Feedback 99
9. Myths and Realities of 360 Degree Feedback 112
10. Conditions for Successful 360 Degree Feedback 131

PART 3. LESSONS FROM EXPERIENCE AND RESEARCH

11. 360 Degree Feedback: Indian Experience 143
12. Life after 360 Degree Feedback: Lessons for the Future 156
13. Getting ROI on 360 Degree Feedback 169
14. Lessons from 100 Impact-making Managers 177
15. Experiences from Other Countries 185

PART 4. 360 DEGREE FEEDBACK TOOLS FOR OTHER SECTORS

16	360 Degree Feedback Tools for School Principals	211
17	360 Degree Feedback Tools for Teachers, Students and Parents	218
18	360 Degree Feedback Tools for Non-governmental Organizations	228

Appendix: Organizations Using 360 Degree Feedback	240
References and Select Bibliography	244
Index	249
About the Authors	255

List of Tables and Boxes

Tables

5.1	Leadership styles, their impact and appropriateness	48
5.2	Characteristics of the three leadership styles	56
5.3	Impact of leadership styles on subordinates and their appropriateness of use	58
8.1	Sample highlights of assessment—Production manager	104
8.2	Sample highlights of assessment—Human resource manager	106
8.3	Sample highlights of assessment—CEO	107
8.4	Sample highlights of assessment—Finance manager	109
13.1	Benefits of 360 Degree Feedback	174

Boxes

1.1	Action and results	5
1.2	Still movement	13
2.1	Ability	19
4.1	Leadership strategy: Attention through vision	36
6.1	Do not use feedback for appraisals	72
6.2	Trust the process	80
17.1	Teacher effectiveness questionnaire: Some items	221
17.2	Questionnaire for parents	223
17.3	360 Tool for postgraduate students	225

Preface to the Second Edition

It is nearly a decade since we have presented the first edition of this book. In the last 10 years a lot of experience has been generated in our country, but the theory and approach remained the same. In the last ten years, we are convinced that our approach to 360 Degree Feedback is the most appropriate approach. Since the time of our last book we have worked with at least another hundred organizations in implementing 360 Degree Feedback and have gained a lot more experience. This experience increased our conviction that this is a powerful tool. It provokes even a pessimist of the approach to become more sensitive to his/her idiosyncrasies and leads to enhanced awareness and lays the path for growth. Such a powerful tool is being misused or being put to a limited use by a few ambitious and ruthless consultants and even human resources (HR) managers. This tool loses its power once you use it as a performance appraisal tool and hits at the very root of human resource development (HRD). HRD has got to be self-initiated and self-motivated. At best for an unaware candidate, one can lead him/her to get a 360 Degree Feedback done by an organizational initiative but without compulsion.

Another lesson we learnt is that Indian managers take things more seriously if the organization reviews the outcome and makes change as one of the targeted key performance areas (KPAs). We kept conducting biannual conferences on 360 Degree Feedback and the last one was on 'Life after 360 Degree Feedback'. We have included in this second edition lessons from this conference as well as lessons from our own experience in the last decade. We have also included research we have done using over 8000 top-level managers whose leadership roles and qualities we profiled using our Roles, Styles, Delegation and Qualities (RSDQ) model. We selected a hundred of them on the basis of their 360 Degree Feedback profiles and published a book of their stories. Lessons from their stories and practices of some of the HR award winning organizations are presented in this edition. We hope this gives an update of the 360 Degree Feedback the Indian way. We have dropped some basic chapters giving a lot of data, and interested readers could always refer to the first edition. We felt that we have come a long way since the first edition and hence took the liberty of dropping the obvious.

16th July 2014

T.V. Rao
Raju Rao

Preface to the First Edition

The concept of 360 Degree Feedback is becoming very popular. A few years ago most organizations and their top management would merely acknowledge but dare not attempt using this tool. Today, at least over 100 organizations are actively implementing it and another 500 or more, roughly, are trying to experiment with it. In the last five years at TV Rao Learning Systems Pvt. Ltd. (TVRLS) alone, we have facilitated the use of 360 Degree Feedback with more than 50 organizations. If we include those who attended our public programmes, then the number of organizations that have had at least one exposure, or at least one of their managers exposed, exceeds 200.

At TVRLS, in the last five years alone, we have covered the profiling of around 3000 senior managers. They were assessed, in turn, by 10 candidates at an average; each amounting to around 30,000 assessments. This provided plenty of data to determine the well-performed roles, as well as the not so well-performed roles, and the leadership qualities that seem to make a difference. While research is underway at TVRLS to find the differentiating competencies, and competencies that seem to make a difference for getting results and producing outstanding performance, we have gathered enough insight and have discovered the tremendous potential this tool offers for growth, individual development, and building leadership competencies. Our research and work indicate that this is an experience every individual must go through.

Since the time we launched 360 Degree Feedback, we have applied this to Chief Executive Officers (CEOs), top-level managers, middle managers, young managers, Human Resource Development (HRD) managers and a variety of other categories of managers. We have also covered the heads of educational institutions, particularly school principals, and have developed tools for teachers, parents and non-governmental organizations (NGOs). We have also held three biannual conferences on 360 Degree Feedback and got organizations to share their experiences. We started a new newsletter exclusively for those interested in 360 Degree Feedback and brought out three issues of the same. It is the repeated successes with this tool and continued interest shown by students, managers and management teachers that have prompted us to write this book.

This book is inspired by the potential of this tool to build future leaders in all sectors. It should be used more as a developmental tool than as an appraisal tool in Asian countries and the other way round in the West. We strongly believe that in relationship-oriented and relationship-valuing countries like those in the Asian region (India, Sri Lanka, Malaysia, Indonesia, Philippines, Thailand, etc.), and even in the African region where we had the opportunity to work in the recent past, pushing 360 Degree Feedback as an appraisal tool will not work. However, its potential to strengthen leadership competencies is tremendous. If we define leadership as social phenomena and as a game of influence, what alternative does a leader have than to find out what impact he/she made or what influence he/she had? Such a potential tool cannot be ignored or avoided for fear of negative feedback. Yet we are amazed to see sometimes, how some of the top-level leaders dread 360 Degree Feedback. They are either misinformed about it or have not been able to manage their own insecurities. The same can be said for HRD managers, who are supposed to promote development themselves, but may not have the right awareness of its potential.

What adds to the amazement is that the 360 Degree Feedback is not an invention from the West. Much before someone in the US had coined the word 360 Degree Feedback, the methodology had been reasonably well-perfected and used in the beginning of 1986 at the Indian Institute of Management, Ahmedabad (IIM[A]). In fact in late 1970s itself, the first author of this book had seen this first being attempted by innovative managers in Bharat Earth Movers Ltd., Bangalore. We were also once informed by Dr Udai Pareek, one of India's leading thinkers and writers in the field of organizational behaviour, that when Dr Rolf Lynton tried to apply this methodology at the Small Industries Extension Training Institute (SIETI) in Hyderabad for evaluating Ford Foundation consultants he nearly lost his job. Those who say that it is a Western concept and is not likely to work in India or that Indian organizations are not yet mature or that it is meant for elite groups or for top management are only revealing their ignorance in this knowledge-based era. We found an abundance of this ignorance and hence we thought it appropriate to write this book to clear all doubts about 360 Degree Feedback.

Another form of ignorance about the potential of 360 Degree Feedback can be seen in the opinion of some researchers and consultants that 360 Degree Feedback affects shareholder value, and sometimes negatively!

In this book, we want to show that 360 Degree Feedback is an awareness-building tool and lay the foundation for leadership development. To the extent that such an awareness of impact and possibilities for impact will lead to performance improvements and organizational success is a logic that one can apply and we wish to clarify that one should not expect anything more than enhancing talent through 360 Degree Feedback.

We have been highly influenced by the recent book *The Extraordinary Leader: Turning Good Managers into Great Leaders* by Zenger and Folkman (2003) where they surveyed the 360 Degree Feedback assessments made by over 200,000 people who assessed around 20,000 managers. Their study indicated the potential of this tool to transform a keen manager into a leader.

Our work with the students at the Indian School of Business (ISB) where over 50 of them went through peer appraisal and with the CBSE school principals (as a part of the programme offered by the Ravi Matthai centre at IIMA), where we designed and used an exclusive 360 Degree Feedback tool for them and our experiments with NGOs have only increased our conviction that this is a great tool.

We acknowledge the influence of many individuals and organizations in helping us reach this stage. The senior author learnt a few lessons from this and introduced a multiple feedback methodology for the first time in the management development programmes at IIMA in the year 1986. We started a programme on leadership styles and organizational effectiveness in 1986 in which the participants had to register three months in advance and give us the names and addresses of a group of 15 to 20 colleagues, subordinates, seniors and others who can comment on leadership styles and other qualities. These programmes were a great success. The term '360 Degree Feedback' was not invented by that time. The people who went through those programmes include: K.L. Chug (at that time with Bhadrachalam Paper Boards), M.K. Agarwal (TCI, now Managing Director of Gati); Harsh Mariwala, Bhuvan Chaturvedi, Anil Sachdev (Eicher); H.N. Arora (Reliance), M.K. Sinha (SRF); Hrishikesh Mafatlal and his entire top-management team.

We would particularly like to acknowledge Professor Pradip Khandwalla who provided a lot of support when Dr T.V. Rao first designed a Management Development Programme (MDP) with such a methodology and proposed it in the organizational behaviour area for approval in IIMA on his return from Xavier Labour Relations Institute (XLRI) in the year 1985. Khandwalla not only supported this but also joined in as a faculty member to offer the programme. We used his management style inventory besides other individual tools. It is Pradip who came up with the idea of measuring 'roles' performed by the managers which we later developed into the R of the RSDQ model. We must acknowledge the support of IIMA which encourages innovativeness. There are many innovations in IIMA that do not get adequate recognition until they are imported from the US. The potential of this great institution is underestimated most of the time.

We would also like to acknowledge many individuals and organizations that have taken the risk and that have dared to experiment with 360 Degree Feedback when no one else dared to do so. Significant among these are Santrupt Mishra of the Aditya Birla Group, Bhaskar Bhatt and Ramadoss of Titan and many others from the Tata Group and IL&FS, Deepak Chanrai of Chanrai Group of Nigeria, G.V. Prasad and Satish Reddy of Dr Reddy's Laboratories, and several others who tried this out.

Our experience with 360 Degree Feedback indicates that if one can overcome the initial fear of feedback, one will get to know a lot about oneself. Many Indian CEOs have gone through this: Kumar Mangalam Birla, Chairman, AVB Group; Agarwala of Hindalco; V.T. Moorthy of BMC; Krishna Kumar of Taj Group; Korakhiwalla of Wokhardt; Ravi Venkatesan of Tata Cummins; Ajit Nambiar, Anju Nambiar of BPL; MK Agarwal, Managing Director, Gati; Pradeep Dhobale of ITC, Bhadrachalam; Samir Inamdar, Managing Director, Tyco International; S.M. Kidwai, Managing Director, Tata Tea; Milind Desai of Tata Finance; Vimal Bhandari, Arun K. Shah; Hemang Raja and Hari Shankaran of IL&FS; Vikram Shah of Novell Software; A. Mahendran of Godrej Hi-Care; Arun Bewoor of Bush Boake Allen; Ashok Agarwal of IIHMR; Satish Reddy, G.V. Prasad of Dr Reddy's Labs; Gautam Hari Singhania of Raymond Ltd.; Y. Radhakrishna of SBI; Shrikanth Gathoo, M.B. Lal of BPCL; Deepak Chanrai, Managing Director, Kewalram Chanrai Group Nigeria; Ravichandran of Afprint, Nigeria; K.N. Agarwal, Managing

Director, Alexandria Carbon Black, Egypt; Adi Godrej of Godrej & Boyce and Narayan Murthy (Infosys) etc. Besides them, hundreds of senior and middle-level managers have been going through 360 Degree Feedback programmes to know and improve their effectiveness.

Our staff at TVRLS have been a great support in this journey: Merlin George heading the Centre for 360 Degree Feedback at TVRLS, and Gopal Mahapatra and Nandini Chawla for trying our experiments and spreading and adding to our knowledge base in 360 Degree Feedback.

Dr Udai Pareek has been a great companion and mentor for us by joining us at every possible opportunity.

We hope the reader will find this work useful in nurturing human talent.

Ahmedabad   **T.V. Rao**
July 2004   **Raju Rao**

Introduction

> **NEED FOR CONSTANT AWARENESS**
>
> No student of Zen would presume to teach others, until he had lived with his master for a minimum of 10 years.
>   Tenno, having completed 10 years of his apprenticeship, acquired the rank of teacher.
>   One day, he went to visit the master, Nan-in.
>   It was a rainy day, so Tenno wore wooden clogs and carried an umbrella.
>   When he walked in, Nan-in greeted him with, "you left your wooden clogs and umbrella on the porch", didn't you?
>   Tell me, did you place your umbrella on the right side of the clogs, or on the left?
>   Tenno was embarrassed for a minute, for he did not know the answer.
>   He realized he lacked awareness. So he became Nan-in's student, and laboured for 10 more years to acquire continual awareness.
>
> (From the collections of Anthony deMello, 1987b.)

Varun, Senior Vice President (SVP) in an Asian multinational, is a chartered accountant (CA). He became SVP in that company at the age of 37. He has received six promotions in the last 10 years and the average promotion rate in that company has always been more than 3 years. He is considered very sincere, meticulous, honest, hardworking, loyal, attentive to details and highly analytical. He has saved a lot of money for the company, manages its collections well and is a prudent administrator.

However, no one likes to work with him. There are 30 executives and managers in his department, mostly postgraduates in Commerce and some CAs. Whenever the human resources (HR) department has posted an executive to work in the commercial department, there have either been resignations or requests of transfers from the plant. Employees often complained that Varun works very hard, comes an hour or more early and expects everyone in the department to do the same and also work late regularly. No mistakes ever escape his attention, and upon detection he loses his temper and yells at employees. Employees admit that they do learn a lot while working with him, but have to pay a heavy price in terms of their peace of mind and psychological energy. No one dares to give him feedback as he is thought of highly by the top management and has been promoted rapidly over the years. His output and loyalty have always been unquestionably high. The average tenure of his junior staff is about six months, and every year at least about 50 per cent of them request transfers or leave the department. Most of the time these departures are written off as a result of a high demand for CAs and Commerce graduates from outside the department. Only a few internal people know the truth of the matter.

When the HR Chief suggested to him that a 360 Degree Feedback assessment should be conducted, his response was, "You see how hard I work and how much I give to this company. And look at the employees you post in my department and their commitment to work. They can't even stand hard work for a few days. Tell me who needs 360 Degree Feedback, them or me?"

The HR Chief convinced the SVP nonetheless, and the latter attended the 360 Degree Feedback workshop. Through the 360 Degree Feedback process, he understood his strengths and weaknesses for the first time. While he was happy to see that his strengths were noticed and acknowledged by everyone, the discovery that his interpersonal competence was rated as extremely poor, teamwork within the department was bad and his juniors' morale low shook him. Some of his juniors even stated in their feedback that he creates tension and fear in the department. First, he found it very difficult to reconcile his department's high regard for his abilities and the results he helped bring about, with their assertion that he was very poor at teamwork and at maintaining interpersonal relations. The question he asked during the workshop was: "How is it that I am delivering results year after year and getting promoted faster than anyone else, if my team work is poor and interpersonal competence low?"

Within a few days of the 360 Degree Feedback workshop, back in the organization, the SVP initiated a number of changes. Everyone noticed the change in him and he no longer behaved as formally as before. He stopped insisting that people come early or leave late as long as they completed their work and made corrections themselves. Gradually, he also cultivated the practice of holding informal departmental meetings. In three months, the SVP had changed visibly. According to some of the juniors, "He smiles now, which he rarely ever did before, and we are no longer afraid to approach him. He even sits with us to have a cup of tea though at times he continues to throw papers at us in anger". A couple of years later he was adjudged one of the best Presidents of the company.

This is a good example of what 360 Degree Feedback can do. It has made SVP Varun recognise the impact he is making on others and helped him enhance his positive impact.

Effective Leaders Are Effective People

All leaders exhibit qualities of effective people. Effective people have a high degree of self-awareness. They know largely what they are capable of and what they are less capable of, what can be considered their strong points and what areas they are weak at, and where they are more likely to succeed and where they may have difficulties succeeding. They choose the right path on the basis of this self-awareness.

They do things and make things happen. They undertake a large number of activities and create an impact.

They continuously seek feedback from others, on the impact of their actions. They enrich and empower themselves with the feedback they receive from their own actions, and the impact they create on others. They strive to create a positive impact on a continuous basis so as to enhance their self-confidence and empowerment, and build their self-confidence and leadership qualities. Effective managers also do not feel shy of getting feedback from others to enhance their self-awareness.

You can build yourself as a leader by discovering your own qualities of effectiveness as a person, manager and as a leader. Managers can build themselves as leaders, with the help of others, by their actions and through the study of the impact of their actions.

360 Degree Feedback or multi-dimensional feedback or multi-rater feedback is a good tool to enhance effectiveness as an individual, as a manager and as a leader—in whatever setting you may be. You can enhance your effectiveness as a parent, teacher, manager, chief executive

officer (CEO), minister, civil servant, doctor, salesman, police officer, etc.—whatever role that is important for you. Most successful organizations use multi-source assessment and feedback to enhance the leadership competencies and effectiveness of their employees.

Multi-source feedback is a process by which an individual gets his/her aggregated feedback from different categories of individuals —seniors (boss, reporting officer, reviewing officer), subordinates, direct and indirect reporters, peers (colleagues and internal customers), external customers and suppliers, and other role/set members with whom he/she is interacting.

This feedback is obtained on a pre-determined instrument or questionnaire of relevance and significance to both the individual and his/her organization. It is obtained anonymously, by an external agency or through a credible internal facilitator. The feedback is presented in aggregates (averages or percentages), for each category of feedback givers.

The feedback is intended to help the individual to:

- Recognize his/her strengths and leverage them,
- Recognize areas needing improvements and work on them or enhance effectiveness by avoiding situations that may bring down effectiveness,
- Enhance awareness of others through communication and
- Explore new areas to make an impact.

Feedback is a sensitive issue. Effective use of feedback requires adequate preparation to bring down defences and create the right attitudes. This book aims at motivating you to seek such feedback, and enabling you to understand, interpret and use such feedback to empower yourself. This book enables you to prepare well for both receiving the feedback and preparing the action plans.

TV Rao Learning System (TVRLS) specializes in this methodology, and its chairman, Dr T.V. Rao, the first author of this book, has evolved this methodology while at the Indian Institute of Management, Ahmedabad (IIMA). He has been using it since 1985.

This book also presents the Roles, Styles, Delegation and Qualities (RSDQ) model—which has been well tested out in the last 15 years.

The Power of 360 Degree Feedback presents the experiences of various individuals and organizations, and offers tools for those in various settings ranging from schools to non-government organizations (NGOs) and large multinational corporations (MNCs). It is a book intended to present the various ways in which an organization can use 360 Degree Feedback experiences as well as systems to enhance the organizational effectiveness.

This book is also intended to caution you that 360 Degree Feedback can be as subjective as any other assessment. However, it is the aggregate feedback and consistency in feedback that tend to make it more objective about people. All the assessments of people by other people are subjective.

There are many approaches to 360 Degree Feedback. Some of the organizations have started using it for performance appraisal. While it has utility as an appraisal tool, 360 Degree Feedback can also be an extremely limiting step for an organization to take—if it uses this tool mainly to assess the performance of an individual, especially when better tools for performance appraisal are available.

360 Degree Feedback has tremendous potential to enhance the effectiveness of an individual and to build him/her as a leader, or the competencies and organizational values he/she would like to develop. 360 Degree Feedback assessment should be taken as indicative and should be reflected upon by the individual—rather than as being conclusive and be acted upon by the organization.

At times, 360 Degree Feedback can be very provocative. The candidate should use this for review, reflection and action—rather than to identify those who have given feedback, and react to the feedback.

In a study conducted by the authors at TVRLS, it was found that, on an average, there is an 80 per cent chance that the guesses are wrong and only a 20 per cent chance that they are correct. It is, therefore, a futile attempt to find the source of feedback, and a lot more beneficial if the individuals use the feedback for their growth. Hence, it should be used more as a developmental tool, and action plans should be prepared on the basis of this feedback.

The action should be primarily directed at empowering the self and changing oneself where necessary. After all, even if you have to change others, it requires change in one's own self, approach, attitude, communication, etc.

Our experience also indicates that it is but natural to become defensive in the event of negative feedback. We, therefore, recommend that 360 Degree Feedback be used to empower yourself. Such an enhanced awareness helps you become a more effective leader, just as implementing action plans after a reflection of the feedback puts you well on way to leadership.

360 Degree Feedback Is an Awareness-building Tool

> **AWARENESS-BUILDING TOOL**
>
> *When you seek feedback, always start with self-assessment in the areas where you sought such feedback.*
>
> *In many areas your self-assessment may be similar to the assessment by others. These areas indicate your 'open self'. If they are strong points, you should learn to use them more, or look for occasions to use them more. If they are weak points, you may like to reflect upon them and work out methods to improve them.*
>
> *In a few areas, the feedback you get may be different from your perceptions of self—sometimes in the positive direction, and at other times in the negative. These differences are likely to give you more insights about yourself, and the impact of your behaviour on others. A good reflection may help in planning to enhance your effectiveness in your role, and in the organization.*
>
> *Sometimes, you may already be aware of the areas where such differences exist.* This indicates a high degree of your empathy and perceptiveness. In such cases you may focus your reflection on the consequences of such perceptions of others and if you would like in any way to change their perceptions. Perceptual changes normally occur if there are behaviour changes. Sometimes, perceptions can also be changed through more communication and dialogue. However, such dialogue should not be to justify your behaviour—but should aim at better understanding yourself and your impact.
>
> *Sometimes, you may find the perceptions of others to be varied and conflicting. Sometimes they may even be opposite. For example, some may perceive you to be good in communication, while others may see you as withholding information and being secretive. Some*

(Contd.)

(Contd.)

> may perceive your sociability as a strength, while for a few, it may be a weakness. Some may perceive you as 'dynamic', 'active' and 'aggressive', while a few may see this very behaviour as 'dominating' and 'manipulative'. This is a result of the chemistry you have generated. Chemistry depends as much on the perceived as on you, yourself. In other words, some people have looked at that part of the pot that is full, while others may have looked at the empty part of the half-filled pot. It is the empty part that is likely to help you more.
>
> This could also mean one or more of the following:
>
> *You may be behaving differently with different persons or groups.* If it is planned, it is an indication of flexibility. If you are aware of this and feel it is needed, then it is fine. You only need to reaffirm to yourself the desirability of such flexibility. Sometimes, it may also indicate biases in your approach such as favouritism, etc. Just ensure that it is more your flexibility and not your bias, and make sure that the differential impact is in the desired direction.
>
> *It may also be a reflection of differences in perceptions of the same behaviour rather than the behaviour itself.* People are different. Every person sees us through his/her own eyes. What is reflected could be a perception, which is influenced by the perceivers' own experience and expectations. Sometimes, low or poor assessment reflects high expectations or unfulfilled expectations. Every assessor has his/her own perspective.
>
> *360 Degree Feedback is provocative and, at best, indicative. It is not conclusive. It is a starting point. Self-discovery is a continuous process. Others can merely help us. The final awareness is within us.*
>
> (Source: Leadership and Organizational Effectiveness Through 360 Degree Feedback: Workbook, TVRLS, Ahmedabad, 2002.)

From various studies described in this book, it is not only clear that 360 Degree Feedback has had a great impact on individuals, team and organizations, but also the extent of this impact differs from individual to individual, as well as from organization to organization.

Who Benefits the Most?

Impact at an individual level appears to be more when the individual was very open, keen and motivated for self-awareness and growth. The impact of the feedback was low for those participants who did not take charge of their own development. They may seem to have held a belief that the data was not their own (but was owned by someone else!). This dependence orientation on the organization, or on the consulting firm, may have resulted in a restricted impact of the 360 Degree Feedback.

In the case of organizations, greater impact was felt when the organization-wise data was used and followed up with some focused interventions or programmes for developing competencies that were important and had come out as areas of focus. For example, in one company, the vision and articulation of vision was an area of focus—based on the 360 Degree Feedback. This organization took immediate steps to conduct a focused vision exercise—and true enough, their scores on this parameter had increased during the reassessment. It is indeed sad that many companies just leave it to the individual, and do not really make use of the organization-level data by backing it with training programmes.

It is this potential of 360 Degree Feedback that prompted our research, study and work for nearly 18 years now available to the readers. Of these 18 years, the last five years' work by TVRLS is filled with richness in experiences and saw the expansion of this tool—taking it to schools and NGOs. It is gradually also beginning to reach and see application in the government sector and with the families, too.

We hope that this book will help spread the message and help a number of people who are not yet aware of the power of this potential tool. May they use it for their own benefit and for the good of the society.

This Book...

Intended to help all those interested in 360 Degree Feedback. This book is presented in four parts.

The first part deals with the background needed for effective leadership and management. It explains *what* constitutes effective personality in the first chapter and, in the second chapter, what makes managers effective. The third chapter deals with qualities of leaders, the fourth

Introduction **xxvii**

with the roles performed by leaders and the fifth with the leadership styles that make them effective.

The second part of this book explains the process of the 360 Degree Feedback or Multi-rater Assessment and Feedback Systems (MAFs). In the sixth chapter, we explain the process of 360 Degree Feedback or MAFs and in the seventh, the most popularly used RSDQ model for developing leadership and other competencies. Over the years, we found this approach to be the most suitable for change and development. This 360 Degree Feedback tool is the heart of MAFs. The eighth chapter presents some insights into coaching. Coaching is a useful part of 360 Degree Feedback and some case studies are presented in this chapter. In the ninth chapter, we present some myths about 360 Degree Feedback, and in the tenth chapter, we present some of our experiences of its impact and the various conditions required to make it successful.

The third part of the book is the new addition to this second edition. Except one chapter which reproduces the experiences from other countries on 360 Degree Feedback, this part attempts to give deep insights into the way the 360 Degree Feedback is being implemented in India, and also deals with issues like the returns of investment (ROI) and research on 360 Degree Feedback. Out of around eight thousand 360 Degree profiles available of senior managers with the authors, about a hundred top scoring individuals have been selected and studied for their life histories and success stories in the work place. Based on the biographic details, some of their outstanding characteristics responsible for their success were deciphered in a study at TVRLS. The fourteenth chapter reproduces the lessons from these 100 managers. This part also reproduces data from the fourth workshop held by TVRLS on the life after 360 Degree Feedback and assessment centres—another HR intervention of the recent times. The relevant chapter summaries from this conference as well as study conducted by one of the authors for HR awards at IIMA along with his colleagues from IIMA and Steel Authority of India are presented in these chapters. In the last chapter of this part (Chapter 15), we conclude with a summary of some international experiences taken mainly from published literature. Through this chapter we intend to give our readers a flavour of the global scenario.

The fourth part is devoted to providing the actual tools for headmaster or principals of schools, teachers, parents and students as well as NGOs. Instead of describing the process, we have preferred to reproduce the actual tools for these groups. It is our desire to make these tools available, with due acknowledgements to TVRLS, in our commitment to the nation and the people who help shape our society.

We believe that 360 Degree Feedback can be a high-potential tool for building leaders and leadership for the future, a tool useful for all. We hope that inspired readers will contribute to its usage and build further on the knowledge base so as to make our society a better place.

TEACHING TO LEARN

"I wish to learn. Will you teach me?"
"I do not think that you know how to learn", said the Master.
"Can you teach me how to learn?"
"Can you learn how to let me teach?"

To his bewildered disciples, the Master later said: "Teaching only takes place when learning does. Learning only takes place when you teach something to yourself".

(From the collections of Anthony deMello, 1987a.)

PART 1
Developing Managers into Leaders

CHAPTER 1

How to Be an Effective Person?

An effective person is one who has a high degree of self-awareness. Such awareness is characterized by a good insight into one's own strengths and weaknesses. In addition, effective individuals are constantly searching for opportunities to test themselves in new situations, gain more insights into their own personality, improve upon their strengths and overcome their weaknesses.

Every individual's personality and psychological world (attitudes, values, habits, knowledge, abilities, etc.) can be considered as consisting of four parts in terms of her/his self-awareness and the awareness of others. These include the following:

1. **An open or public self which consists of those aspects that are known to one's self and also known to others:** Some of our strengths, as well as peculiarities, are known to us as well as to those who keep observing and interacting with us. Someone may be an expert in information technology (IT) and everyone else around him/her may know the same. A good dancer knows what he/she is, just as those who are around him/her. A talkative person, an introvert, a sociable person, etc. are all examples of how some of our qualities cannot be hidden and constitute our public self.
2. **A closed or a private self which only the individual is aware of and others are not:** There may be several strengths, weaknesses, habits, etc. which are not known to others as we may not prefer talking about them. For example, most people with religious attitudes and prejudice are not likely to go around sharing their views. Interestingly, modesty also prevents most people from sharing, with others, their strong points. As a result, talents exhibited in the early years go unnoticed in later years, unless a situation is created wherein they have to share their existence with others and create opportunities to use them. A human

resource development (HRD) manager in a company may have worked in an earlier company as a materials manager and would have done a great job of vendor development. However, as he/she has been recruited to head HRD, he/she may never get an opportunity to apply his/her talent in vendor development.
3. **A blind spot or the part which the individual is not aware of but others are aware of:** Some or many of what is perceived to be our strengths and inadequacies may not be known to us. In relationship-valuing societies and cultures like the Asian cultures, people will normally tell you things that please you and refrain from giving negative feedback. In such societies people may have a sizeable chunk of blind spots. An individual may pride himself/herself on being flexible and creative, while the same behaviour may be interpreted or experienced by his/her subordinates as inconsistent and unreliable (as he/she keeps changing his/her stand and views due to creativity, while others affected by it may perceive an inconsistency behind the change of ideas, etc.).
4. **A dark or hidden part which neither the individual nor others are aware of:** This is because we never get an opportunity to try ourselves out and discover what we are truly capable of. During our entire lifetime we may get an opportunity to discover only a small part of our potential.

The following points may help enhancing personal and leadership effectiveness:

- Having a large area of blind spot impedes effectiveness.
- Discovering more of the dark area helps bringing out latent talent.
- A high degree of awareness of one's strengths, weaknesses and qualities helps in making conscious choices and enhances effectiveness.
- Blind spots can be reduced by seeking feedback from others, accepting it, reflecting on it and using it to improve.
- A high degree of privacy could mean non-availability of your talents to others as they will not be aware of your strengths. You may need to enhance your communication and let others know your competencies.
- The dark area can be reduced by undertaking new tasks, activities, exploring new methods of working, experimenting,

job rotation, etc. High action orientation, experimental and risk-taking attitudes are needed. Proaction and initiative are the most important prerequisites.
- Leaders, effective managers and effective people constantly explore their dark area and attempt to reduce blind spots.
- *360 Degree Feedback is one of the effective tools to reduce blind spots, put to use hidden talents and capabilities and initiate actions to discover new areas or competencies.*

> **BOX 1.1 ACTION AND RESULTS**
>
> No one climbs a mountain just by gazing at it. It is through commitment and action that one can climb the tree of success.

Other Dimensions of Personal Effectiveness

It matters very little whether you are an extrovert or introvert, whether you are reserved or gregarious, a reasoning type or intuitive type, etc. It is important to be aware of what your qualities are, how they affect you and how they contribute to the outcome of your actions. In other words, self-awareness is an important component of effectiveness. In addition to a high degree of self-awareness and continuous striving to enhance it, certain qualities contribute immensely to personal and managerial effectiveness. These include:

1. Action orientation or exploratory orientation,
2. Self-disclosure,
3. Receptivity to feedback,
4. Interpersonal sensitivity,
5. Self-confidence,
6. Internality and inner directedness,
7. Trustworthiness,
8. Inner core values such as honesty, sincerity and truthfulness,
9. Goal orientation and
10. Drive and passion (this includes passion for results, innovations and achievement).

Exploratory orientation

A person who takes initiative to keep experimenting with himself/herself in new situations is action-oriented, is not afraid of making mistakes, can take risks, is restless in his/her work, has high activity levels and likes variety, and change is likely to discover more and more of his/her potential. (S)he constantly applies herself/himself and does things. Such a person may be called an action-oriented explorer. It is such explorers who can discover more and more of their talents and benefit themselves and their organizations.

Self-disclosure

People who communicate with others about themselves rather freely, and who express and share their views, opinions, knowledge, feelings and personal experiences with others (including subordinates, colleagues and bosses) can be considered as the self-disclosing type. These people communicate with others and make an impact on others. Such communication or self-disclosure helps in generating data and has more of an open and public self than private self. Without an optimal amount of self-disclosure we deny others the opportunity to know us, and ourselves, appropriate feedback. Low scorers are private individuals who may have difficulty discovering themselves fully. At least, it is difficult for them to see themselves fully from the eyes of others. Not only that, they also make a limited impact on others.

Receptivity to feedback

Those who seek feedback constantly or periodically and try to find out what impact they and their behaviour have on others, those who take criticism sportingly, examine themselves and their behaviour and try to learn from such feedback, and those who value what others say about them, their actions, behaviour, etc. are good learners from feedback. They are likely to develop themselves more and become more effective in the process. Those who are not willing to listen to the views, opinions and feedback from others, and those who become defensive and closed to feedback, are likely to develop less.

CHAPTER 1 How to Be an Effective Person? 7

Receptivity to feedback is therefore an essential element of managerial effectiveness and growth.

Interpersonal sensitivity

Those who are sensitive to the cues and non-verbal communications of others, those who are perceptive of the impact of their behaviour on others and are therefore sensitive in not saying and doing things which may be out of place, those who are sensitive to the needs and feelings of others and those who make efforts to understand the other person or group before saying anything can be called perceptive persons. Such individuals are likely to utilize their time properly and make an impact on others. This also makes them effective in most managerial settings.

Test your propensity for effectiveness using the four dimensions in the test given below.

Self-test 1.1: Personal Effectiveness (© T.V. Rao Learning Systems Pvt. Ltd. Reproduced with permission)

Rate yourself on each statement using the following 5-point rating scale:

0 = Not at all characteristic of you or you normally do not do this (nearly '0' or less than 10%)

1 = Not characteristic of you and you may do this rarely (less than 25%)

2 = Somewhat characteristic of you and you do this sometimes (50%)

3 = Fairly characteristic of you and you may do this most of the time (75%)

4 = Highly characteristic of you and you do this almost always (90% and above)

8 THE POWER OF 360 DEGREE FEEDBACK

Please use the preceding rating scale to indicate your rating on each of the 40 items. Please do not think too much for each item. Indicate the rating that comes to your mind first.

S. No.	Statement	Your Rating
1.	I like to keep testing myself in new situations.	
2.	I like to keep trying out new methods of work wherever possible.	
3.	I like to keep undertaking new activities.	
4.	I enjoy changing my roles and work responsibilities.	
5.	I like to have variety in my work from time to time whenever possible.	
6.	I am restless until I complete whatever I undertake.	
7.	I am not afraid of making mistakes in my work.	
8.	I enjoy taking risks in my work and carry out new things.	
9.	Most of the time I am occupied with some activity or the other.	
10.	I am high in initiative taking.	
11.	I like to be open and frank with all people I interact with.	
12.	Generally, I don't hesitate to express my feelings to others.	
13.	I am quite quick and strong in expressing my opinions in a group or to a person even if this may be unacceptable to them.	
14.	When someone discusses his/her problems, I also share spontaneously my experiences and personal problems of a similar kind with him/her.	
15.	I enjoy talking with others about my personal concerns and matters.	
16.	I freely share my views and opinions with my juniors.	

(Table Contd.)

CHAPTER 1 How to Be an Effective Person?

(Table Contd.)

17.	I freely discuss my opinions and feelings with my boss or other officers above me.	
18.	I am known to be a fairly open (not reserved) person in my communications and interactions with others.	
19.	I freely share my knowledge and ideas with others as I am not afraid that others will steal them.	
20.	I go out of my way to let people know my reactions to important decisions and events in the organization.	
21.	I listen carefully to the opinion of others about my behaviour.	
22.	When someone directly tells me how he/she feels about my behaviour, I tend to take it and reflect on the same.	
23.	I take steps to find how my behaviour has been perceived by the person with whom I have been interacting.	
24.	If someone criticizes me, I hear him/her and try to discover more about my own behaviour and how it is being perceived.	
25.	I value what people say about my style, behaviour, qualities, etc.	
26.	I actively keep seeking feedback on my actions and behaviour from my subordinates.	
27.	I keep seeking feedback from my superiors.	
28.	I am highly receptive whenever a colleague of mine shares his/her views and opinions about me.	
29.	I feel that most people around me give right feedback when asked for their opinion about me.	
30.	In the recent past, I have become aware of many of my blind spots, strengths and weaknesses.	
31.	I tend to say things that are appropriate for the situation and they don't turn out to be out of place.	
32.	I don't come across situations wherein I had to regret saying something tactlessly.	

(Table Contd.)

(Table Contd.)

33.	I am particular to observe how a person will take what I am going to tell him/her and I communicate to him/her accordingly.	
34.	Most often I pick up cues about others' feelings and reactions even when I am involved in arguments or conversation.	
35.	I can sense easily when people are put off or bored or annoyed when they are interacting with me.	
36.	I am quite sensitive to non-verbal cues offered by others in interpersonal or group discussions.	
37.	Often my perceptions of others regarding their interest in the topic of discussion tally accurately with their subsequently expressed feelings and views.	
38.	I feel that I am very tactful and diplomatic in saying things that my colleagues may not like in acceptable ways.	
39.	I am sensitive to the moods of my boss and am reasonably sure of the right time, to communicate things.	
40.	I am sensitive to the moods of most of my colleagues and subordinates.	

Scoring Personal Effectiveness

Score your responses in self-test 1.1 using the scoring system presented below.

Exploratory orientation

A person who takes initiative is action-oriented, is not afraid of making mistakes, can take risks, is restless in his/her work, has high activity level and likes variety and change is likely to discover more and more of his/her potential. He/she constantly applies himself/herself and does things. Such a person may be called an action-oriented explorer. The first 10 items in self-test 1.1 deal with this. Add the scores in all the 10 items. Scores between 30 and 40 represent a high activity level and exploratory orientation. Scores below 10 indicate very low activity level and exploratory orientation. If your scores are below 20, then there is a good degree of scope for improvement. You may not be discovering much of your hidden talent.

Self-disclosure

Items 11 to 20 in self-test 1.1 deal with self-disclosure. Add the scores in items 11 to 20. Scores between 30 and 40 indicate that the person is highly self-disclosing type. The 'open' part may be high for these individuals. Scores below 10 indicate a reserved and closed personality. Others do not get to know him/her much. Such people may have a high private world and may even have more blind spots. Others fall in between, depending on their scores. Low scorers may reflect about the opportunity they deny to themselves by not being open and free with others.

Receptivity to feedback

Items 21 to 30 deal with receptivity to feedback. Add the scores in these 10 items. Scores above 30 indicate a high degree of receptivity to feedback. Scores below 10 indicate that the individual is more closed than open to feedback. Openness to feedback helps reduce blind spots and increase self-awareness. It also helps in discovering more and more of one's potential.

Perceptiveness

Items 31 to 40 deal with perceptiveness or being sensitive to the feelings and reactions of others through verbal and non-verbal cues. Add the scores in these 10 items. Scores above 30 indicate a high degree of perceptiveness and scores below 10 indicate low perceptiveness.

Other Dimensions That Make You Effective

Self-confidence

It is the self-concept or self-worth that an individual carries with him/her all the time. A confident person is able to accomplish a number of things. Self-confidence enables you to apply what you have as strengths, and also makes you more open to feedback and experimentation. Self-confidence puts a glow on your personality and makes you attempt to do things and also take risks. There is an approach orientation by confident people and avoidance orientation by less confident people.

Internality and inner directedness

This relates to the tendency to do things out of one's own initiative and direction rather than merely doing something to comply with others or the role expectations of others. An inner-directed person is dictated by his/her inner self and is likely to put more of his/her talents to use.

Trustworthiness

Trustworthiness or reliability and sincerity are hallmarks of effective people. They honour their promises and make statements which they always mean. Trustworthiness enhances the reliability of a person and creates a healthy society. It enhances confidence, and both the inner and outer image of a person. Trustworthiness promotes trust and trusting society is more enjoyable and liveable.

Inner core values such as honesty, sincerity and truthfulness

It is values that give a direction to life and also a sense of joy. They are essential for creating a healthy society, essential for healthy living. Effective people are characterized by the values they possess.

Goal orientation

A goal-oriented person is clear about what he/she wants to do, where to put his/her efforts and consequently reduces wastage of time. Goal-oriented people are likely to remain focused. If you know what you want to achieve, you have already succeeded halfway. Most people do not know what they want to achieve and, as a result, remain unfocused and waste a good part of their lives.

Drive and passion

This includes passion for results, innovations, achievements, etc. While goal directedness gives direction, drive gives intensity. It reduces time and enhances the value of life. A person with drive and passion can achieve the same things in less time as compared to the person with less drive and less passion. In other words, he/she has more time available to do other things.

These are just a few qualities and attitudes that make an effective person. These are, by no means, exhaustive. There may be many more. Qualities such as emotional intelligence, emotional maturity and psychosocial maturity also contribute to effectiveness.

BOX 1.2 STILL MOVEMENT

Four persons got totally drunk. While returning home, it was pitch dark and they had to cross a river. They looked out for the boatman but he was not to be seen anywhere and the boat was tied to the mooring. They decided to row themselves home. So they got into the boat and began rowing. Soon it was dawn but they were yet to reach the bank. Their intoxication was slowly receding. Only then did they realize that the boat was still tied to the mooring!

Similarly, preconceived notions and agitation blind our minds on several occasions. This prevents us from seeing the truth and reality 'as it is'. To solve a problem, one must first understand the problem with a calm and composed mind. This will facilitate seeing things objectively.

(Swami Sukhabodhananda, *Oh Mind Relax Please!*, 2002)

CHAPTER 2

What Makes Managers Effective?

Managers and Leaders

A manager is one who manages things, while a leader is one who leads. He/she may lead an organization, teams or other people. While sometimes the distinction is very thin, it is becoming thinner as managers are increasingly being required to play leadership roles. Consider the following roles that a manager is required to play:

1. Conducting performance review discussions,
2. Ensuring that management information systems (MIS) and other systems are implemented well,
3. Articulating the vision for the department or unit,
4. Communicating the top management vision to other members of his/her team,
5. Inspiring subordinates with vision and values,
6. Setting a personal example by following all the requirements of the job,
7. Understanding the expectations of customers,
8. Meeting the expectations of his/her seniors,
9. Influencing the thinking of his/her seniors and
10. Creating new opportunities for the growth and development of subordinates.

Of these roles, 1, 2, 4, 7 and 8 are managerial activities. While the person who performed these activities may show his/her leadership in the way he/she carries them out, they are essentially managerial in nature as they are job requirements and there are standard ways of doing things. Without these, managerial tasks are not complete and organizational goals cannot be achieved. Performing these and other such activities is essential for the survival of any organization.

However, the rest of the roles 3, 5, 6, 9 and 10 are the activities that take the organization or the department into the future. They require a higher degree of initiative, and that is what makes a leader different from a manager.

Every manager today is required to play both leadership and managerial roles. A manager's effectiveness has to be both in terms of leadership and managerial roles.

Tremendous changes have taken place in the global economic environment in the last decade. Today, the world is of a different order. The corporate world can be characterized as highly competitive, technology- and systems-driven, customer-centred, speedy, cost- and quality-conscious, fast-changing and highly competitive. In this changed situation, to be able to survive, one has to compete with those who have technological advantages, financial advantages, systems advantages, communication advantages, and, above all, people advantages in terms of their competencies, attitudes and work culture. In such a situation, organizations need to have highly competent, top-level managers to lead them. Hence, the topmost team of each company becomes important. It needs to perform leadership and institution-building roles very effectively, balance short-term targets with long-term organization-building concerns, inspire and develop the staff, and be customer- and quality-driven. Each individual manager plays a critical role in the company. He or she can be a good change agent by constantly improving himself/herself in relation to the roles he or she is playing, and the styles in which he or she is playing those roles, delegating and making the right impact on others through his/her behaviour.

What Makes Managers Effective?

The following types of competencies are required to be an effective manager and to make an impact as a leader–manager:

- Technical or functional and business competencies,
- Managerial competence,
- Leadership styles and human relations competence and
- Conceptual competence.

Each of these competencies includes knowledge, attitudes, values, motives, self-awareness and skills. The combinations that make a manager effective may vary from time to time and depend on the nature of business or organizational activity, environment, etc.

Technical and business competence

This competence is essential to understand, design, plan and conduct business. Without this, business does not get started and business activities do not get appropriately undertaken. This competence essentially deals with an understanding of the business—its technology, market, customers, finance, etc. This could, at times, be called 'entrepreneurial competence'.

This includes knowledge/attitude and skills relating to the following areas:

- One's own business and product line,
- Environment,
- Competitors and their strategies,
- Customers and markets,
- Technology,
- Finance,
- Research and development,
- Manufacturing processes,
- Quality requirements, etc.

Managerial competence

Managerial competence is required to put business plans into operation and manage operations effectively. Managerial competence, again, has two perspectives: current and future. The current perspective deals with managing the operations effectively and efficiently at a given point of time. The future perspective deals with management for the future and includes creating a sustainable organization and managing change. The current operations involve managerial roles and skills; the future operations require leadership roles and skills. Managing current operations requires transactional competence, while future activities require transformational competence. The following are some of the roles a manager is required to perform:

Roles associated with managerial or transactional competence

- Short-term goal setting,
- People management (subordinates, colleagues, seniors),
- Customer management,
- Unions and associations,
- Team management,
- Technology management,
- Systems management,
- Resource management,
- Public relations,
- Environment management,
- Quality and customer care,
- Safety management,
- Financial and cost management and
- Boss management or managing his/her seniors.

Leadership or transformational competence

- Articulating and communicating vision and values,
- Formulating and managing strategies or strategic thinking,
- Long-term planning and policy-making,
- Setting challenging and achievable goals,
- Values and culture building,
- Mobilizing and creating a resource base,
- Exploring new markets and new technologies,
- Inspiring and empowering people and
- Influencing the thinking of seniors, customers and other stakeholders.

Leadership styles and human relations competence

Managerial effectiveness also involves not merely performing roles, but also performing them in ways that build others and the organization. These ways of building or developing people, systems, culture, values, etc. make a lasting impact. The manner in which various leadership and managerial roles are performed is a significant determinant of the effectiveness of a leader–manager. The style of the person and human relations skills matter a lot in making an impact. To make the best impact, the performer (leader–manager) should use appropriate styles, should have the right kind of beliefs and attitudes, and should be able to exhibit a high level of sensitivity.

The empowering style or developmental style essentially builds a lasting organization, which has self-regulating and self-sustaining mechanisms. This should be accomplished through a continuous use of a developmental style. Flexibility should be adopted till the time the organization is fully mature and an appropriate culture is built and institutionalized.

Leadership styles get reflected in general beliefs of dealing with employees, assignment of tasks, communicating vision, providing support, managing mistakes, conflict management, decision-making, communicating business and other information, giving significance to others, etc.

The impact of the styles gets reflected in morale, job satisfaction, work commitment, dependence and the empowered feelings of the juniors who work with the person.

Learning orientation

- Effective managers are effective persons.
- They apply themselves in new situations. They are proactive and risk takers.
- They have a high degree of sensitivity to information. Their antennas are sharp.
- They are more often good listeners.
- They continuously seek feedback from others. They use the feedback for self-improvement than for self-aggrandizement.
- They delegate. They are empowering. They build the competencies of others to spread their areas of influence and allow them to make time for higher level tasks.
- They are hard-working and set examples for others. They are organizational achievement-driven, though their influence motivation is higher.

- They have larger community (society, nation, humanity, etc.) and organizational interests dominating their thinking; they are willing to sacrifice their personal interests.
- They are continuous learners. They reflect continuously, and learn from themselves and from others. They use multiple sources of learning to develop their competencies in various areas.
- They try to reduce their *blind spots* through seeking feedback continuously.
- They have a high degree of self-awareness. They are aware of their strengths and try to discover more.
- They have high degrees of self-confidence and self-esteem.

Conceptual competence

- Ability to integrate information and link parts,
- Ability to look into the future,
- Ability to visualize the invisible,
- Ability to take a global view of things,
- Ability to anticipate environmental changes,
- Ability to think abstract,
- A concern for society and its future,
- Understanding the economic environment,
- Understanding the global environment and issues,
- Ability to anticipate changes,
- Ability to initiate changes,
- Focus on values and institution building,
- Having concerns about sustainability and
- Ability to reflect.

BOX 2.1 ABILITY

Ability is an alertness to cash in on the opportunity.
(Swami Sukhabodhananda, *Oh Mind Relax Please!*, 2002)

CHAPTER 3

What Makes a Good Leader?

What Is Leadership? Some Contemporary Observations

There are more than 3000 empirical investigations on leadership and over 70 definitions. Almost all the definitions of leadership imply that it is some form of social influence. All definitions and studies imply two types of leadership:

1. Traits or behaviour and
2. Impact of those individuals who are assigned formal authority to direct others.

Factor analysis studies indicate three factors of leadership:

1. Individual performance and achievement,
2. Aiding attainment by the group and
3. Sociability.

Ghoshal and Bartlett's (1997) lessons from case studies for the role of top management indicate that it may be true that risks can be reduced by introducing strategies, structures and systems, but it should be recognized that the diversity of human skills and the unpredictability of the human spirit make initiative, creativity and entrepreneurship possible. The basic role of top management, they argue, is to recapture valuable human qualities by individualizing the corporation. To individualize the corporation and to obtain organizational effectiveness, the top management should adopt a philosophy based on purpose, processes and people.

There have been many studies highlighting the qualities and characteristics of Indian leaders (Sinha, 1995; Singh and Bhandarkar,

1990; Piramal, 1996; Pandit, 2001; Srivastava, 2003; Chary, 2002, Pareek 2001).

Pareek (2002a) emphasized that leaders should be institution builders. They should focus their attention on the following eight roles:

1. Identity creation,
2. Enabling (resource creation),
3. Synergizing,
4. Balancing (conformity and creativity),
5. Linkage building,
6. Futuristic,
7. Impact making and
8. Creating superordination.

The implication of Pareek's studies for leaders is to build institution-building capabilities of top-level managers and senior executives.

Lala's (1986) study of an analysis of Indian leaders has indicated 13 qualities of leadership: communication, compassion, competence, courage, decision-making, humility, love, integrity, man management, stamina, teamwork, training and vision.

Pandit (2001) studied 22 Indian leaders from various fields. These included entrepreneurs such as Bhavarlal Jain, Deepak Kanegaonkar, Ravi Khanna, Kiran Mazumdar Shaw and Ronnie Screwala; entrepreneur managers such as H. Dhanrajgir, V. Kurien and Deepak Parekh; manager entrepreneurs such as N.R. Naryana Murthy, Ashok Soota and Pramod Chaudhuri; family entrepreneurs such as B. Kelkar and R. Chitale; and exceptional managers such as Anu Aga and R. Mashelkar. The common traits he found among them include the following:

1. Commitment (drive, dedication, passion, obsession and zeal),
2. Persistence (doggedness, determination, hard work, insistence and tenacity),
3. Difference (distinctness, differentiation, innovativeness and talent),
4. Curiosity (creativity, clarity of thought and intelligence),
5. Persuasiveness (negotiation, influencing and presentation skills),
6. Risk-taking or entrepreneurship,
7. Focus (concentration, goal orientation and centring),

8. Values (honesty, integrity, honouring commitment, truthfulness, etc.),
9. High energy (spiritedness and stamina),
10. Learning,
11. Humility (modesty and unpretentiousness) and
12. Non-listening (firmness and not obstinacy).

Chary (2002) studied seven Indian business leaders: Kiran Mazumdar Shaw, Azim Premji, N.R. Narayana Murthy, Venu Srinivasan, Deepak Parekh, Dr V. Kurien and Mukesh Ambani.

The following emerged from his study:

1. They are passionately committed to their goal.
2. They are visionaries rewriting management principles—they are ahead of their times.
3. They are missionaries of the world.
4. They have exalted goals and social concerns.
5. They had a mission and then acquired core competence making us revisit the core competence theory.
6. They had a firm foundation of values (integrity, humility, compassion, honesty and customer service being some of these).
7. Simplicity and humility characterize most of them.
8. They share love for people.
9. They all practice out-of-the-box thinking.

Leadership has been defined in so many ways and by different authors and experts. Tichy and Cohen (1997), the authors of *The Leadership Engine*, point out:

> The most scarce resource in the world today is the leadership talent capable of continuously transforming organizations so as to win in tomorrow's world. The individuals and organizations that build leadership engines and invest in leaders developing other leaders have a sustainable competitive advantage. (p. 8)

According to Tichy and Cohen:

- Winning leaders, with a proven record, take direct responsibility for developing other leaders.

CHAPTER 3 What Makes a Good Leader? 23

- Winning leaders can articulate and teach others how to make the organization successful. They tell stories about their past and explain their learning experiences and beliefs.
- They have well-developed methodologies for teaching others.
- Leadership talent can be nurtured and it is never too late or early to develop one's own leadership abilities and the talents of others.
- Leaders are normally viewed as those people who motivate one or more people to do a specific thing.

Warren Bennis says that the basis of leadership is the capacity to change the mindset or framework of the other person (Tichy and Cohen, 1997). Lee (1997) of Franklin Covey, after reviewing a number of studies on leadership and its modern definitions, states that leadership is:

> An intensely human enterprise, and does not fit neatly into definitions and boxes. Leaders have all the spontaneity, unpredictability, frailty, vulnerability and potential that is possible in the human race. If we are to lead with honor, we must start with the premise that flexibility, adaptability, and wisdom are possible, that we have seeds of greatness in us, and if we care deeply about the lives of others, we can work together to accomplish worthwhile things. (p. 265)

Peters (1997), quoting Warren Bennis, points out that one thing in common in most leaders is that they all make mistakes but bounce back from them. They use failures as building blocks.

The ability to spend more time framing contexts and less time defining the content, more through coaching and supporting rather than directing and controlling, becomes the model for middle managers (Ghoshal and Bartlett, 1997).

Hesselbein and Paul (1999), of the Drucker Foundation, say that leaders exist at all levels of the organization. They identified the following traits of leaders:

- They excel in seeing things with clarity and they challenge status quo.
- They are energetic and seem to be able to run through obstacles.
- They are deeply interested in a cause or discipline related to their professional arena.

- They can tap convictions of others and connect them to the organizational arena.
- They help everyone see what their everyday work means for a larger purpose.
- They have a high quest for learning.
- They are open to people and their ideas.
- They are driven by goals or ideals that are bigger than what an individual can accomplish.
- They are willing to push themselves from comfort zones even after they have achieved success.

Smart (1999) in his book *Top Grading* lists 50 critical competencies for top graders. Some of these include intelligence; analytical skills; judgement and decision-making; conceptual ability; creativity; strategic skills; pragmatism; risk-taking; integrity; initiative; excellence; self-awareness; adaptability; listening; being a team player; assertiveness; communications; political insight; running meetings; vision; change management; conflict management; energy; ambition; enthusiasm; tenacity and balance in life.

Goleman (1998) considers emotional intelligence as central to leadership. In his chapter on the competencies of stars, Goleman identifies personal and social competencies as constituting the emotional competence. The following characteristics have been included in his framework:

- Personal competencies determine how we manage ourselves. These include:
  1. Self-awareness (knowing one's internal state, resources and intuitions). This includes emotional awareness, accurate self-assessment and self-confidence.
  2. Self-regulation, including managing one's internal states, impulses and resources. These include self-control, trustworthiness, conscientiousness, adaptability and innovation.
  3. Motivation, including the tendencies that guide or facilitate attaining goals. These include achievement drive, commitment, initiative and optimism.

- Social competencies determine how we handle relationships. These include:

1. Empathy or awareness of others' feelings, needs and concerns. These include understanding others, developing others, service orientation, leveraging diversity and political awareness.
2. Social skills dealing with adeptness at inducing desirable response. These include influence, communication, conflict management, leadership, change catalyst, building bonds, collaboration and cooperation and building team capabilities.

Goleman (1998) observes,

> Emotional competence is particularly central to leadership, a role whose essence is getting others to do their jobs more effectively. Interpersonal ineptitude in leaders lowers everyone's performance: It wastes time, creates acrimony, corrodes motivation and commitment, and builds hostility and apathy. A leader's strengths or weaknesses in emotional competence can be measured in the gain or loss to the organization of the fullest talents of those they manage. (p. 32)

Goleman indicates that the traits of outstanding leaders transcend cultural and national boundaries. The most effective CEOs have been found to have three main clusters of competencies. The first and second clusters fall under the category of emotional intelligence. They include personal competencies such as achievement, self-confidence and commitment; the second consists of social competence such as influence, political awareness and empathy. The third cluster competencies are cognitive: they think strategically, seek out information with a broad scan and apply strong conceptual thinking. They blend all these into an inspired vision and influence the thinking of others.

Pfeffer (1998) observes three qualities of most successful transformations:

- Build trust,
- Encourage change and
- Measure the right things and align the incentive system to new practices.

Pfeffer argues that a people-centred approach can increase profits and give itself a competitive advantage.

Implications for Organizations

The various studies and points of view from researches, reviewed earlier, indicate the following:

- Leadership is critical for business development or for any form of development.
- Leadership is not anymore limited to a few people in an organization.
- Each one's leadership competencies can be developed.
- Leaders need to be developed and multiplied for growth and survival.
- It is imperative for managers to explore their talent and develop their leadership competencies for their own good and the good of their organizations.
- Self-awareness is a very critical first step in developing their leadership talent.
- Organizational programmes and plans are required to develop leadership talent, and leadership development programmes do help in developing the same.

If leadership is so critical, and the future of organizations depends upon having as many leaders as possible, it is critical for organizations to develop a large pool of leadership talent.

Many leadership programmes focus on specific traits, rather than on any comprehensive qualities. This is because it is difficult to have any one quality focused upon. Team-building exercises help develop team-building skills. It is for this reason why many organizations have attempted, in the last decade, to use the 360 Degree Feedback as a leadership development tool. In India, too, it is becoming popular. This topic is indeed widely spoken and written about. Given below are excerpts from the highly readable book, *The Circle of Innovation* by Tom Peters (1997), and an article on 'Leadership' by Marwin Bower in *The McKinsey Quarterly*, 1997, No. 4:

> Leadership scholars define a leader as a person who sets attractive goals and has the ability to attract followers, or constituents, who share those goals. Above all, a leader must be trusted and respected. Trust between a leader and constituent opens up two-way communication, making it possible for them to realize their common goals. (*The McKinsey Quarterly*)

CHAPTER 3 What Makes a Good Leader? 27

The one who wants to become a leader has to possess some attributes and some qualities. Qualities may be harder to imbibe, but in successful leaderships, the number of attributes far outnumbers the qualities.

Some of these qualities, as outlined by Marwin Bower in *The McKinsey Quarterly*, are as follows:

Trustworthiness is integrity in action. Integrity is honesty carried through the fibres of the being and the whole mind into thought as well as action, so that the person is complete in honesty. Leadership scholars have put trustworthiness at the top of the list of qualities required by any leader.

Fairness that is defined as being equitable, unprejudiced, impartial, dispassionate and objective.

Unassuming leaders are not ostentatious; they do not need big titles nor a bungalow or a Mercedes to prove their power or authority; they let their actions to speak for themselves. Arrogance, haughtiness and egotism are poisonous for leadership. Leaders are unassuming in their behaviour. Unpretentiousness can be learned and it suits, quite well, the examples that chief executives should set. Having a servant leadership point of view helps any chief executive to focus on the company's performance and on the needs of the constituents, rather than on his/her own performance or image. The kind of informality and warmth practised by the leaders would percolate down the organization, to create a highly cohesive and interesting place to work in.

Listening behaviour: Leaders always like to preach. They realize that by only speaking and not listening, they lose touch with the frontline or where the action actually takes place.

> Of all the skills of leadership, listening is one of the most valuable and one of the least understood. Most captains of industry listen only sometimes and remain only ordinary leaders. But a few, the great ones, never stop listening. They are hear-aholics—ever alert, bending their ears while they work and while they play, while they eat and while they sleep. They listen to advisers, to customers, to inner voices, to enemies, to the wind. That is how they get word of unforeseen problems and opportunities, before anyone else. (Nulty, 1994)

Leaders are open-minded: Excessive self-confidence can lead to egotism and even arrogance; it certainly closes minds. Egotism on the part of the leader creates a bunch of 'yes' men and executives—who have stopped thinking and let their boss do the thinking. Even when in doubt about the grandiose plans made by their chief, they keep their mouths shut—for they know from experience that whatever may be their point of view, it would get stonewalled. Instead of hundred brains we have just one, single brain working.

Sensitivity to people and situations: The reality is that leaders cannot motivate nor can they persuade effectively—be it constituents or others—without having some sense of what's on their minds. So, unless they are always forthcoming about what is on their minds (which is unrealistic to expect), they must try to discern what they are thinking and feeling. Marwin Bower calls this attribute 'sensitivity to people'. Leaders should be polite, considerate, understanding and careful that what they say to someone is not dispiriting, unless criticism is intended. Leaders, especially chief executives, must also not be overheard discussing someone's job performance with another person. The fact is simple: leaders cannot persuade people, nor can they get people to do what is right for the organization—until they understand what the people are thinking and feeling.

Situations are created by people and must be dealt with by people. The leader of a company, who is called on to resolve a dispute or disagreement, must combine a careful analysis of the facts with an acute sensitivity to the feelings and attitudes of the people involved.

Some of the other qualities, which are pretty self-explanatory, are as follows:

1. Initiative,
2. Judgement,
3. Broad mindedness,
4. Flexibility and adaptability,
5. The capacity to make sound and timely decisions,
6. The capacity to motivate and
7. A sense of urgency.

Zenger and Folkman (2003), on the basis of their study using 360 Degree Feedback data of about 20,000 managers assessed by over

CHAPTER 3 What Makes a Good Leader? 29

200,000 assessors using 20 different instruments, have identified 20 insights on leadership. These remarkable insights are as follows:

1. Great leaders make a huge difference as compared to merely good leaders.
2. One organization can have many great leaders.
3. We have been aiming too low in our leadership activities. We should aim at producing outstanding leaders, rather than merely leadership improvement programmes.
4. The relationship between improved leadership and increased performance outcomes is neither precisely incremental nor linear.
5. Great leadership consists of processing several building blocks of capabilities, each complementing the other. These include character, personal capability, a focus on results, interpersonal skills and the ability to lead organizational change.
6. Leadership culminates in championing change.
7. All competencies are not equal. Some differentiate good leaders from great leaders, while others do not.
8. Leadership competencies are closely linked together.
9. Effective leaders have very varied personal styles. There is no single, right way to lead.
10. Effective leadership practices are specific to an organization. Leaders must fit the organization.
11. The key to developing great leadership is to build strengths.
12. Powerful combinations produce exponential results. For example, focus on results and interpersonal skills have powerful combinations. Improving interpersonal skills may be the best way to improve technical skills.
13. Greatness is not brought about by the absence of weakness.
14. Great leaders are not perceived as having major weaknesses.
15. Fatal flaws must be fixed. These include inability to learn from mistakes and develop new skills, being interpersonally inept, being closed to new ideas, failure to be accountable to results and not taking initiative.
16. Leadership attributes are often developed in non-obvious ways.
17. Leaders are made, not born.

18. Leaders improve their leadership effectiveness through self-development.
19. The organization, with the help of an immediate boss, provides significant assistance in developing leadership.
20. The quality of leadership in an organization seldom excels that of the person at the top.

From the study of this research on leadership using 360 Degree Feedback, the following implications can be drawn for building leadership competencies:

1. **Display high personal character:** Everything about great leadership radiates from character. Personal character improves the probability of exhibiting strong interpersonal skills. Character is based on innate values and high self-awareness.
2. **Start small:** Do something now that has immediate impact. Small things lead to big things. Identify some quick and readily visible things.
3. **Excel at something:** Zenger and Folkman (2003) indicate that the impact of one perceived strength moves leaders to the 64th percentile. Three strengths move them to the 81st percentile. They also suggest the candidate to figure out what he/she is good at and improve it to the 90th percentile.
4. **Connect competencies and leverage combinations:** See the power of combinations. For example, focus on results and interpersonal skills have powerful combinations.
5. **Use a non-linear approach to becoming a better leader:** Improving interpersonal skills may be the best way to improve technical skills.
6. **Build on your strengths:** Figure out what you do well and magnify it. It only takes strengths in a few areas to make an impact. Find what you do well and then figure out what combinations are required to be seen as more effective.
7. **Remedy fatal flaws:** These include the inability to learn from mistakes and develop new skills, interpersonal ineptness, being closed to new ideas, failure to be accountable to results, not taking initiative.
8. **Work on these fatal flaws fast and furiously.**

CHAPTER 3 What Makes a Good Leader? 31

One of the most moving quotes from the book *The Circle of Innovation* is: "I set as the goals the maximum capacity that people have—I settle for no less. I make myself a relentless architect of the possibilities of human beings."—Benjamin Zander, Conductor, Boston Philharmonic. Yes that is what leadership is all about:

"Relentless Architect of the Possibilities of Human Beings"

CHAPTER 4

Managerial and Leadership Roles

To be an effective manager, the most important first step is to learn to perform managerial roles that are appropriate to the managerial level, position and function. Top-level managers should be spending a significant part of their time on the following:

- Visualizing the future of the global economy and the local economy;
- Identifying opportunities (business opportunities, including new markets, new products, new technologies, new management practices and systems, new competencies, etc.) where the organization could make an impact;
- Thinking strategically, generating alternative business scenarios and making strategic choices in technology, markets, finance, customers, people and talent, processes, etc.;
- Benchmarking with the best and being sensitive to business information;
- Initiating processes in the organization to make use of these opportunities, by developing or revisiting the vision for the organization in the context of the new opportunities;
- Inspiring and enthusing employees with vision and opportunities, and enabling them to translate the vision into action and results;
- Generating resources and making them available;
- Being sensitive to the performance support and motivational support needs of the staff and providing them the same;
- Continuous competence building of the employees at individual and team levels so that they can make the organization perform;
- Setting standards, providing information, setting the direction for change and monitoring the same and
- Paying attention to the long-term interests of the organization by creating an appropriate culture and periodically drawing the attention of all employees to the organizational processes and systems.

CHAPTER 4 Managerial and Leadership Roles

These are just a few illustrative tasks. Every manager needs to identify, periodically, the most important tasks and set of roles he/she should perform on the basis of the needs of the organization, opportunities and other contextual factors.

Managers at middle levels and junior levels should be more concerned about:

- Understanding the organizational requirements;
- Making operational improvements;
- Setting short-term goals;
- Supervising, monitoring and motivating staff;
- Identifying developmental needs and providing for training;
- Understanding internal customers' needs and serving internal customers;
- Ensuring that teams work together and
- Ensuring that systems, norms and values are followed.

They are required to perform more of executive roles and less of roles in policy planning, conceptualizing, strategizing, change management, etc.

It is important for every manager to review the role requirements periodically and plan for improving his/her effectiveness. Such planning may include identifying important tasks that are not being performed at all or are being performed inadequately at present, identifying tasks that need not be performed at his/her level and are being performed (time wasters), identifying the time requirements for the new tasks and planning his/her time, processes and review mechanisms.

Most Neglected Roles and Tasks of Top Management

From the experience of the authors who were associated with the 360 Degree Feedback of over 8,000 senior and top level managers from different organizations, the following emerge as the most neglected roles:

- Articulating vision and values for one's unit or department or function,
- Inspiring and developing subordinates,

- Understanding and meeting internal customer needs and requirements,
- Teamwork and team building and
- Culture building and institutionalization.

Articulating Vision, Communicating and Inspiring Employees

> *A vision is a statement or group of statements having clear and compelling imagery that offers an innovative way to improve, which recognizes and draws on traditions and connects to actions that people can take to realize the change. Properly conveyed and presented, it creates enthusiasm and brings in commitment and energy to the workplace.*

Visionary leadership is the ability to create and articulate a realistic, credible, attractive vision of the future for an organization/organizational unit that grows out of, and improves on, the present. This vision, if properly selected and implemented, has an energizing effect and jump-starts the future by calling forth the skills, talents, motivation and resources to make it happen.

It is vital that the vision should have the following properties:

1. Inspirational possibilities which are:
   - Value-centric,
   - Realizable,
   - Of superior imagery,
   - Articulate,
   - Unique and
   - Offering a new order that can produce organizational distinction.

2. Clear imagery which offers new ways to improve and
3. Connects to actions that people can take to realize change.

A survey comprising 1500 senior managers and CEOs was conducted in the USA in the year 2000 to find the key traits desirable for a CEO. The survey was spread over 20 countries, and, out of the 1500 top-level managers surveyed, 870 were CEOs in large-sized organizations. Around 98 per cent of all respondents listed a 'strong sense of vision' as the most important trait responsible for success. Another study of 18 visionary companies versus 18 non-visionary companies, over a period of 65 years, showed that the financial positions of the 18 visionary companies were higher than the non-visionary ones by over 15 times.

Srivastava's (2003) study of transformational leadership of 10 Indian leaders indicated the following roles:

1. They showed courage in taking on challenging jobs and assignments.
2. They managed their relationships well, with peers, bosses, customers, suppliers, press, etc.
3. They communicated well with others.
4. They sought and encouraged feedback and did not get upset with negative feedback.
5. They motivated others.
6. They established direction for others.
7. They developed people and planned succession.
8. They articulated vision, developed commitment for the new vision and institutionalized the vision.
9. They planned their work well and set challenging goals.
10. They managed their time well.
11. They were result-oriented.
12. They managed change well.
13. They innovated.
14. They involved others in decision-making.
15. They had good track records, and the initial years of their careers were successful.
16. They were influenced by their bosses.

Examples of vision

'To be the single-source software provider to the financial services industry'.

'To be the leading African American car-owned promotional and public relations firm in the USA'.

'To become the most customer-responsive producer of an automobile interior firm in North America'.

BOX 4.1 LEADERSHIP STRATEGY: ATTENTION THROUGH VISION

Bennis and Nonus (1985) have emphasized the strategic role of vision in their book. In their study, the leaders seem to have involved themselves over and over again, in the following things when they took charge of their organizations: they paid attention to what was going on, they determined what part of the events at hand would be important for the future of the organization, they set a new direction and they concentrated the attention of everyone in the organization on it. Bennis and Nonus found that this was a universal principle of leadership, as true for orchestra conductors, army generals, football coaches and school superintendents as for corporate leaders.

A vision articulates a view of a realistic, credible and attractive future for the organization—a condition that is better in some important ways than what exists now. With a vision, the leader provides the all-important bridge from the present to the future of the organization.

There is a clear-cut distinction between the leader and the manager. By focusing attention on a vision, the leader operates on the *emotional and spiritual resources* of the organization, on its values, commitment and aspirations. The manager, by contrast, operates on the *physical resources* of the organization, on its capital, human skills, raw materials and technology. In leadership, leaders appeal to one of the most fundamental of human needs—the need to be important, to make a difference, to feel useful, to be a part of a successful and worthwhile enterprise.

To be able to shape a meaningful vision for an organization, the leader would need to critically look into the past and present needs and challenges facing an enterprise, as well as future possibilities. All of the leaders in the study by Bennis and Nonus seemed to have been masters at selecting, synthesizing and articulating an appropriate vision of the future.

Leaders require *foresight*, so that they can judge how the vision fits into the way the environment of the organization may evolve; *hindsight*, so that the vision does not violate the traditions and culture of the organization; *a world view*, within

(Box 4.1 Contd.)

(Box 4.1 Contd.)

> which to interpret the impact of possible new developments and trends; *depth perception*, so that the whole picture can be seen in appropriate detail and perspective; *peripheral vision*, so that the possible responses of competitors and other stakeholders to the new direction can be comprehended; and a process of *revision*, so that all visions previously synthesized are constantly reviewed as the environment changes.
>
> Leaders make a difference only when the vision has been successfully communicated throughout the organization and effectively institutionalized as a guiding principle. They are only as powerful as the ideas they can communicate.
>
> (Discussion based on the study by Bennis and Nonus, 1985.)

Articulating and developing organizational culture and values

Culture is defined as a system of shared meaning held by the employees of an organization, which differentiates that particular organization from the others. The 'system' is, in turn, a set of key principles and values shared by the members or employees of the organization. It gets reflected in the norms, behaviour patterns and habits of the people. If articulated well it becomes easier to promote.

Culture is a system which holds the organization together by providing standards for the behaviour of its members and hence directing their efforts towards the objectives. It is an informal code of conduct and control mechanism which guides attitudes and behaviour of the employees/members. Culture is the set of intangible standards which governs behaviour at the workplace.

Functions of culture

- Culture defines the boundary of the organization, thereby differentiating one organization from another.
- It establishes the identity of the organization and its perceived personality.

- It generates commitment towards a goal higher than any individual members.
- It lays down acceptable standards of performance and actions of the members.
- It is the control mechanism that guides and shapes the attitudes and behaviour of employees towards a common goal.
- It enhances organizational commitment and increases consistency of behaviour of members, thus reducing ambiguity.

Sustaining/maintaining culture

Practices and functions within the organization tend to reinforce the existing culture by giving the members a similar experience. Functions such as selection, performance appraisal procedures, training and career planning tend to ensure that members complying with it are rewarded. Some culture could also hand out punitive measures to members challenging or not complying with it.

Three forces are mainly responsible for maintaining culture in any organization:

1. Selection practices,
2. Top management behaviour and
3. Socialization methods.

Selection: The goal of any selection process is to choose a potential member for the organization with the necessary skills, knowledge and ability to perform certain tasks effectively. These factors apart, the decision-maker is also required to judge how well the potential member can fit into the organization. It is essential that the values of the potential member and those of the organization be properly matched, or at least as much as possible, to ensure organizational success. The core values of the potential members should not be against the values of the organization.

Top management behaviour: The culture of an organization is also influenced, to some extent, by the actions of the top management. The behaviour and actions of the top management get filtered down the hierarchy of an organization and establish informal norms and practices amongst the members. Consistency in the top management's actions, time and again, reinforces these intangible set standards and maintains them.

Socialization: It is the process which helps a new member gets adapted to the culture of an organization. The new member may not be aware of the culture, standards and norms specific to the organization. This unfamiliarity could cause him/her to challenge or disturb the culture.

Developing culture

The most effective ways of communicating culture across the organization's members are stories, rituals, material symbols and language.

Stories: Stories are specific to organizations. They are narratives or events and incidents about the organization's founders, rule breaking, rags-to-riches stories, reductions in the workforce, relocation of employees and organizational coping. These incidents or events would be a reflection of the culture and values of the organization. They would reinforce the principal values and provide explanations and legitimacy for current practices.

Rituals: These are repetitive in nature. They are a sequence of activities and practices that express the priority of goals, where people are important, and reinforce the key values of the organization. These need not necessarily exist as formal rules and could evolve through consistency.

Material symbols: These are those material goods that convey the importance of the member who has them. They express which behaviour is appropriate and desirable by the top management.

Language: Every organization has unique terms to describe and denote particular equipment or people or products related to the business. Assimilation of these terminologies is the language of that specific organization. The language is specific to the organization and could even exist as a subculture or a part of it. By learning this language, members signify their acceptance of the culture and help in maintaining it.

Inspiring, motivating and developing staff

Competent and motivated staff can make many things happen. Without capable people, all other resources lose their value. Technological advantages, financial advantages and other material resource advantages are time-bound and are amenable to change. Employee competencies, once developed, have continuing value. Enterprising people and entrepreneurial competencies can generate new technologies and new resources, but not vice versa. It is people who can make things happen. They have unlimited power, which only needs be brought out, brought up and used. This is possible through appropriate personnel policies, leadership styles and attitudes of senior and top-level managers. Investing time and effort on understanding, developing, motivating, guiding, empowering and supporting employees is a very crucial step for organizational effectiveness.

Recent literature on successful organizations has revealed that it is through people that organizations can build a sustainable competitive advantage. This can be done through the following:

- Senior managers and top-level managers spending sufficient time and effort in understanding, motivating and empowering their employees;
- Having performance management systems and practices that have an empowering value and implementing them seriously with appropriate time investments;
- Having good HRD policies, practices and systems;
- Investing time and effort on training and applications of knowledge gained through training;
- Providing continuous guidance and counselling to staff;
- Offering interesting work, giving clear-cut work directions and fixing accountabilities;
- Recognizing and rewarding desired behaviour;
- Having appropriate personnel policies;
- Being sensitive to discriminatory practices and establishing a sense of equity and justice on a continuing basis;
- Promoting values that show respect for people and their contributions and
- Having appropriate leadership and managerial styles.

CHAPTER 4 Managerial and Leadership Roles **41**

Robins (2002) has offered the following insights for managing people. These may be useful to remember:

1. The best predictor of a person's behaviour is his or her past behaviour.
2. Employees who exhibit good citizenship behaviour outperform those who do not.
3. Never underestimate the role that an organization's culture plays in an employee's success or failure.
4. People are happiest when employees are put in jobs that align with their personality.
5. The most powerful workplace motivator is 'recognition, recognition and recognition!'
6. No matter how motivated an employee is, his or her performance is going to suffer if there is no supportive work environment.
7. Leadership: It is impossible to lead people who do not trust you.
8. Too often, 20 years of experience is nothing more than one year of experience repeated 20 times.
9. No matter what a leader does, if the followers do not respond, then the leader fails.
10. Your job as a leader is to compensate for things lacking in the employee or the work environment.
11. Most leadership theories have a US bias.
12. Much of a company's success or failure is due to factors outside the influence of leadership.
13. Actions do speak louder than words.
14. Teams do often create negative synergy.
15. To perform well as team members, individuals must be able to communicate openly and honestly, to confront difference and resolve conflicts, and to sublimate personal goals for the good of the team.
16. Employees are increasingly recognizing that work is squeezing their personal lives and they are not happy about it.
17. Nearly 90 per cent of Fortune 1000 firms use 360 Degree Feedback for their employee appraisals.
18. It is difficult for employees to resist a decision in which they have already participated.

19. Older workers want to learn and are just as capable of learning as any other younger employees.
20. Managers often ignore the impact downsizing has on the survivors.

All these require proper attitudes, styles and behaviours to be shown by senior managers. Some of these are further discussed in the subsequent sections.

Internal customer orientation, collaboration and teamwork

Organizations that are quality conscious, customer oriented, cost conscious, technology driven, continuously changing and those that act with speed are likely to survive in a competitive world. As the people have become highly cost conscious, quality conscious and would like services to be delivered at their door step, it is inevitable for organizations to continuously improve their products and services. Producing products or offering services at a low cost depends not only on the technology but also on the internal efficiencies, overheads, processes and systems. Good quality products can be produced if everyone in the organization becomes quality conscious. Costs can be reduced if people do not have to waste their time in follow-ups and monitoring. Overheads will be less if internal customer orientation is high. Therefore, internal customer orientation is an important quality for managers at all levels. Senior executives and heads of departments should be highly customer driven (internal customer) in order to ensure quality, low costs and efficiency.

Experiences in most countries have indicated that departmentalization promotes managers to serve their own department's needs—this very often at the cost of other departments. Managing internal customers by continuously understanding their needs and expectations and attempting to meet them is an important role senior management should play. The following activities help them in the same:

- Strategic thinking,
- Culture building,
- Communication,

CHAPTER 4 Managerial and Leadership Roles   43

- Corporate principles and code of conduct,
- Periodic internal customer satisfaction surveys,
- Planned interdepartmental meets,
- Role negotiation exercises,
- Periodic informal get-togethers and social gatherings,
- Joint training programmes,
- Job rotation, interchangeability, attachments, etc. and
- Cross-functional teams.

Top Management Roles

Top management and other senior executives of any corporation are required to perform both leadership and managerial roles. The various activities that a manager undertakes are indicative of the roles he/she is playing. These roles can be broadly classified as managerial and leadership roles. Managerial roles normally deal with operational issues and managing for the present. Leadership roles deal with building for the future. Both are equally important and they need to be continuously balanced. Without managing the present, there may be nothing left for leading in the future. Without an eye on the future, mere management of the present may not lead to progress. Hence, both sets of roles need to be played effectively. Most managers tend to forget this and overemphasize or overplay some of them against the other.

Leadership roles

- Preparing a vision for future,
- Formulating long-term policies and strategies,
- Culture building,
- Inspiring and developing employees,
- Setting example,
- Mentoring and coaching,
- Empowering,
- Synergizing and
- Creating new technologies.

Managerial roles

- Short-term planning and goal setting,
- Monitoring systems,
- Performance monitoring,
- Setting standards,
- Co-coordinating,
- Networking,
- Managing technology and systems and
- Managing customers.

Institution-building role of top executives

- Building uniqueness and identity for the organization,
- Developing resources,
- Synergizing role,
- Balancing creativity and conformity,
- Building linkages between organization and external systems and society,
- Taking the organization into future,
- Making an impact on external environment and
- Providing superordination and a sense of fulfilment.

CHAPTER 5

Managerial and Leadership Styles

One of the most important tasks of a manager is to manage human resources. Effective management of human resources requires an understanding of the capabilities of subordinates, assigning them appropriate tasks, helping them acquire new capabilities, maintaining their motivation level and structuring the work so that people can derive some satisfaction from doing it. As one goes up the managerial ladder, he or she is required to spend an increasing amount of time interacting with people. These interactions may be on the shop floor, in group meetings, in dyadic transactions, through telephone conversations or in formal or informal gatherings. Many managers spend more than 50 per cent of their time interacting with their subordinates.

The effectiveness of the manager depends on both the content of the interaction and the manager's style. The manager's technical competence, functional knowledge, skills and information are very important in determining his or her effectiveness in managing subordinates. A capable manager is able to influence a subordinate by providing technical guidance and clear directions when needed. However, if the manager is not sensitive to the emotional needs of subordinates and does not use the appropriate styles of supervision and leadership, there is a great danger of crippling the growth of subordinates. For example, an authoritarian manager may arouse strong negative reactions by continually dictating terms to capable subordinates, but may do extremely well with subordinates who are dependent and who are just beginning to learn their roles. Similarly, a democratic manager may be liked by capable subordinates but seen as incompetent by dependent subordinates. It is necessary, therefore, for managers to interact differently with different people.

Styles of Managers and Leaders

Although all managers are unique in some way, certain styles are characteristic of majority of managers. Any manager may adopt more than one of these styles depending on the situation.

Authoritarian and democratic styles

As early as 1943, behavioural scientists Lippitt and White, at the University of Michigan, identified two types of leaders: authoritarian and democratic. The authoritarian leader determines all policies and strategies, decides on the composition and tasks of the work teams, is personal in giving praise and criticism, and maintains some personal distance from employees. In contrast, the democratic leader ensures that policies and strategies are determined by the group, gives technical advice whenever the group needs it, allows freedom to group members to choose their work teams, tries to be objective in providing rewards and punishments, and participates in discussions.

When Lippitt and White compared these two styles of management in their experimental studies, they found that authoritarians produced: (a) a greater quantity of work; (b) a greater amount of aggressiveness towards the leader; (c) less originality in work; (d) less work motivation; (e) more dependence; (f) less group feeling and (g) more suppressed discontent.

Task-oriented and employee-oriented styles

Blake and Mouton, in the year 1964, developed the concept of task-oriented and people-oriented leadership. The following sections explain the differences between these styles.

Task-oriented manager or leader

A task-oriented manager lays emphasis on the task, often believes that ends are more important than means and thinks that employees need to be supervised closely in order to accomplish their tasks. This type of manager becomes upset when tasks are not accomplished. The concern for accomplishment of tasks is so high that the human aspect is likely to be neglected in dealing with subordinates. This type of supervisor is likely to have difficulty in human relations and may appear to be a 'tough' person. A task-oriented supervisor may frequently question or remind subordinates about their tasks, warn them about deadlines or show a great deal of concern about details.

Employees who work with an excessively task-oriented manager often develop negative attitudes about their work and their manager. They may be motivated only by fear and may feel dissatisfied with their job. They may develop shortcuts that, in the long run, affect the organization's performance.

Employee-oriented supervisor

In contrast, the employee-oriented manager believes that concern for the needs and welfare of subordinates promotes both quality and quantity of work. This concern may be reflected in attempts to keep subordinates in good humour and in frequent inquiries about their problems (even those unrelated to work). On the other hand, this type of style may also lead to inefficiency. Subordinates may perceive this type of supervisor as too lenient and may take advantage of his/her concern.

The task-oriented and employee-oriented styles may not be present in pure forms, and a manager may demonstrate combinations of both styles. The effectiveness of the styles may also depend on factors such as the nature of the task or the nature of the subordinate.

Subsequent work by Fiedler, in the year 1967, indicated that the effectiveness of task-oriented on people-oriented styles is contingent on situational factors such as the power of the leader, acceptance of the supervisor by subordinates and the way in which the tasks are structured.

Goleman's Leadership Styles

Goleman (2002) identified six styles as the basic leadership styles: visionary, coaching, affiliative, democratic, pace-setting and commanding. He also indicated the effect each of these styles has on the work environment. He even suggested, on the basis of his studies, the appropriate usage of these styles. The results of his work are summarized in Table 5.1.

TABLE 5.1 Leadership Styles, Their Impact and Appropriateness

Leadership Style	Resonance	Impact on Climate	When Appropriate	
1	Visionary	Moves people towards shared dreams	Most strongly positive	Need for a new vision or a clear direction
2	Coaching	Connects what a person wants with the organizational goal	Highly positive	Help an employee improve performance by building long-term capabilities
3	Affiliative	Creates harmony by connecting people to each other	Positive	Heals rifts in a team, motivates during stressful times or strengthens connection
4	Democratic	Values people's inputs and gets commitment through participation	Positive	To build consensus, or get valuable inputs from employees
5	Pace-setting	Meets challenging and exciting goals	Frequently executed poorly, often highly negative	To get high-quality results from a motivated and competent team
6	Commanding	Soothes fears by giving clear direction in an emergency	Often misused, highly negative	Best in crisis, to kick-start a turnaround, or with problem employees

Nurturant Task Leader

J.B.P. Sinha has been doing a lot of research in the area of appropriate styles of leadership in the Indian scenario. His studies indicate that the nurturant task (NT) leadership style is the most appropriate style in Indian settings. Given the Indian culture which is characterized by dependence and relationship orientation, leaders who nurture people can be more effective (Sinha, 1980, 1984).

The results of a study conducted by Sinha revealed that Indian executives are more positively inclined to accepting NT leadership than to authoritarian (A) or participative (P) type of leadership. The NT leader was found to be perceived by the respondents as 'active, strong, dominant, firm, independent, alert, encouraging and extrovert'.

He is strict and can get work done. He is different from the A type leader who was found to be autocratic, influential, insecure, impractical, dissatisfying and hence not respected by others. The two types of leaders, i.e. NT and A, however, do have some overlap. Both are strict, both push their ideas through and try to dominate subordinates' activities. The NT type leader was found to be closer to the P type leader who was reported to be democratic, respected, satisfying, secure and skilful, though weak. NT as well as P type of leaders were found to be encouraging and gave due credit to members, without losing control.

The foundation of human relationship lies in the family system and socio-cultural norms of a society. The Indian home provides a good deal of affection, warmth and stimulation for the growth of its children. A child, when grows up and joins an organization, carries highly personal and emotional ties with him. He forms his relationships in the organization on the basis of these ties. An Indian, as a leader, carries an image of a benevolent father or elder brother in his organization. This image is not relevant to Western countries where a radically different type of family structure and relationships exists. The following expectations of the subordinates must be kept in mind to be a successful leader in an Asian setting:

- Nurturing, personal attention and help from superiors in learning and problem-solving similar to what they received in their family lives.
- Acceptance of an individual as an extension of oneself in a family-like network of affiliations. That is, the relationship has

to be personalized rather than contractual. It must reflect his/her prestige and power and he/she must be recognized by his/her superior.
- Reward for loyalty along with efficiency and other qualities. Disregard or discouragement to loyalty may be taken as betrayal of personal confidence and trust. It might demoralize or affect behaviour.

The implication of Sinha's studies is that the leader should not underplay the importance of relationships and the need for nurturing, and should bear in mind India's history of feudalism, paternalistic management and the need to be nurtured. Sinha's study has stimulated a lot of research in India. Even recent studies of forest officers have indicated a preference for NT leadership styles by village folks, as contrasted with the preferred (P) style by forest officials (Parul, 2002).

Benevolent, Critical and Self-dispensing Styles

Another way of looking at managerial and leadership styles by T.V. Rao in the mid-1970s has been used in various countries with satisfactory results. This classification was influenced by the writing and work on institution builders and institutional managers by David McClelland of Harvard University and by Stewart's concept of psychosocial maturity (Rao and Stewart, 1975).

While working with David McClelland and Abigail Stewart, Rao was analysing the Thematic Apperception Test (TAT) stories written by Indian managers. In these stories, they found that four different orientations of managers were depicted by the story writers. These four styles were further condensed on the basis of later observations by Rao. In this concept, leadership or managerial styles stem from three mutually exclusive orientations: benevolent, critical and self-dispensing.

Benevolent style

This style helps protect subordinates, continually tells them what they should and should not do, and comes to their rescue whenever needed. Such managers cater to their subordinates' needs for security and are generally liked by them. They are effective as long as they are physically present. In their absence, workers may experience a lack of direction and motivation. Such managers tend to have dependent followers, and initiative-taking behaviour may not be reinforced.

Critical style

This style takes a critical approach towards employees and does not tolerate mistakes, for quality of work, undisciplined behaviour or individual peculiarities. Finding mistakes, criticizing subordinates and making them feel incompetent are characteristic behaviours of critical managers. Subordinates may produce acceptable work out of fear, but they do not like this type of manager.

Self-dispensing style (developmental)

This style inspires confidence in subordinates, helps them set broad goals and allows them to work on their own. Guidance is provided only when requested by subordinates. Competent workers who have this kind of supervision are likely to feel confident about their work. They are free to work both independently and interdependently with their colleagues.

Institutional manager

Closely related to a self-dispensing manager is what McClelland and Burnham (1995) refer to as an institutional manager, because this type of manager is involved in developing the department or unit. Such managers are also called institution builders because they ensure the growth and development of their units and subordinates by incorporating processes that help people to give their best and to grow with the organization. McClelland and Burnham identified the following characteristics of institutional managers:

1. They are organization-oriented and tend to join organizations and feel responsible for building them.
2. They are disciplined in their work and enjoy their work.
3. They are willing to sacrifice some of their own self-interests for the welfare of the organization.

4. They have a keen sense of justice.
5. They have a low need for affiliation, a high need to influence others for social or organizational goals and a disciplined or controlled way of expressing their power needs.

Such managers often aim at a self-dispensing style, but are flexible in their own use of styles. They are likely to create highly motivating work environments in their organization.

Implications of Styles

No single style is universally effective. The effectiveness of the style depends on the employee, the nature of the task and various other factors. If a new employee does not know much about the work, a benevolent manager or leader is helpful, a critical manager or leader may be frightening and a self-dispensing manager or leader may cause bewilderment. On the other hand, a capable employee may feel most comfortable with a self-dispensing style of management and resent a benevolent manager who continually gives unwanted advice.

Employees with low self-discipline probably could be developed best by critical style, at least on an intermittent basis. Continual use of critical style, however, is unlikely to be effective. Flexibility and perceptiveness regarding when to use each style are useful attributes for leaders or managers.

Leadership Styles and Motivational Climate

The effectiveness of any leadership lies in the kind of work environment that is created in the organization. Managers may find the following suggestions helpful in creating a proper motivational climate.

Create a climate of independence and interdependence rather than dependence

A self-dispensing or developmental manager promotes an independent and interdependent climate for subordinates and does not interfere unless it becomes necessary. Subordinates are trusted and given freedom to plan their own ways of doing their work. They are expected to solve problems and to ask for guidance only when it is needed. By providing freedom of work, encouraging initiative and supporting experimentation and teamwork, a manager also helps in satisfying the subordinates' needs for belonging, affection and security.

Some managers allow their subordinates to come to them continually for advice and guidance and, in extreme cases, may not allow them to do anything on their own. If every subordinate should check with the manager and obtain approval before taking any action, the manager is creating a climate of dependence and the subordinates will not be able to take any initiative. When problems arise, they may hesitate to look for solutions, and when something goes wrong, they may not accept responsibility. Learning from experience becomes difficult for them because they have always turned to their manager for advice. Thus, the manager becomes burdened with responsibilities and problem-solving. Not only are the manager's energies wasted, but so are those of the subordinates.

Create a climate of competition through recognition of good work

Employees look forward to being rewarded for good or innovative work. Financial rewards are not always necessary; even a word of appreciation has great motivational value. Although appreciation given indiscriminately loses its value, a manager should not withhold appreciation until the formal appraisal reports. Many other ways of recognizing good work can be very rewarding. Giving praise in the presence of others, giving increased responsibility and writing letters of commendation and recommendation can be used in addition to financial rewards. Such recognition and public acknowledgement help employees to value work and to derive a sense of satisfaction and a feeling of importance. These go a long way in motivating them to perform better. They even create a sense of competition among employees.

Create a climate of approach and problem-solving rather than avoidance

Some managers approach problems with confidence, face them squarely, work out mechanisms to solve them (often with the help of others) and constantly work to overcome problems. They derive satisfaction from this struggle—even if the outcome is not always positive—and they inspire subordinates to imitate their initiative.

Some managers, however, see everything as a headache and postpone solutions to problems or delegate them to someone else. Workers also are quick to imitate this avoidance.

Create an ideal climate through personal example

Just as managers are imitated in their approaches to problem-solving, they are viewed as models for other work habits. In fact, the manager's styles may filter down the hierarchy and influence employees several grades below. Therefore, good supervision and good work habits make the manager's job easier in two ways: his or her own tasks are done more efficiently, and a climate is created for making the department or unit more efficient.

Motivate people through guidance and counselling

The following discussions point out some general strategies that managers can use in creating the proper motivational climate for their subordinates. However, because individual workers have individual needs, individual counselling also can motivate subordinates. Within a group of workers, a manager may find very efficient workers, poor workers, problem creators, cooperative employees and so on. Therefore, the manager should be sensitive to their individual differences.

Khandwalla (1995) identified and used top 10 management styles: conservative and entrepreneurial styles, professional and intuitive styles, participative and authoritarian styles, organic and bureaucratic styles, and the familial and paternalistic style and the altruistic style. These 10 are proposed as pure styles. Khandwalla did a lot of work using these styles of the top management and proposed that each of these styles can be used both effectively and ineffectively. The measurement of each style is not on the basis of one individual but on a group of top-level managers who have knowledge of the company. They are expected to assess the top management as a group and, on the basis of the responses, the management style is identified for the organization.

CHAPTER 5 Managerial and Leadership Styles 55

In the 360 Degree Feedback workshops conducted earlier, this tool was also used. The results of the study of top-level managers attending the leadership styles and organizational excellence programmes at the Indian Institute of Management (IIM) indicated that developmental style was found to promote pure management style and impede defective management styles. It was also found that critical leadership style impedes the pure management style and promotes defective management styles (Khandwalla, 1995). Many other relationships emerging from the 360 Degree Feedback data were discussed by Khandwalla in his book on management styles.

A research study at TVRLS has indicated that the three different Indian styles (benevolent, critical and developmental) have different impacts on subordinates as well as the work environment (Rao and Rao, 2002). This study of 48 managers, from one company, using their 360 Degree Feedback indicated that the benevolent style produced dependence and resentment while critical style also resulted in limited learning and, at the same time, resentment towards the boss. The developmental style was found to result in feelings of job satisfaction as well as learning. The impact of the three different styles found from the research study at TVRLS is summarized in Table 5.2 (see Rao and Rao, 2002 for more details). Table 5.2 gives the characteristics of the three leadership styles.

Impact of Leadership Styles and Appropriateness of Their Use

Sustained use of leadership style leads to the effects depicted in Table 5.3.

TABLE 5.2 Characteristics of the Three Leadership Styles

Task Area	Leadership Style and Its Characteristics		
	Benevolent	Critical	Developmental
Goal setting or task allocation	Assigns tasks on the basis of likes and dislikes to people	Assigns tasks in an impersonal way, without consideration for the person and his/her competencies, in a purely rule-oriented and bureaucratic way	Assigns according to competencies with a view to provide challenges and experiences of success in a planned way. Recognizes and respects individual differences and builds people
Management of mistakes	Comes to the rescue and salvages the situation. Protects subordinates	Has very low tolerance. Loses temper, reprimands, criticizes and even punishes for mistakes	Helps employees to learn from mistakes, encourages the use of mistakes as learning opportunities
Articulating vision	Has personal vision and shares them with those close to him/her	Short-terms goal-oriented. Not so much vision driven	Shares vision and enthuses others with vision. Helps them to internalize and feel a part of the vision. Builds on the vision of others and incorporates the same into his/her vision
Managing failures	Rescues subordinates. Favours particularly the loyal ones by showing more affection and warmth as a response to deal with failures	Cannot tolerate failures. Reprimands and punishes	Helps people to learn from failures

Managing conflicts	Decides who is right and who is wrong and resolves conflicts amicably	Calls both parties and expresses irritation or shows the rule book or loses temper or rules by fear	Encourages the conflicting parties to come together and resolve their conflicts and build capabilities of conflict resolution
Rewarding and recognizing	Rewards those close to him and rewards selectively	Does not reward or recognize easily. Feels that it may spoil employees	Rewards and encourages all deserving cases as and when needed. Uses recognition and various forms of rewards as empowering tools
Communicating and sharing information	Share information selectively with those close to him/her	Does not share information. Feels powerful by keeping information with him/her and fears the misuse of information by others	Shares information with a view to build others. Shares it freely
Empowerment	Empowers those close to him/her	Does not empower any one. Keeps all power to himself/herself	Empowers all
Delegation	Delegates selectively to those loyal to him/her	Does not delegate but closely supervises and monitors and controls all the time	Delegates and develops people to exercise discretion
Systems use	Uses systems but modifies them to suit the favoured ones	Strict disciplinarian. Follows systems meticulously for their own sake	Systems driven. Uses systems to empower and build a lasting culture

TABLE 5.3 Impact of Leadership Styles on Subordinates and Their Appropriateness of Use

Style	Sustained use of this style leads to....	Use this style when....
Benevolent or paternalistic or relationship-oriented	• Personal loyalty to the leader	• The employee is new
	• Enjoyment of work due to relationship with or pleasing the boss	• Task is new and relationships are important
	• Dependence on the leader	• With employees who are accustomed to a paternalistic leader till such time they get adjusted
	• Feeling of loss in his/her absence or exit from the scene	• With dependent employees who need care and affection
	• Inability to get along with other professionals or systems-driven managers	
	• Learning is by those who are close or loyal to him/her	
Critical leadership	• Feelings of incompetence on the part of the subordinates	• With undisciplined subordinates
	• Resentment towards the boss	• When norms are being violated and personal goals have taken precedence over the organizational goals

	• Preference for leaving the boss or situation	
	• Job tensions	
	• High energy levels spent on the job due to tension and fear	• Indiscipline is on the rise
	• Low self-esteem	• Turnaround is needed and some short-term goal orientation and systems are important
Developmental leader	• Independence or interdependence	• With competent employees
	• Teamwork, provided it is moderated well	• Mature organization
	• High degree of learning	• Technical and R&D departments
	• Professionalism and systems orientation	• Those who need to be kept independent and protected from other transactional costs
	• High satisfaction culture building	
	• Empowerment	

PART 2

Designing and Implementing a 360 Degree Feedback Programme

PART 1

CHAPTER 6

360 Degree Feedback: The Power Tool

The CEO of a company is told that he is not visiting his units enough and spending as much time as was expected. Consequence—the employees are self-sufficient and independent but feel directionless at times. They would be inspired to do many more things if they had more interaction with him. After this feedback, the CEO decides to increase the frequency of meetings with his unit heads. Since there were too many places to visit, he decides to initiate a communication mechanism which will enable him to keep in touch more frequently with his unit heads.

Another CEO gets feedback that he is a visionary and a developmental leader. His short temper, however, creates frequent fear of him and demotivation, thus affecting their work. Satisfaction levels could be far higher if he can manage to keep cool. This CEO was already aware of his temperament and now knows the consequences it is creating. He decides to explore ways of controlling his temper or at least minimizing it in case he is not able to control himself.

Yet another top-level manager gets feedback that he is an idea man and also imposes his ideas. As a result people feel stale, feel that they are merely there to follow instructions and, in effect, their creativity is getting killed.

Another divisional head gets feedback that he is sincere, loyal, meticulous, highly committed, hard-working, disciplined, has a lot of technical knowledge, but people do not like working with him as he lacks human touch.

Here is what the HRD manager of one of the Birla Group companies had to report about his line managers: One of their senior executives had undergone the 360 Degree Feedback exercise.

64 THE POWER OF 360 DEGREE FEEDBACK

Before the 360 Degree Feedback exercise, the senior executive was perceived as:

1. A task-oriented person,
2. Working in isolation,
3. Not sharing information with other team members,
4. Highly cost-conscious in nature,
5. Giving less importance to people-development-related matters,
6. Always speaking about profitability/productivity and
7. Less involved with local government officials/political leaders/ other local people.

After the 360 Degree Feedback exercise, he was found to be:

1. Sharing all information with his team members and all staff/ workers,
2. Team-working, i.e. involvement of all senior managers/other concerned people,
3. Always talking about people-development-related matters,
4. Always attending training programmes/workshops and addresses the gathering,
5. Believing that company's image building is with people and their attitudinal aspects and
6. More involved with union leaders/local government officials/ other leaders, etc.

Each one of us has some strength or the other. We also have some idea of what we may be weak at. We may be right or wrong but we do carry self-perceptions. Is it not common that we discover our potential in new areas sometimes to our own surprise? We take a lot of our strengths and weaknesses for granted and do not bother to spend time to explore and discover them. What we think as our strength also has limitations and what we see as our weak area has a brighter side. We may also not be aware that we have some strengths which are noticed by others and one or two weak areas which affect our effectiveness.

When the four persons, mentioned above, found out the impact of their behaviour, or qualities, on others, they decided to do something to bring about change. Two of them said that they were aware of some lacunae and the 360 Degree Feedback that they obtained confirmed

CHAPTER 6 360 Degree Feedback: The Power Tool 65

the truth in their feelings. One of them was taken by surprise. He did not know that people were averse to working with him. All along he was being praised for his loyalty, sincerity and technical knowledge, and it never occurred to him that he had a negative impact on others. He now started seeing the reason why people joining his department wanted to be transferred frequently. He was all along attributing it to the hard work he expected them to put in and did not realize his lack of human touch.

Some of us are more aware of our strengths only and take our weaknesses, and their negative impact on others, for granted. Others are more aware of their weaknesses but take them for granted as a part of their personality and even consider them as 'God-given'. This affects their self-worth and they unknowingly carry a small part of this with them. These kinds of persons point out the weak areas of others, set low expectations for themselves so that they do not have to face failures, or blame others for their inadequacies (parents, teachers, some seniors who taught them and society at large).

How do we work on their failings? The first prerequisite for working on these weaknesses is to recognize how we come across to others and use this learning for correcting or preparing more accurate self-concepts. Self-awareness does not mean accepting everything the other person says. We often found, in our 360 Degree Feedback, that some individuals create different impressions on different individuals. Surprisingly, in some cases, a particular quality or behaviour, seen as a strength by some, is seen as a weakness by others.

We came across one head of department in a company who was assessed for his 'sociability' as a strength by some and as a weakness by others. When he investigated further, it became clear that sociability was a characteristic trait of this person. He gave parties, socialized well with people in the colony where he lived, mixed without being conscious of status, was jovial, etc. Some of his subordinates felt that they were easily able to get things done from other departments as he had a good equation with his colleagues. A few others felt that they were able to get things done as he was respected. However, he was known to talk loosely about some of his colleagues in social gatherings that he organized and this damaged the reputation of those individuals. All this was not known to him prior to his 360 Degree Feedback. After the feedback he investigated to find out more about the darker and brighter sides of his sociability. Today he is wiser. He continues to build his strengths on his sociability trait. People may not have noticed this change in him, but he says, 'I am aware about my change. I am very happy that I got my 360 Degree Feedback, which has prompted me to discover more of the impact I am making on others'.

All the other persons mentioned above have made changes in their roles or styles to some extent. In two cases, these were noticed and complimented on by their juniors and other colleagues. In two other cases, the individuals prepared action plans and implemented them, but this may or may not have been noticed immediately. In the long run, however, they were confident about the better impact they were likely to have. At least there was a change in their sensitivity and confidence levels.

Objectives of 360 Degree Feedback or Multi-rater Assessment Feedback (MAF)

It is possible to aim at the following through 360 Degree Feedback or MAF:

- Providing insights into the strong and weak areas of the candidate in terms of the effective performance of roles, activities, styles, traits, qualities, competencies (knowledge, attitudes and skills), impact on others, among others;
- Identifying developmental needs and preparing development plans, more objectively, in relation to current or future roles and performance improvements for an individual or a group of individuals;
- Generating data to serve as a more objective basis for rewards and for taking other personnel-related decisions;
- Reinforcing other change management efforts and interventions for organizational effectiveness, which may include total quality management (TQM) efforts, customer or internal customer satisfaction-enhancing interventions, flat structures, quality-enhancing and cost-reducing interventions and decision process changes;
- Aligning individual and group goals with organizational vision, values and goals;
- Culture building;

CHAPTER 6 360 Degree Feedback: The Power Tool **67**

- Leadership development;
- Potential appraisal and development;
- Career planning and development;
- Succession planning and development;
- Team building;
- Planning internal customer satisfaction improvement measures and
- Role clarity and increased accountabilities.

Advantages of the 360 Degree Feedback or MAF

The 360 Degree Feedback appraisal systems have certain advantages. These advantages are not substitutes for traditional appraisal methods but supplement them. Normally MAF should be viewed as supplements to the regular key performance area (KPA)- or key result area (KRA)-based appraisal systems rather than as replacements of the same.

Additional advantages offered by MAF are as follows:

- It is more objective than a one-person assessment of traits and qualities.
- It adds to objectivity and supplements the traditional appraisal system.
- It provides feedback which is normally more acceptable to an employee.
- It can serve all the purposes met by a traditional appraisal system like identifying the developmental needs, reward management, performance development, etc.
- It helps focus on internal customer satisfaction.
- It has the potential of pointing out managerial biases in traditional appraisal systems.
- It is a good tool for enhancing customer service and quality of inputs to internal customers.
- It provides scope for the candidate to get multiple inputs to improve his/her role, performance, styles and ideas and enhances the acceptability of the individual.
- It is more participative and enhances the quality of HR decisions.

- It is suitable for new organizational cultures being promoted by most world-class organizations (participative culture, learning culture, quality culture, competence-based performance culture, teamwork, empowering culture, leadership culture, etc.).

Prerequisites for Participation in 360 Degree Feedback or MAF

360 Degree Feedback systems can be very sensitive. A person who is not well prepared for it can be thrown out of balance. It can also create some new issues in an organization. If not designed and conducted well, it has the potential danger of developing wrong perceptions or notions in the candidate about one or more of his/her assessors and could also make him/her develop new attitudes towards himself/herself. It is therefore necessary and important to manage the process well and make it foolproof. The first important step is to determine if the organization is ready for it. The second important step is to determine if the candidate is ready for it. The following are the indicators of an organization's readiness for MAF:

1. The top management of the organization is committed to develop the competencies of employees on a continuous basis.
2. There are a number of HRD systems operating in the organization and they are being taken seriously in implementation.
3. The top management is serious about creating opportunities for employees to learn from each other and learn from their mistakes.
4. The top management is willing to invest its time and effort in giving feedback to its own subordinates.
5. The top management and senior managers take the current appraisal system seriously and do all that is required to ensure its effective implementation.
6. The top management and senior managers conduct their performance review and organization sessions regularly.
7. The top management is adequately committed to competence building through multi-rater feedback.
8. The top management is willing to subject itself for an assessment by its subordinates and colleagues.
9. There are not too many status barriers and ego problems in the organization.
10. People take feedback supportively and use it for development.

11. There is not too much of politics in the organization.
12. People are not likely to use the feedback for playing politics.
13. There is a high degree of systems orientation being attempted by the organization.
14. The organization already is in the process of becoming a customer-driven organization.
15. There is a good degree of team work being practised in the organization.
16. The HRD department has a high level of credibility.
17. Top management interventions are not seen with suspicion by the employees.
18. Managers are interested in learning about themselves.
19. There is a high degree of process orientation in the organization.
20. The organization is value-driven.
21. Softer issues of management, such as managing people, professionalism and development, are handled well in the organization.
22. Managers take their jobs seriously and learn.
23. There is a high degree of emphasis on competence building.
24. The organization has a history of taking all change management tools seriously and implementing them till the end.
25. People in the organization take feedback seriously and try to benefit from the same.

The following are indicators to assess the readiness of a candidate for MAF:

1. The candidate has a desire to know himself/herself through the eyes of others. He/she is willing to receive feedback from others and does not become over-defensive.
2. The candidate desires to be better.
3. The candidate is receptive and respects the views of others.
4. The candidate should be a learning-oriented individual.
5. The candidate has an attitude for healthy competition.
6. The candidate should have at least one and a half years of experience (except in the case of management trainees).
7. The candidate should have a direct working relationship with at least six individuals who can rate him/her.
8. The candidate should have no history of any previous psychological or psychiatric problems.

Maximizing the Value of 360 Degree Feedback or MAF

Tornow and London along with CCL Associates (1998) have outlined a number of suggestions for maximizing the value of 360 Degree Feedback. A 360 Degree Feedback survey, which collects inputs from superiors, subordinates, peers and even customers, offers a complete picture of people's performance, pinpointing where improvements need to be made. In the rest of this chapter we summarize the main points from their book.

Based on 360 Degree Feedback, you can:

- Create an organization-wide performance management system for all employees and managers. This system communicates, on a continuous basis, the skills and behaviours that your company expects from its managers and employees. It also helps people manage the many relationships that form the core of your organization's performance. Successful working relationships mean success for the company.
- Link individual and group goals to company strategy. Individuals, teams and departments can focus too much on their performance and not enough on the performance of the company as a whole. This summary shows how 360 Degree Feedback surveys can prevent that error.
- Create a culture of continuous learning. A 360 Degree Feedback programme can transform your company into a learning organization in which learning is as important as the daily performance of the work.

Performance Evaluations: Why Everyone's Input Is Needed

A 360 Degree Feedback programme gathers information, usually through a questionnaire, about the performance of employees or managers from people all around them—including peers, subordinates and even customers. This type of multi-perspective evaluation is more complete and accurate than the traditional top-down evaluation. Superiors see only a portion of a manager's performance. They need other perspectives to fill in the blanks. Subordinates, for example, can provide important information on the leadership qualities of a manager. Customers are in a better position, than anyone, to evaluate how employees perform with customers.

A 360 Degree Feedback evaluation is also valuable because people do not act the same towards everyone. The interpersonal skills of a manager are probably more accurately reflected in feedback from subordinates or peers than in feedback from a manager's superiors.

Another important aspect of 360 Degree Feedback is the inclusion of self-evaluations. Ratings by others will probably be more accurate, but self-evaluations force employees and managers to sit down and think about their strengths and weaknesses.

Finally, 360 Degree Feedback evaluations have the advantage of confidentiality. Top-down evaluations are usually not confidential. Managers must be prepared to defend their evaluations, which may cause them to soften or in some way alter what they might have said anonymously. Since 360 Degree Feedback involves groups of raters, the results are anonymous. These results are therefore less likely to be based or skewed either positively or negatively. Needless to say, raters should be asked to evaluate the dimensions, or elements, of a person's performance that they know best.

Drawbacks

Not every process is perfect and 360 Degree Feedback programmes are no exception. For example, subordinates may rate bosses high because they are afraid of retaliation. Peers tend to evaluate each other positively as well, perhaps to avoid disrupting the group. On the other hand, peers who are competing against each other for promotions may tend to rate their colleagues on the lower side. Nevertheless, the number of people and variety of perspectives involved in a 360 Degree Feedback process should ensure a generally unbiased and accurate view of a person's performance.

Create a Performance Management System

Do not just use 360 Degree Feedback piecemeal on individual performance improvement programmes (see Box 6.1). Maximize the value of 360 Degree Feedback by using it as the foundation of an organization-wide performance management system that applies to

> **BOX 6.1 DO NOT USE FEEDBACK FOR APPRAISALS**
>
> A 360 Degree Feedback programme should be used to help managers and employees identify weaknesses in their performance and develop their skills and competencies. Many experts discourage using 360 Degree Feedback for purposes other than performance development—purposes such as performance appraisals, salary action or promotion decisions, for example.
>
> When ratings affect a person's salary or job assignment, raters might be less inclined to honestly express their opinion of another's performance. In addition, when money is at stake, recipients of the feedback could get defensive instead of focusing on how they can improve their performance.
>
> Thus, using 360 Degree Feedback for performance appraisal destroys its effectiveness as a personal development tool.
>
> Tornow and London believe that 360 Degree Feedback should be used solely for development purposes at first. Only when employees and managers are fully comfortable collecting and using feedback for performance improvement, should the process be carefully expanded to include appraisal.

all individuals and groups in your company. This performance management system will:

- Help your people focus on the skills and competencies which the organization believes are important and
- Reinforce the working relationships throughout your company that define an organization's performance.

Focusing on what is important

The items in a 360 Degree Feedback survey distributed throughout the company enable employees and managers to focus their attention on the skills and competencies that their company expects from them. For example, a 360 Degree Feedback survey developed by the Centre for Creative Leadership includes the following three items:

1. This person patiently allows good people to develop.
2. This person makes direct reports more visible to higher management.

3. This person sets a challenging climate to encourage individual growth.

These items send the clear message that the company considers the development of skills and experiences of subordinates as a key leadership role for managers.

Since feedback surveys must be distributed to both raters and the people being rated, the message is widely disseminated.

Connectivity

The performance of an organization depends on how well individuals and groups within the organization relate to each other and to customers—what the authors call 'connectivity'.

At the individual level, 360 Degree Feedback connects employees and managers to their 'constituencies', which include superiors, peers, subordinates and external customers. The stronger the connection, the better people can understand and meet the various needs and expectations of their constituencies and, thus, the better they are at performing their jobs.

The link between relationship management and performance applies at the functional level as well. Any function or department in your company must meet the needs of various constituencies, including top management, other functions, customers and employees within that function.

In the past, the importance of these relationships was not always recognized, especially among different functions. A product design group might create a new product without consulting with production on its manufacturing feasibility or with marketing on whether customers wanted the new product.

Maintaining close working relationships between departments or functions is challenging because their needs and expectations are often in conflict. Marketing has one set of needs, engineering another and production a third. Somehow, functional managers must find a way to balance the needs of their own functions with the expectations of other functions.

To sum up, you must encourage individual employees and functional groups throughout the organization to take charge of getting feedback from their constituencies on a regular basis. This ensures an organization-wide performance management system that is not only ongoing but also decentralized. People will no longer have to wait for performance improvement programmes to be launched at top management's will.

Align Individual and Company Goals

You can use 360 Degree Feedback to determine whether individuals and departments are achieving their assigned tasks by meeting the needs of their constituencies. But are those tasks relevant to the goals of the company? Do they add to the company's competitive advantage? Are managers focused on the issues and priorities that the company considers important to its survival?

A second way in which 360 Degree Feedback adds value to your company's organizational development is by aligning the goals of individuals and groups to the goals of the company.

Link to strategy

A 360 Degree Feedback programme communicates the company's direction or strategy and the behaviours and values required to implement this strategy. This is especially valuable when the strategy is changing and employees or managers are unclear on how (or even if) they should change their behaviour.

For example, in response to competitive pressures, a company decides that it is not in the business of manufacturing computers but rather in the business of helping customers find solutions. This means convincing its hard-core engineers to become customer-oriented problem solvers. By emphasizing interpersonal and customer-response behaviours in its 360 Degree Feedback performance feedback surveys, the company can send engineers the message that technology no longer dominates the company's culture.

Monitoring change

A 360 Degree Feedback programme will not only help you communicate new strategies and expected behaviour to employees, it will also help you monitor how well the company and its employees are accepting and adapting to the changes.

CHAPTER 6 360 Degree Feedback: The Power Tool 75

A 360 Degree Feedback survey of employees, six months after you launch an organizational change effort, will tell you whether employee behaviour is moving in the direction of the change. You can also look at aggregate results—that is the combined results of groups of individuals—to see if certain teams or departments are lagging behind in performance.

Business-related feedback

In conclusion, development programmes based on 360 Degree Feedback must be tied to business results. Employees or managers will not learn new skills and behaviour for which they see no purpose. 'We are losing our creative edge' or 'We are changing our production process' are clear examples of business reasons for learning (and being assessed on) new skills.

Customer Input Adds Strategic Value

The ultimate goal of your corporate strategy is to satisfy a targeted group of customers and keep it loyal. Customer input in the 360 Degree Feedback process is vital in making the process strategically relevant.

Design phase input

When designing a 360 Degree Feedback survey for your employees, involve your customers to ensure that the questions on the survey are tuned to their needs, expectations and priorities.

Customer involvement reinforces the important link between customer requirements and the ultimate success of the company in the minds of your employees.

Customer-oriented items in the survey will also focus your employees' attention on the specific skills and competencies that give you a competitive advantage in your customers' eyes.

Customer feedback

Customer-oriented survey items usually generate either process feedback or outcome feedback. In other words, the questions in the survey help your company get feedback on how your customers view the way the product or service was delivered (the process) or whether they were satisfied with the end product or service (the outcome).

At the organizational level, customer feedback will help you assess your strategic decisions. Are you offering the products or services that your customers find valuable? Have you put into place processes for delivering the product or service that customers need and appreciate? Customer feedback will also help you assess the performance of your employees. Do they have the skills and competencies that customers demand? Is your employee performance development programme getting the job done?

At the individual level, customer feedback will help employees adjust their behaviour, on a regular basis, based on the changing requirements of customers. Listen to what your customers say. They are, after all, the ones who pay your bills.

Create a Culture of Continuous Learning

A third contribution that 360 Degree Feedback can make at the organizational level is to help you create a corporate learning culture. In a company with a learning culture, learning is seen as a task as vital to the company as producing products or services. The reason is that through continuous learning, your company is prepared better to adapt to and even anticipate a complex and often-changing business environment.

Performance is still the focus; you must still create the right products and services for your customers. But the sustained performance of the company depends on learning. To create a learning organization, you must use 360 Degree Feedback to help managers and employees develop not only their work skills, but also their learning skills. Here is how:

1. Provide feedback on learning skills and abilities. Most 360 Degree Feedback is concerned with performance skills and competencies. Create feedback programmes that focus on people's learning skills as well.

    For example, 360 Degree Feedback survey questions can reveal whether people seek feedback on a consistent basis or take advantage of opportunities to do new things. Some of your

CHAPTER 6   360 Degree Feedback: The Power Tool

people might realize that, although they are good managers, they are poor learners.
2. Provide on-demand feedback. To support learning, your company needs a system that gives employees more control when they get feedback. For example, feedback is particularly important when a person is tackling new challenges or when things are not going well. This is when he/she could use 360 Degree Feedback.
   More and more feedback programmes are available through online technology. Managers can decide when they need feedback on their performance, choose the dimensions on which they want feedback and zap the custom-made survey to the people from whom they want feedback. The filled-in surveys eventually come back anonymously.
3. Rate groups and the organization, not just individuals. Usually, 360 Degree Feedback involves rating the performance of individuals. Let groups or teams receive feedback from raters outside the team so that they can learn how well they are performing as groups. These outside raters could be drawn from customers, other groups or teams that interact closely with the targeted group, or management.
   You could apply the same process to your company as a whole. After all, your company also needs to understand how its performance is perceived by its various stakeholders, both inside and outside the organization, including customers, employees and shareholders.
4. Link individual and group development to the organization's developmental needs. A traditional 360 Degree Feedback process helps people fulfil the current responsibilities of their jobs in a better manner.
   Learning requires a broader focus. People cannot anticipate or prepare for a change by concentrating on their current responsibilities. They must look up from their jobs, so to speak, and see what is happening in the business environment that could bring changes to the company. Make sure the feedback items on your surveys are linked to your company's long-term strategic needs, not the narrow short-term requirements of employees' jobs.

Concrete and Clear Survey Items Make Feedback Believable

A 360 Degree Feedback process is built around a detailed questionnaire delivered to a group of people who are familiar with the performance of the manager or employee to be rated. Items on the questionnaire can relate to traits (for example, 'unhurried', 'dependable'), skills ('speaks effectively'), behaviour ('praises people for a job well done') and attitudes or values ('believes in democratic participation in decision-making').

When determining items for your questionnaire, use items that are as concrete and observable as possible. The less observable an item or the more an item requires an opinion on an internal state, the easier it is for a ratee to reject the feedback if it is negative. 'The raters got my values all wrong!' a ratee might retort.

Other rules for determining items on a questionnaire are as follows:

- Make them clear. An ambiguous item may confuse raters to respond differently from what they had intended.
- Make them one-dimensional. Items should never lead to two possible answers. For example, an item that says 'is perceptive of the influence he has and works to enhance that influence' involves two dimensions: understanding the influence and enhancing that influence.
- Make them valid at face value. Raters must immediately see the relevance of all items.
- Make sure that the raters can observe the item. If you ask the raters to assess a certain behaviour, make sure that they are in a position to see that particular behaviour.
- Keep out the qualifiers. Forget words such as extremely or very. They only confuse the issue. For example, a rater faced with the item 'This manager has extremely good management skills' marks 'slightly disagree'. What does he/she mean? Does he/she mean that the manager has good management skills but not extremely good management skills? Or that the manager shows extremely good management skills some of the time and not all the time?
- Make sure that items have adequate test/retest reliability. That is, if raters see a question one day and the same question a few days later, they will respond the same way. If an item is unclear

or poorly written, raters might respond differently even though no real change occurred.

Different ways to score items

Most 360 Degree Feedback questionnaires ask raters to score items in one of two ways. The most common method is based on frequency. For example, an item such as 'Pays attention to detail' can have a response scale running from '1 = not at all' to '5 = very frequently'.

Another type of response scale, called the mastery scale, asks raters to score how well the item is performed. In this case, the response scale might run from '1 = poorly' to '5 = very well'.

The advantage of a frequency scale is that it is easier to determine when something was performed rather than how well it was performed.

However, frequent is not always better. 'Pays attention to details' can be obsessive if it is overdone. Also, the correct frequency might depend on the person involved. One subordinate may need constant attention from the manager, while another needs little attention. Therefore, frequency scales used by themselves may not prove as valid or useful as mastery scales.

Another issue: how long a scale should you have? Two-point scales are easier to interpret. If a rater has to choose only between '1 = strength' and '2 = needs work', it is hard to misunderstand the response. However, in the following year, the manager may have made progress but still needs work. How can you show this progression? Five-point scales are the most common but present their own problem. They leave a mid-range response (neither satisfied nor dissatisfied) that lets raters get away with a vague or noncommittal response. A six-point scale, some experts say, is a better choice.

The first step in presenting the information is to take an average of groups of questionnaire items to create scale scores. Each scale refers to a specific skill or competence.

For example, one feedback survey offers four items to measure 'decisiveness':

1. Displays a real bias for action,
2. Is quick and approximate rather than slow and precise,
3. Is action-oriented and
4. Does not hesitate when making decisions.

When transforming the data from the surveys into a feedback report, average the scores from these separate items to calculate the scale score for 'decisiveness'. A scale score is only as good as the choice of items that formed the scale together. Choosing which items will be used to measure each skill determines the validity of the responses to the questionnaire.

Presenting the data

Calculating scale scores is only the first step in creating the feedback document. The next step is to bifurcate the ratings by groups of raters. This helps managers see how their skills and behaviour are seen by people with whom they have different relationships. How direct reports rate the manager on his/her leadership of subordinates is more important than how peers rate those same skills. Bifurcating the raters also brings out discrepancies between the self-image of the person being rated and the image that others have of that person.

Another way to enhance the interpretation of the information is to compare individual scores to norms. This helps people compare their scores with those of other people.

BOX 6.2 TRUST THE PROCESS

Managers and employees will use the feedback to improve their skills and competencies only if they trust the process and the information that comes from it. To create this trust, let people know the following facts:

- The information is going to be used to help them become better managers and employees and not to decide whether they will get a raise or promotion.
- The company considers the capacities and skills assessed in the survey as critical.
- Support for improvement will be forthcoming after the feedback process is completed. People should know that the company will be helping them translate this information into a plan for improvement.

The final tip: Let participants choose the people who will be rating them. But give them guidelines so that they choose a good balance and number of raters.

Many reports highlight certain items of importance. High and low items and scales are often highlighted, for example. This helps people focus on areas that they must prioritize for improvement.

Make Sure People Use the Feedback

A 360 Degree Feedback process yields raw data and information. Just throwing this information at employees or managers will not necessarily lead them to improve their performance, enhance their working relationships or acquire a learning mindset. The organization needs to step in at this time and help participants accomplish two things:

- Accept the feedback (see Box 6.1).
- Translate the feedback into actionable steps for improvement.

Accepting feedback

It is not always easy to accept the information that emerges from a 360 Degree Feedback process. Many people have a very set view or image of themselves. When feedback from others clashes with that self-image, people will tend to ignore it. A low rating may be discounted as 'sour grapes' or ignorance ('he doesn't know what I do').

To help employees and managers accept the feedback, make sure the information is clear and well organized. It is easier to discount confusing or badly organized data. Some characteristics of the ratings themselves will make them hard to ignore. For example, if many different sources offer the same rating on an issue—a rating that conflicts with a participant's self-image—the participant will have to acknowledge that the self-image might be wrong. Extreme ratings—a two out of ten, for example—and consistency of ratings across different dimensions also reinforce the legitimacy of the information. People often attempt to block or distort negative information emerging from the feedback process. A well-designed process with specific criteria and different evaluators minimizes this blocking action.

From information to action

A well-designed 360 Degree Feedback process will highlight the weaknesses (and strengths) of your employees or managers. Now you must help them use that information as the foundation on which to build a personal development plan.

The most effective way to ensure that people learn from the feedback process is through some type of formal development programme. Development programmes can range from feedback meetings with the boss and subordinates, in which you create a performance improvement plan to attend week-long, off-site training programmes. These off-site programmes can include both indoor and outdoor exercises to help people develop new attitudes and skills.

Whatever may be the type of development programme you offer to employees and managers, the first step is to pinpoint the areas that they should focus on. As they review the information, people should ask themselves these three questions:

1. Is it accurate?
2. Is it of value to me?
3. Is it important?

With a well-designed feedback process, the question of accuracy should not be doubted. The value and importance, however, is a judgement call that depends on the person. A person may not place a high value on building teams but may believe that completing assignments on time is very important. That person will be more concerned with a rating of four (out of five) on completing assignments than a rating of two on building teams.

CHAPTER 7

Competence Building through 360 Degree Feedback

Tremendous changes have taken place world-wide in the last two decades. These changes have had a strong impact on Indian industry. The world is very different today from what it was a decade ago. Today's corporate world can be characterized as highly competitive, technology- and systems-driven, customer-centred, quick, cost and quality conscious, fast-changing and highly competitive. In this changed situation, to survive, one has to compete with those who have technological advantages, financial advantages, systems advantages, communication advantages, and, above all, those with people advantages in terms of their competencies, attitudes and work culture.

In such a situation, organizations need to have highly competent top-level managers to lead them. The top team of each company becomes important. They need to perform leadership and institution-building roles very effectively. They need to balance short-term targets with long-term organization-building concerns. They need to inspire and develop their staff. They need to be customer-driven and quality-driven. Each individual manager plays a critical role in the company. He/she can be a good change agent by constantly improving himself/herself in relation to the roles he/she is playing, styles with which he/she is playing those roles, delegating and making the right impact on others through his/her behaviour.

TVRLS has developed a model for the top and senior management in terms of managerial and leadership competencies which is termed the RSDQ (Roles, Styles, Delegation and Qualities) model. This model of leadership and managerial effectiveness views effective management and leadership as a combination of four sets of variables.

Roles

In order to be effective, every manager has to play a number of roles. These are transformational roles (leadership roles) and transactional roles (managerial roles), some of which are as follows:

- Articulating and communicating vision and values,
- Formulating long-term policies and strategies,
- Introducing and managing new technology and systems,
- Inspiring, developing and motivating juniors,
- Managing juniors, colleagues and seniors,
- Culture building,
- Managing internal customers,
- Managing external customers and
- Managing unions and associations.

Styles

While effective managers recognize all the leadership roles and perform them well, it is not only the roles or activities that determine the effectiveness but also the way in which they are played. The model envisages that managers may play most roles well, and devote time and effort, but they could be insensitive to the style in which they carry out those roles. The leadership styles have been classified, on the basis of previous research done at the Indian Institute of Management by T.V. Rao, into the following:

- A benevolent or paternalistic leadership style in which the top-level manager believes that all his/her employees should be constantly guided and treated with affection like a parent treats his/her children, is relationship-oriented, assigns tasks on the basis of his/her own likes and dislikes, constantly guides them and protects them, understands their needs, salvages the situations of crisis by active involvement of himself/herself, distributes rewards to those who are loyal and obedient, shares information with those who are close to him/her, etc.
- A critical leadership style is characterized to be close to the Theory X belief pattern where the manager believes that employees should be closely and constantly supervised, and directed and

reminded of their duties and responsibilities, is short-term goal-oriented, cannot tolerate mistakes or conflicts among employees, is personal power dominated, keeps all information to himself/herself, works strictly according to norms and rules and regulations and is highly discipline-oriented.
- A developmental leadership style is characterized as an empowering style where the top manager believes in developing the competencies of his/her staff, treats them as mature adults, leaves them on their own most of the times, is long-term goal-oriented, shares information with all to build their competencies and facilitates the resolution of conflicts and mistakes by the employees themselves with minimal involvement from him/her.

It has been found that the developmental style is the most desired organization-building style. However, some individuals and some situations require, at times, benevolent and critical styles. It has also been found in the research that some managers are not aware of the predominant style they tend to use and the effects their style is producing on their employees.

Delegation

The RSDQ model considers level of delegation to be an important part of a senior executive's effectiveness. This dimension has been included because most senior managers seem to have difficulties delegating, especially those effective managers who get promotions fast in their career. In view of these experiences, delegation has been isolated as an important variable of leadership. Those who delegate release their time to perform higher level tasks and those who do not continue to do lower level tasks and suppress their leadership qualities and managerial effectiveness.

Qualities

The model envisages that managers should exhibit qualities of leaders and world-class managers (e.g. proaction, listening, communication, positive approach, participative nature, quality orientation, etc.). Such qualities not only affect effectiveness with which top-level managers

86 THE POWER OF 360 DEGREE FEEDBACK

perform various roles but also have an impact on the leadership style and hence are very critical.

The TVRLS instrument for 360 Degree Feedback for managerial and leadership development is based on the RSDQ model. In the case of *managerial qualities*, there are about 75 activities identified under each of the roles mentioned above. It is an instrument (two versions: one consisting of 55 items for senior managers and another consisting of 75 items for top-level managers) developed to assess these measures and the extent to which the manager is perceived as performing these roles. In the case of *leadership styles*, a 51-item instrument assesses the extent to which the aforementioned styles are exhibited across 12 different situations or activities and the impact the person makes on his/her subordinates in terms of five variables: feelings (dependence, incompetence, independence, interdependence, resentment, etc.), job satisfaction, work commitment, morale and extent of learning by the subordinates. Through this instrument the participant gets to know his/her styles as benevolent, critical or developmental (dominant and back-up) as well as their impact. The *delegation* questionnaire assesses the extent to which the participant is delegating and releasing his/her own time for higher level roles and tasks. There is a 10-item questionnaire that measures the various symptoms of delegation or non-delegation. In the case of *behavioural qualities*, 25 qualities are included, at present, using a semantic differential technique. Three open-ended questions at the end try to find out most dominant strengths and weaknesses of the respondent along with suggestions for improvement.

The instruments developed on the basis of the RSDQ model are updated periodically depending on dimensions important to top management roles and positions with changes in the business environment.

RSDQ Model—Applications and Variations

The 360 Degree Feedback instrument based on the RSDQ model is being used in a large number of organizations in India, such as the Aditya Birla Group, IL&FS, Gati Corporation, Mafatlal Group, Goodlas Nerolac and the State Bank of India, and in other countries such as Nigeria and Egypt by the Chanrai Group, Alexandria Carbon Black, Infosys, Taj Group of Hotels (India Hotels), Titan Industries,

CHAPTER 7 Competence Building 87

Cummins India, Dr Reddy's Laboratories, Wockhardt, Fulford, Linde Engineering, etc. The main purpose of using the RSDQ model in these organizations has been to provide insights to top-level managers on others' perception and the impact they create in the organizations due to the effectiveness with which they perform various managerial roles and leadership styles. The data generated are used as the basis to aid them formulate action plans.

The model has also been used as the basis for developing customized instruments for various organizations. Variations of the model depend on:

- Level/position to which 360 Degree Feedback is being provided and
- Purpose of 360 Degree Feedback.

A few illustrative variations are briefly described in what follows.

NTPC

In the case of NTPC, the 360 Degree Feedback instrument was prepared and used as part of the company's development centre. The instrument was role-based and focused on critical managerial and behavioural competencies of that particular role. The dimension of quality was also included. Since it was positioned at middle management, delegation and leadership styles were not included as part of the instrument. Items were generated by interviewing role incumbents as well as their role set members (peers, subordinates and boss). The basic purpose was to help in-house assessors understand the dynamics of 360 Degree Feedback and its effectiveness in providing developmental inputs to the individual.

Tata cummins

The instrument used in Tata Cummins was RSQ for which items were generated through individual interviews. The model was used not only to provide 360 Degree Feedback for development, but also a task force worked on it to make it a part of ongoing appraisal by integrating the feedback, in the annual performance appraisal, in the form of KPAs.

GVFL

In GVFL, 360 Degree Feedback was used for both senior and lower management. In the case of senior management, the focus was mainly on helping them understand the impact they were creating on the entire organizational culture. For this purpose, the complete RSDQ model was used. In the case of junior and middle management, the focus was on providing developmental inputs to the role incumbents by providing feedback on all critical managerial roles and qualities. An instrument was specially designed with only RQ. Through individual interviews, two separate instruments were designed—one for internal customers and the other for external customers.

Indian group of hotels

An instrument very similar to that used for Tata Cummins, i.e. RSQ, was developed for the Indian Group of Hotels (Taj). However, here it was used purely for developmental feedback and has not yet been incorporated into their performance appraisal.

Our studies using this model indicate the following general trends.

Indian CEOs seem to be good at boss management and weak at managing unions and also at performing transformational roles. They seem to perform transformational roles less effectively. Among the transformational roles, their strengths lie in articulating vision for the unit and influencing the thinking of their seniors. In a large number of other areas such as culture building and inspiring and developing staff, they need to improve a lot more. Future leadership programmes should focus on their change management skills. Their styles are predominantly developmental. They seem to delegate a good deal. High activity levels, positive thinking, communications and change orientation are some of the notable strengths. Proactivity, cool and composed nature, empathy, patience and participative nature could be developed more to make an impact. Some of these roles and qualities could be developed to make an impact.

We also found that there is a great degree of variation in the effective performance of roles, styles, delegation and qualities. This indicates the need for 360 Degree Feedback as a tool to create more self-awareness. They are not yet taking direct responsibility for developing others as leaders. They seem to do little to inspire and develop their juniors.

CHAPTER 7 Competence Building **89**

While they are good at articulating their vision and communicating the same to their juniors, the impact of this gets limited and they are not able to teach others about how to make the organization successful. They are still operating at conceptual levels and are reluctant to share their past and explain their learning experiences and beliefs.

They are not spending adequate time and effort to develop their own leadership abilities and talent of others. Their investment in 360 Degree Feedback is just a beginning.

The RSDQ model provides an effective framework for profiling managerial roles in organizations—both in India and other countries. It not only recognizes important dimensions of managerial effectiveness but also highlights critical activities, styles and qualities. When 360 Degree Feedback is given against such a backdrop, it provides very meaningful insights to managers with regard to the effectiveness with which they perform various roles, and their overall impact on the organization. While the focus is largely on providing developmental inputs to managers, the model can also be used to effectively integrate 360 Degree Feedback with performance appraisal since it focuses on the effectiveness of overall managerial performance.

Developing Competencies through 360 Degree Feedback

TVRLS has been associated with the task of designing and developing 360 Degree Feedback-based programmes since its inception and has gained a lot of experience. The most significant learning from all these years is that the RSDQ model has evolved as a powerful model of behaviour change and leadership development. This model is well known and very popular. The model gives feedback on more manageable aspects of behaviour to less manageable aspects.

The following have been found to be the advantages of the RSDQ model over the other models available from the West.

1. It is based on Indian experiences and indigenously evolved. It is therefore more relevant to Indian organizations and suits Indian psyche.
2. It provides feedback in a gradual manner from simple to complex issues.

3. It provides feedback on changeable areas which are easier and faster than less amenable and slow.
4. It is a comprehensive leadership-building tool.
5. It has flexibility to incorporate any aspects within the RSDQ framework.
6. It has been incorporated and tried out successfully with top management, CEOs, senior and middle-level executives, youth, sales and marketing persons, headmasters, principals, family heads, and all other categories of persons.

These advantages are explained next.
It is based on Indian experiences and indigenously evolved. It is therefore more relevant to Indian organizations and suits Indian psyche.
The work on the RSDQ model began in the 1980s at the Indian Institute of Management Ahmedabad (IIMA). The first programme on Leadership Styles and Organizational Effectiveness, offered in 1986 at the IIMA, did not have such an effective RSDQ model. It merely focused on leadership styles, managerial styles, decision-making styles, delegation and other personality and managerial effectiveness variables. It is out of the experiences of those attending these programmes that the roles part of it was added. It was the discussions in the initial programmes that have led to the formation of the focus on roles and activities. The participants of these programmes generated these activities. Professor Pradeep Khandwalla added a lot to the listing of these tasks and roles. Over the last decade and half, the roles list got enhanced, tested and retested, consolidated and experimented. Reliability studies conducted (test–retest reliability studies with a two-month gap) indicated that these are relatively stable across a two-month period with no feedback and any other significant intervention taking place. Recent studies of a service organization also indicated that feedback can help change the nature of performance of these roles in Indian settings.

The Indian mind is a little role bound. Roles are incorporated into the performance appraisals. Roles and activities are measurable and manageable. Given these considerations, the roles part of the RSDQ model is clearly more suitable and powerful for Indian managers and leaders. The styles questionnaire is based on long years of experience and research by the senior author. The three styles identified are very much Indian and at the same time have a research base. The three styles correspond to the four-stage maturity model of Abigail Stewart. This model is based on the premise that the psychosocial maturity of an individual is an indication of the corresponding maturity and growth stages envisaged by Sigmund Freud and Erick Erickson (Rao and Stewart, 1975). Both the author and Abigail Stewart worked with David McClelland who got his data of TAT stories written by Indian and other country managers and analysed for their maturity and depiction of leadership styles. The three leadership styles therefore have both a theoretical base and insights based on the observation of Indian managers across the last two decades. The three styles are benevolent (corresponding to the oral stage and dominated by the use of mouth—charismatic leaders use their oral skills to influence people and enjoy loyalty), critical (corresponding to anal and phallic stages where order and assertiveness are the qualities and discipline is the focus) and developmental (corresponding to the Freudian genital stage of differentiated ego formation). Interestingly, working over the last two decades, another former student of David McClelland, Daniel Goleman, recently came up with a six-style model of leadership. These six styles of leadership envisaged by Goleman (2002) are as follows:

1. The visionary leader who moves people towards shared dreams and creates a strongly positive climate. This style is considered appropriate when changes in vision or direction are needed.
2. The coaching leader who connects what people want with the organizational goals. This style helps build employee performance by building long-term capabilities.
3. The affiliative leader who creates harmony by connecting people to each other. This style of leadership has healing effects, heals rifts in teams, strengthens connections and motivates during stressful times.
4. The democratic leader who values people's inputs and gets contributions and commitment through participation. This style is useful in building participation and synergy.
5. The pace-setting leader who meets challenging and exciting goals. This style is useful to get high-quality results from a motivated and competent team.
6. The commanding leader who soothes fears by giving clear direction in an emergency. It has negative effects but is suitable in crisis situations.

Of these types, the visionary leader is a combination of benevolent and developmental styles. The coaching style leader is purely developmental, the affiliative style leader is benevolent, the democratic style leader is developmental, the commanding style leader is critical and a pace-setting style leader is a combination of the developmental and benevolent leader. Although the distinctions and overlaps are not as clear, the theory has a lot of commonalities and differences. The Indian styles are applicable in various settings such as managing mistakes, goal setting, managing rewards and managing conflicts. Our own research has established that there is high correlation between the style and the impact on the subordinates.

The benevolent style has been found to create dependence (negative) and loyalty (positive), the critical style has been found to create counter-dependence (negative) and incompetence (negative), and the developmental style has been found to create interdependence and learning. The style questionnaire focuses on the situations, rather than style, after indicating the effects of each style on people.

Our experience has indicated that 360 Degree Feedback does lead to participants identifying situations where they could use a different style to maximize their effectiveness. In the 360 Degree Feedback workshops, the focus is on enabling one to understand one's own styles, rigidity or flexibility and identify the situation, as well as individuals, where, and with whom, the participant may experiment with different styles. Our experience says that participants do try to change their style. One area where heightened awareness leads to good results is the management of mistakes. It has also been found that the style links up well with other qualities.

Delegation is a major issue in Indian organizations. In an insecure culture, continuous successes need to be reported. Familiarity and experience ensure security. Most managers use their success as the building block for growth but are unable to try new areas to generate new successes. Most organizations have found benefits coming out of this section. Several participants thought that they delegated a lot until they were told, through 360 Degree Feedback, that they do not even leave routine divisions for their subordinates to manage. This is one area where changes have been observed.

Any number of qualities can be incorporated. Qualities include three categories: those which are lasting traits and more difficult to change (e.g. being cool versus being short tempered or irritable, trusting

CHAPTER 7   Competence Building   **93**

versus suspicious, etc.) and those that are relatively easy to change (e.g. organized versus disorganized, listening to others versus preoccupied with own concerns, etc.). Here the candidate can chose and work better on those that give long-term results as well as short-term results.

These experiences make it clear that indigenously created and developed tools are more relevant and the return on investments is high from these. *They provide feedback in a gradual manner from simple to complex issues.*

The most important part of the competence development strategy is the feedback workshop. If we simply profile 360 Degree Feedback and pass on to the individual, it may be informative and enhance self-awareness but may not result in any great changes. Our experience indicates that if the individual is prepared to receive the feedback and then the feedback is presented, it will have a better effect. Such preparation would cover various aspects, including a good understanding of the feedback tool, leadership qualities required for the contest of the organization and the business realities faced by the individual, scope for exhibiting the competencies and methods of demonstrating the competencies one has and developing those that one does not have. Such a strategy of feedback is possible in workshop format with adequate follow-up and review mechanisms. The subsequent part of this chapter presents some details of the way in which such workshops are conducted to facilitate the development of managerial and leadership qualities.

A typical design of the 360 Degree Feedback workshop conducted by TVRLS proceeds in the following way.

Session 1

In this session, the chemistry of 360 Degree Feedback is explained. It is emphasized that the feedback one gets is an indication of the chemistry one generates and should not be taken to mean that the participant has all the qualities (positive or negative) pointed out by the person giving feedback. The feedback sometimes could be an indicator of the perceiver's mindset and is as much the feedback about the giver of feedback as that of the receiver. One should normally look for consistencies and the common chemistry generated by the candidate and his/her behaviour. It is also emphasized that contradictions are common and opposites are expected depending on the eye of the beholder. For example, the behaviour of the candidate may be perceived as assertive and dynamic by one person and as 'dominating and aggressive' by another. It is as much an indication of the giver's preference as an indication of the receiver's behaviour. The reasons for inconsistencies in feedback are examined.

This session prepares the candidates to be emotionally ready to take feedback and not to get puzzled over inconsistencies. It also talks about the role of the receiver of feedback and emphasizes the need to understand how a person generates a particular type of chemistry. The emphasis of this session is also that 360 Degree Feedback is to be taken as more a provocative intervention rather than a prescriptive intervention.

Session 2

This session is devoted to roles. The participants examine the questionnaire and give their assessment of the importance of each of the items on a three-point scale. They assess each item as very critical for the effective performance of their role, to not at all critical and somewhat critical. This is intended to generate an expectation that draws their attention to essential items when they receive feedback rather than to look at all the 50 of 75 items. The session prepares them to focus on the important areas. They are then explained the methods of presentation of data, and a sample profile is projected on the screen. They learn to interpret their own data. It is only after this that they are given their feedback individually. After they receive the feedback, they get an hour time to reflect on their feedback and draw preliminary action plans. Some of them may share their plans and the data may be presented in terms of group trends. The facilitator then gives the benchmarking data to help each participant assess where he/she stands in relation to the group. These data are fairly provocative.

Session 3

In this session, the theory behind leadership styles is explained. The style tools are revisited and the rationale is discussed. After the theory is discussed, the participants are given their feedback. The emphasis is on the impact created by their styles (e.g. Are people learning? Do they

CHAPTER 7 Competence Building

enjoy working with the participants? Do they report high morale and growth?). There are questions to this effect. These are followed by an examination of styles, feedback and action plans. The session ends with each participant identifying one or more situations where he/she likes to experiment with changed styles and one or two individuals with whom he/she likes to try a new style to get better results and create better impact.

Session 4

This session focuses on delegation and a similar sequence is followed: theory, examination of the tool and preparation for feedback, reflection and action plans on areas to delegate, more people to delegate more, etc.

Session 5

This session focuses on qualities. It starts with the review of literature on qualities of successful leaders (e.g. Jack Welch, Narayana Murthy, etc.), followed by an examination of the tool and assessment of the relative importance of the qualities by each participant, feedback, reflection and action plans. The action plans emphasize on the methods to use, existing strengths and identification of qualities to be improved.

Session 6

The last session may focus on sharing of group work and planning action.
Individual counselling is followed by this.
Thus, the way the sessions are scheduled and the way they progress are considered very absorbing and gradual. When the open-ended feedback is received at the end, the participant is well prepared to absorb any unpleasant feedback he/she may get.

It provides feedback on changeable areas which are easier and faster than those which are less amenable and slow.

The merit of the RSDQ model is that it offers a wide area of choice for change. The roles or tasks are the easiest to change. For example, a person received the feedback that he was not clearly communicating the company's vision. The person could make this change in himself immediately after the programme. Similarly, improvements in performance feedback, introduction of systems, becoming more sensitive to internal customers, are all 'easy to act' areas. Delegation has been found to be the most 'easy to act' area. Several participants who have attended our workshops have spent their time on delegating more and releasing their time for higher level tasks to be performed.

A few of them have also worked on personality-based areas like 'controlling their short temper and irritability' and reported some success after some time. The areas to choose from are wide and the RSDQ model offers such wide choices.

It is a comprehensive leadership-building tool and has flexibility to incorporate any aspects within the RSDQ framework.

In view of the inclusion of styles, roles, delegation and qualities, the tool is comprehensive and offers scope for incorporating any other areas in these. Leadership is treated as a role, style, empowerment (delegation) and as a set of qualities. Due to its multidimensional nature it is a superior tool.

It has been incorporated and tried out successfully with top management, CEOs, senior- and middle-level executives, youth, sales and marketing persons, headmasters, principals, family heads and all other categories of persons.

Many questionnaires have been developed using this model for a variety of categories of participants. Some of these are highlighted in the following sections.

RSDQ model is more amenable to a change and is more amenable to be incorporated or integrated into the appraisal systems of organizations.

On the four components of the questionnaire the more manageable aspects are those dealing with the roles. The roles identified so far are as follows:

1. Vision and values,
2. Strategic thinking and leadership,
3. Technology and systems management and leadership,
4. People management and leadership,
5. Culture building,
6. Internal customer management and leadership,
7. Team work and team leadership,
8. Managing seniors (boss management),
9. Ceremonial roles including liaison with government and other agencies,

10. External customer satisfaction and management,
11. Performance management and
12. Organizational values and discipline.

This list can be expanded. Under each of these roles the activities are to be listed. The activities may be more specific or broad. The roles may vary from organization to organization and the importance attached to the activities may also vary.

Feedback on how well the individual is performing these roles helps him/her to recognize the areas where he/she needs to improve his/her performance. The areas will, in turn, help the individual to plan performance. Feedback on the performance of any one or more of these activities or tasks may lead to the individual recognizing them, incorporating them and preparing action plans to overcome the weaknesses. The areas may be incorporated into the performance management or KPAs or KRAs.

Competence Building Does Not Occur Merely through Feedback Workshops

While a good part of our work in this area has demonstrated that 360 Degree Feedback workshops do wonders for a few individuals, in most cases they run the risk of leaving them as more self-aware individuals without any concrete observable behaviour changes. Behaviour change requires sustained effort on the part of the individual. It requires the following conditions:

1. The candidate should recognize the importance of the desired behaviour in terms of the activities, styles or qualities in his/her context. For example, how important it is for him/her to articulate vision for his/her section or department or organization. If not how important it is in his/her role to communicate the top management vision and organizational values continuously to his/her juniors, etc. Or the criticality of reading technological journals and updating him/herself with new technological developments or alternately building such tendencies among his/her juniors, etc. Or he/she should recognize the need for and the importance of a developmental style or critical style as his/her situation demands.

2. The individual should then get feedback on the current standing of self as perceived by others and the need for a change—to leverage and strengthen it further or to acquire more or to reduce it to the desired level.
3. The individual should then prepare a plan of action on the change desired and the actual activities he/she would like to undertake to bring in the required change.
4. This should be followed by a public commitment by the individual to exhibit new behaviour or undertake new activities to leverage his/her strengths or to work on areas he/she needs to improve or cultivate.
5. This should be followed by a dialogue or conversation where possible and applicable with his/her seniors and others who may mentor the candidate to further strengthen his/her plans and convictions. Some other processes discussed and decided may be changed. For example, in the case of one CEO, he got the feedback that he should become more patient and listen to others more than carrying only his point of view and showing his impatience. A few months later he practised listening and felt happy but at the same time decided against reducing his impatience as he found his colleagues to be too relaxed and patient and nothing is moving! He concluded that he will continue to be impatient as if he becomes patient there is no drive left in the organization!
6. There should be a scope for review at the end of few months and the review can be for couple of times with a three- to six-month gap. Most people nowadays are accustomed to work with targets and reviews. In such a world if we expect change from 360 Degree Feedback, it should be stated, monitored and reviewed and incentive systems could also be built around them.

Thus, while the individual should take charge of his/her development, the organization could provide a support system required for such a change.

CHAPTER 8

Coaching in 360 Degree Feedback

Most 360 Degree Feedback programmes achieve limited success as they suffer from lack of follow-up as in the case of performance management systems (PMSs). A good 360 Degree Feedback programme has the following characteristics:

1. It uses tools based on the needs of the organization.
2. It uses simple language and makes sure that all the respondents know and use the same language as in the tools.
3. It keeps changing the tools with the passage of time, to keep building newer competencies in the employees.
4. It prepares the respondents for an effective participation in the programme.
5. It prepares the candidates adequately to receive the feedback and use it properly.
6. It is based on the objective of increasing the choices of the employee in terms of his/her decisions, growth, approach, work, productivity, efficiency, cost reduction, etc.
7. It provides coaching and follow-up support to help the candidate to use 360 Degree Feedback and benefit from it the most [ensure a good return on investment (ROI)].
8. It ensures that the candidate receiving 360 Degree Feedback is made accountable to use it by encouraging him/her to incorporate the feedback into annual PMSs (use KRAs, etc.), and prepare development plans.
9. It provides opportunities for the manager to initiate a dialogue with his/her juniors, seniors, internal and external customers, or other stakeholders.
10. It insists on each candidate preparing development plans after receiving the feedback, and ensures follow-up and implementation.

If 360 Degree Feedback is treated as an individual action point and the organization does not do anything about it, most managers are also most likely to do nothing about it once the feedback is completed. After the initial euphoria is over, they may take their feedback and change for granted.

If 360 Degree Feedback is taken seriously and used as a starting point to initiate a series of conversations with internal teams, the ROI is likely to be high. In this process, coaching plays an important role. The coaching could be done by external coaches or internal team members.

The Role of the Coach

The coach in 360 Degree Feedback can play the following roles:

1. Understanding the role of the candidate and the competence requirements to be successful in that role;
2. Identifying with the help of the candidate or his/her seniors the areas from the 360 Degree Feedback tool that are relevant to success in the current role;
3. Interpreting the feedback, assisting the candidate in understanding the feedback and helping him/her take it in the right perspective;
4. Identifying areas which are the candidate's strengths and point out the same to the candidate;
5. Identifying areas he/she needs to improve on to be more successful in that role and building leadership competencies;
6. Helping the candidate to prepare development plans so as to leverage his/her strengths and resources and to improve on his/her weak areas for future growth and effectiveness;
7. Helping the candidate to plan and prepare for a dialogue with his/her assessors;
8. Assisting the candidate in conducting or initiating the dialogue or conversation with his/her juniors and seniors or internal customers (the coach has to take a calculated risk on this issue as some of the candidates may not do any such follow-up work if left on their own, and if the coach takes active part, he/she may be creating dependences on himself/herself);
9. Helping the candidate to prepare milestones for his/her own progress and

10. Helping the candidate to monitor his/her own growth and development.

Competencies Required to Be a 360 Degree Feedback Coach

360 Degree Feedback coaching is a specialized skill and can be easily acquired like any other. It requires a thorough understanding of the limitations of 360 Degree Feedback. Some exposure and experience in T-Group training, psychology, Indian Society for Applied Behavioural Science (ISABS) and Indian Society for Individual and Social Development (ISISD) training, National Training Laboratories (NTL), USA exposure, behavioural science training and training in coaching are essential. The 360 Degree Feedback coach should have the following competencies:

1. An understanding of the 360 Degree Feedback process and its limitations;
2. The ability to interpret the 360 Degree Feedback data with multiple perspectives and meanings, for example, the ability to see the positive side of low ratings and the limits of high assessments, the ability to view how a strong point at one time could become a weak area, or what contributes to success at one time may contribute to failure in another setting;
3. The anatomy, physiology, pathology and the chemistry of behaviour (personal, interpersonal and group);
4. An understanding of the competencies required to perform various roles in an organization, and what contributes to success and failure;
5. An understanding of the theories of leadership, learning, personality, the Pygmalion effect, role of motives, values, attitudes, personality, etc., in behaviour and behaviour dynamics;
6. A positive outlook to people and an ability to empathize;
7. An interest in, and the ability to, understand the organization, its business, competencies and structure;
8. An understanding of behavioural sciences and human behaviour in organizational and group settings (for example, how technology influences behaviour as much as how hereditary and early socialization influences the behaviour);

9. An understanding of the organizational structure, management systems and their impact on people;
10. Coaching skills (attending, listening, action planning, exploring, mirroring, open questions, diagnostic skills, action planning skills);
11. A thorough understanding of changes at individual, group and organization levels, and changes in management and
12. Some expertise in HRD.

Coaching Process

A lot of literature is available on the coaching process (Pareek and Rao, 1990). The following are some of the relevant points for 360 Degree Feedback coaching:

1. Familiarize yourself with the organization.
2. Familiarize yourself with the candidates receiving 360 Degree Feedback, their roles and competence requirements.
3. Understand the leadership and other competency models (if any) that the organization is using. Study the relevant material. Understand where the organization stands, how they like the coaching to be placed and what is intended to be achieved.
4. Set coaching goals and share them with the candidate and the organization in advance. Ensure that you are on the same wavelength as the candidate and the organization with regard to the objectives of coaching.
5. Study the tools and the theoretical background and rationale (if any) behind the tool.
6. Determine, plan and fix an appropriate time needed for the first coaching session. Indicate the preparation needed by the candidate prior to coaching. Most of the 360 Degree Feedback programmes have their own manuals and workbooks (for example, the TVRLS workbook on the RSDQ model of leadership).
7. Start by explaining the objectives, etc., of the coaching session. You could save time by doing this in a group covering all the intended candidates.
8. Build a rapport with the candidate, and begin by understanding his/her unique situation, role, profile, concerns, competencies needed, etc.

9. Give directions (if any) but always point out several interpretations and several possible alternative courses of action.
10. Be flexible during the coaching session. Use your own strategy and use a different approach for each candidate. For example, some candidates are willing to learn and are too eager to change. They run the risk of blindly accepting everything. Others may not be interested in learning at all; past successes may become stumbling blocks in the learning process. Some others may reject the feedback and may become defensive at the slightest provocation, while others may want to prove everyone else wrong. You need to be flexible enough to deal with each type of candidate differently. The case studies given in what follows describe four different candidates and you could use these to train yourself on how to deal with such cases.
11. Have your attitudes, ethics and values on 360 Degree Feedback very clear and keep repeating these for yourself and for others. For example, in TVRLS the following attitudes and values are promoted:

   a. Each assessee has to be respected;
   b. Each assessor is to be trusted;
   c. Contradictions are a part of life;
   d. Never try to identify the assessor;
   e. Always focus on the feedback;
   f. You do not have to accept feedback as it is, feedback is only a starting point (feedback at times may be more a reflection of the giver than the receiver, the receiver should not reject or accept feedback outright);
   g. 360 Degree Feedback comes in a raw form and it needs to be interpreted properly and
   h. Keep revisiting the feedback for some days after you receive it, to benefit from it.

Case Studies

Given in the following are four cases of four top-level managers from one organization.

If you are to coach them, what strategy would you adopt for each of them?

- What will be your coaching objectives for each of them?
- How much time do you think you will need to coach each of them?
- How many sittings may be required?
- What action plans would you recommend for each of them? Or if you are the person, what action plans would you prepare for yourself?

The following four candidates went through the TVRLS 360 Degree Feedback club. They were assessed on the RSDQ model of TVRLS. The highlights of the feedback for each candidate are also given.

Case 1: Production manager

This candidate is 55 years of age. He has been with the company for three years and has rich experience in production (Table 8.1).

TABLE 8.1 Sample Highlights of Assessment—Production Manager

Area	Highlights of Assessment
Roles	*High:*
	• Performance driven
	• Quality driven
	• Technology driven
	• External customer driven
	Low:
	• Cost consciousness
	• Technology drive low
Style	• Developmental (generally)
	• Juniors learn and enjoy working with him
	• Mistakes management critical

(Table 8.1 Contd.)

(Table 8.1 Contd.)

Area	Highlights of Assessment
Qualities	• Trusting
	• Active
	• Reliable
	• Knowledgeable
	• Reactive
	• Irritable and short-tempered
Open-ended feedback	Main strengths
	• Energy and dynamism
	• Vision driven
	• Encourages and empowers subordinates
	• Technical knowledge
	• Proactive and result oriented
	• Transparent
	• Shares information and knowledge
	Areas of improvement
	• Needs to be calm and composed
	• Needs to be fair and unbiased
	• Needs to work on interpersonal relations
	• Needs to improve problem-solving and decision-making
	• Needs to be more sociable and sensitive towards subordinates
Attitude during feedback	I am aware of my strengths. I need to improve on my temper. I have achieved excellent results and have brought a turnaround in this company. I am open to feedback.

Case 2: Human resource manager

This candidate has been with the company for six months. He is 45 years of age, and has rich experience of working in three other companies (Table 8.2).

TABLE 8.2 Sample Highlights of Assessment—Human Resource Manager

Area	Highlights of Assessment
Roles	*High:*
	• Performance driven
	• Interpersonally competent
	• Influences seniors well
	• System oriented
	• Team worker
	• Communicator
	• Change manager, value driven
	Low:
	• Technology savvy
	• Strategic thinker
	• Sets personal example
Style	• People enjoy working with him
	• Somewhat flexible (50%)
	• People learn by working with him
	• Share information
	• Protective and benevolent
	• Treats mistakes with understanding
Qualities	• Trusting
	• Empowering
	• Transparent
	• Authoritarian
	• Passive
	• Knowledgeable
	• Less empathetic
Open-ended feedback	*Main strengths*
	• Communication skills

(Table 8.2 Contd.)

(Table 8.2 Contd.)

Area	Highlights of Assessment
	• Encourages subordinates
	• Job knowledge
	• Friendly and approachable
	• Flexible and adaptable to change and new ideas
	Areas of improvement
	• Improve computer knowledge
	• Needs to be less biased
	• Needs to be systematic and organized
	• Needs to improve listening skills
	• Over-dependence on others
Attitude during feedback	I am new to this place. I am interested in learning. I want to benefit from this feedback.

Case 3: CEO

This candidate is in his mid-fifties, and has been with the company for the last three years. He has made substantial performance improvements (Table 8.3).

TABLE 8.3 Sample Highlights of Assessment—CEO

Area	Highlights of Assessment
Roles	High:
	• Vision driven
	• Performance driven
	• Quality driven
	• Communicator
	• Team worker
	• Value driven

(Table 8.3 Contd.)

(Table 8.3 Contd.)

Area	Highlights of Assessment
	No low ratings on assessment from others. Self-assessment low on the following:
	• Cost consciousness
	• Time and effort spent in building subordinates
	• Being systems driven
	• Communication
	• Being internal customer driven
	• Networking
Style	• Task-centred, people-centred
	• Highly developmental
	• Empowering
	• Tends to rely on a select few
Qualities	All ratings by others high. Self-assessment low on the following areas:
	• Transparent
	• Empathetic
	• Empowering
	• Trusting
	• Delegates
Open-ended feedback	Main strengths
	• Strategic thinker
	• Vision and foresight
	• Approachable
	• Analytical skills
	• Quality conscious
	• Communication skills
	• Positive attitude
	• Encourages and empowers subordinates

(Table 8.3 Contd.)

CHAPTER 8 Coaching in 360 Degree Feedback

(Table 8.3 Contd.)

Area	Highlights of Assessment
	Areas of improvement
	• Needs to be less biased
	• Needs to be less gullible (easily influenced)
	• Be more system oriented
	• Improve technical and engineering knowledge
	• Be more assertive (where required, aggressive)
Attitude during feedback	This is interesting feedback. I am surprised at the positive ratings people have given me. It looks as though I have a differential impact on different people. I need to look into this and pay attention. I will start by initiating a dialogue with some of them.

Case 4: Finance manager

This candidate has been with the company for the last 15 years. He is 45 years of age (Table 8.4).

TABLE 8.4 Sample Highlights of Assessment—Finance Manager

Area	Highlights of Assessment
Roles	High:
	• Vision driven
	• Technology driven
	• Systems driven
	• Cost conscious
	• Performances driven
	• People manager
	• Influences seniors
	• Good at networking

(Table 8.4 Contd.)

(Table 8.4 Contd.)

Area	Highlights of Assessment
	Self-assessment 100% on each
	Low:
	• Business driven
	• Strategic thinker
Style	• More people-centred than task-centred
	• Developmental
	• Highly protective in managing mistakes
	• High style flexibility
Qualities	• Calm and composed
	• Calm and composed
	• Trusting
	• Proactive
	• Flexible
	• Organized
	• Empowering
	• Knowledgeable
	• A little less fair and unbiased
Open-ended feedback	Main strengths
	• Subordinate development
	• Guides and motivates subordinates
	• Good job knowledge
	• Frank and open
	• Helpful and cooperative
	• Good sense of humour and a pleasing personality
	• Quality conscious
	Areas of improvement
	• Needs to be less biased
	• Needs to be more receptive to change

(Table 8.4 Contd.)

CHAPTER 8 Coaching in 360 Degree Feedback

(Table 8.4 Contd.)

Area	Highlights of Assessment
	• Needs to increase interaction with staff
	• Needs to be open to ideas and views of others
	• Needs to spend more time on subordinate development
Attitude during feedback	I am doing everything well. There is very little scope for improvement. I am a people-centred person. All are happy with me. I believe in being a people-centred manager. I have a lot of free time. My way of doing things is perhaps the best. I can listen to you but I am not sure if I need to do anything better. I do not wish to change my beliefs and approach as they are the ones I have built with experience.

CHAPTER 9

Myths and Realities of 360 Degree Feedback

Experiencing the process of 360 Degree Feedback is like experiencing a storm. While the build-up to a 360 Degree Feedback is slow and steady, once it is arrived, it can create a major upheaval in the minds of many young leaders and managers who have undergone this process. The experience with 360 Degree Feedback might seem rough when it is on. However, the end result is just the opposite. It leaves the individual much stronger and better charged not only to manage change but also to lead change.

Over the last few years, there has been a visible increase in the curiosity and willingness of managers towards experiencing the power of 360 Degree Feedback. There are also people who have experienced it themselves and want others to share and experience it for themselves.

360 Degree Feedback is being used to serve multiple objectives ranging from a change management tool for leadership development to a tool for assessing the potential of participants. In many cases, it is also being used as a tool to appraise senior managers.

There is, however, a fair amount of scepticism about the immediate ROI, as well as the other tangible outcome of 360 Degree Feedback. While 360 Degree Feedback does not give immediate, tangible results, the faith in a powerful tool like this is on the rise and there are companies willing to look at it as an investment even if it were to be used purely as a tool aimed at personal growth. This could well be a sign that people are still believed to be the most important resource.

TVRLS has had the good fortune of doing, probably, the maximum amount of work in 360 Degree Feedback with many companies across the country and, hence, got an opportunity to deal with decision-makers who initiate the process, those who participate in the programme for receiving the feedback, as well as the assessors of the feedback.

CHAPTER 9 Myths and Realities of 360 Degree Feedback

Every interaction with a client or a potential client has given us an opportunity to peep into their minds and get an idea of their opinion/views on 360 Degree Feedback and their perception of what it can do. If one has to conclude, purely based on the work done by us, some of these perceptions are a far cry from the truth. Many of these misconceptions or myths are at an individual level, while some of them are at an organizational level. They create dissonance when a participant is about to get the feedback or has got the feedback. The dissonance could be created in the minds of the participants and other employees, either before, during or after the 360 Degree Feedback process. Some of the widely experienced myths are as follows.

Myth I: Success of 360 Degree Feedback Depends on Finding Out the Exact Source of the Feedback

One of the most common phrases that one gets to hear in feedback workshops is 'I know exactly who has said this'. This is just the opposite of what the soul of 360 Degree Feedback stands for. Anonymity and trust are the two pillars that support 360 Degree Feedback. This is not a game of 'match the following'. If one has to accept the feedback, one must trust the givers of feedback as well as their intentions. After all, they have been chosen by the participants themselves.

One cannot help but recall a very interesting incident that happened in one of the programmes that we had conducted. A very senior manager in one of the leading business houses in the country had chosen to participate in the 360 Degree Feedback process. When he was given his feedback report, he was quite stunned because the maximum number of responses was from the boss category, when in reality he had only one boss. As facilitators, we told him that we could offer him little help as we had absolutely no way of finding out who had sent us the forms. While chatting with him, he told us that he had ticked the appropriate category and then forwarded the forms to his assessors. This only meant one thing: Some of those individuals viewed this as lack of trust and a probable way of identifying the source. They must have, therefore, marked the wrong category on purpose to be on the safe side. While such an act might not necessarily result in such an action, it goes against the basis of what 360 Degree Feedback stands for. For all you know, those individuals would have anyway have marked the right category had it not been marked on their behalf.

One has even heard of extreme cases where individuals have marked the envelopes and then given it to certain people, asking them to fill it up and return it to them, after which they have read through the form and only then sent it to consultants for compiling.

To obtain the maximum benefit from this process, the right attitude has to be one of complete trust and belief, that at a basic level all those who have given feedback are interested in the individual and his/her development, and have, hence, taken the trouble to give their comments. Feedback has any way been captured in the report. The decision that we have to make is whether we should be satisfied with what has been said or we should also want to know who has said it.

In many cases, we have seen that self-development-oriented individuals have gone back after the feedback, done more probing/ exploration about the feedback they have received, the root causes behind it as well as some of the remedial actions as perceived by the respondents. This only adds to the seriousness of the feedback.

Guessing is perhaps the next dangerous activity that should be avoided at any cost. Our own experience has shown that there is a high probability that those who are normally very nice could look at the feedback as a mechanism of telling you what they really feel. On the other hand, those who give you a hard time at work could view this as an opportunity to give some positive strokes and decide to highlight some of the individuals' strong points. Hence, it appears worthwhile not to guess. Curiosity and mistrust need to be replaced with trust and acceptance.

Myth II: These Are My Childhood Problems; It Is Too Late to Change Now!

Another common comment that one gets to hear when handing over feedback to individuals is 'I have been born like this' or 'this is my childhood problem'. Comments like this symbolize a defensive attitude and a lack of openness to even the thought or possibility of change itself.

While studies by psychologists have shown that, though genes have an important role to play in one's personality development, an individual's initiative, corrective action (based on scientific feedback), etc. does contribute to the change process and lead to success.

While some qualities, like being reserved, could be inherent and gifts from God, a lot of research has proved that major personality corrections/changes by individual initiative/remedial action are very much possible. For centuries, many great people in various areas have attributed their success, in respective fields, to their hard work, sincerity, zest for learning and continuous improvement. Little has been attributed to luck or destiny. The well-known model AIDA (Awareness, Interest, Desire and Action for the change process) also supports this.

The first step towards change is awareness followed by acceptance. Thereafter comes the willingness to change. We have seen many instances of individuals who have actually gone through the 360 Degree Feedback process and have brought about perceivable changes in qualities such as communication and being more calm and composed.

Examples of individuals who have been able to make a drastic change in areas such as temper management and delegation as an outcome of 360 Degree Feedback are very evident.

Our own experience with managers over the last 15 years, on multi-rater feedback, has reinforced one view that changes are possible in managers. The degree of change, however, depends on the seriousness of the initiative and the follow-up action.

Myth III: 360 Degree Feedback Is Conclusive

Contrary to popular belief, 360 Degree Feedback is only indicative and, at best, provocative. It needs to be viewed as the beginning (if not, at least as a midpoint) and not as the end. It deals with the symptoms and indirectly with the causes.

In one of our 360 Degree Feedback workshops, we came across a particular group, which had a very high non-delegation score. While detailing out the likely reasons for the high score, there was a great amount of discussion and a refusal to accept that there could be an issue with delegation. Time and again it was reiterated that the score was only an indication, and its purpose was to provoke individuals to dig deeper. Yet it was being seen as a final verdict indicating that the group was very weak in delegation and it was detrimental to the image of the group. After much debate and individual counselling, the group finally agreed that there was a great amount of truth in what the scores were trying to point out, though there were other variables that needed to be looked at for finding out the reasons and the solutions.

This might not be the best way to look at data. The fact that the score is high only indicates unmet expectations, which could be due to low focus on subordinate development or due to low trust on subordinates. It does not conclude on any of the two. To reach to a conclusion, each individual will need to probe further and seek additional information. 360 Degree Feedback acts like an antenna; it captures consolidated information. One has to look at the feedback in perspective. 360 Degree Feedback is like a thermometer; it will only measure the temperature. The exact reason for a high or low temperature will have to be found out with more probing and with sincerity and desire to overcome the challenge.

Myth IV: I Am a High Performer. I Am Successful and Fulfil All the Requirement of the Organizations. Why 360 Degree Feedback for Me?

360 Degree Feedback does not directly deal with tangible outcomes like sales target fulfilment or production or delivery numbers. It deals with the qualities and styles required for a good leader and a manager to achieve these outcomes. It focuses on the path and not just on the destination. It tells the respondent about the perception of people at present, based on their interaction in the past, and helps the participant to use this data for the future and for potential growth.

Performance appraisals look mostly at the past and hence the focus is on tangible outcomes. But there is no tool which actually tells us whether a manager is gearing up with the required qualities for performing the role of a leader.

There is an example of a competent functional manager who was promoted to a leadership position in a senior management committee. Being very successful and a high potential manager, he did not think that there was anything amiss in occupying his new role. However, much to his surprise, he had to face issues on his effectiveness in his new role. A 360 Degree Feedback clearly pointed out the key issues. He had actually carried his chair with his role and he was facing difficulty occupying the new chair.

To put it simply, the new role demanded additional competencies of vision, leading a team, cross-functional perspective, in addition to what he was doing in his previous role. However, the individual was not able to focus on these areas and contributed to focusing on the areas of his previous job. He was neither delegating the old nor accepting the new. The senior manager worked on the feedback and was able to bring about a drastic change in his styles and qualities to be more successful in his new role.

360 Degree Feedback offers the right platform to focus on the intangibles that one has to equip oneself with as a person takes on higher roles of leadership.

Myth V: I Already Know What People Have to Say about Me. What Additional Help Will a 360 Degree Feedback Give Me?

There are many individuals who know, to a large extent, what others think about them. They have a high degree of perceptiveness and are able to gauge what people think about them. They are able to read between the lines and know exactly the impact they are having.

However, thanks to the complexity of human beings, it is not possible to make out the perceptions of all individuals. Often even children are not able to understand their parents. In fact, how often do we understand ourselves? Research has pointed out that, across one lifetime, we ourselves get to know and use only 30 per cent of our potential. The balance we might never know.

If this is the case, a person cannot have complete confidence of being able to gauge the impact he/she is having on other people at the workplace. There are sure to be lot of areas that the individual is not aware of and 360 Degree Feedback gives a structure to these areas and offers a systematic way of exploring them.

Even for those who have been blessed with a high degree of confidence on the outcomes, the data from the 360 Degree Feedback should be viewed as a way of reinforcing what they think. It should be used as a tool for self-reflection and correction.

The data from 360 Degree Feedback should be used to look at the linkages that highlight the blind, unknown, public strengths from multiple sources, for reinforcement and correction to derive the maximum of one's potential.

Myth VI: I Do Not Need Counselling after 360 Degree Feedback

It is great to be intelligent. However, the responsibility of how to use this intelligence is up to the individual. Some people use this intelligence for academics, some for making money. It is the same with 360 Degree Feedback. Interpreting the data and using it thereafter is up to the individual. God save others if he interprets in the wrong way and uses it thereafter. This is where counselling of individuals is of great importance. One has to learn to ask the right questions and then seek out the right method of finding out the answers to the questions. Most of the times, the answers can be obtained only after further introspection.

Take the case of this individual who had got substantial feedback that he was playing favourites at the workplace. Each section pointed to this aspect. During counselling the counsellor asked the individual as to whom he had lunch with every day. The answer to that question gave important insights into the issue of playing favourites. As it turned out, that individual would have his lunch every single day only with a certain set of senior managers and no one else. The individual himself was not able to see the connection, but to many, having lunch with a certain set of people was like giving special treatment to these select senior managers and, hence, making a distinction. It often helps to use a neutral party to explore and probe into the data and find out reasons and, hence, methods to correct the same.

Unfortunately, many view the word counselling with some stigma attached to it. It is looked upon as a handicap instead of being viewed as an opportunity to remove blocks or shackles to one's growth and productivity. Though views on counselling are changing, very often the ego and the unwillingness to engage with oneself come in the way of reducing the blocks and enhancing potential.

CHAPTER 9 Myths and Realities of 360 Degree Feedback 119

Let us change gears and focus on the second type of misconceptions/myths that occur at an organizational level. These notions exist in the minds of key role holders who are responsible for implementing such a process in organizations or deriving benefits for the organization. Some of these are mentioned in the following.

Myth VII: We Are a Very Open Organization. What More Can We Get from 360 Degree Feedback?

Many companies know their model of leadership as well as vision and mission for the future. 360 Degree Feedback is a proactive process of seeking feedback in areas which have been identified as crucial for effective managerial and leadership performance. While one can claim of working in a very open organization, it is unlikely that the degree of openness is so high that people will give a colleague feedback on all the areas that are important without the person even asking for it.

Moreover, the cultural background of India being such that it is highly relationship-oriented, and where even bosses find it difficult to tell their juniors what they really feel, it is unlikely that open feedback will be given spontaneously. Further, when feedback is given over the lunch table or on the corridor, the seriousness and impact are very low. Hence, it is always better to have a systematic process to capture the feedback and a systematic method of working out the plan of action. Chances are high that, when a systematic approach is taken, commitment of the giver and the receiver of feedback is much higher and, hence, may be a more desirable outcome.

Moreover, there are also other advantages of the process of 360 Degree Feedback, which cannot be ignored. Very often people who fill the forms are also likely to benefit to a large extent, as they need to pause and introspect (and look at themselves and how well they are performing) before they rate someone else on these areas.

Openness of an organization and a systematic and focused 360 Degree Feedback as an intervention need not always be well integrated. By highlighting the open organization, one might be denying oneself or potential leaders of an opportunity to go through rigorous self-reflection and development.

Myth VIII: Implementing 360 Degree Feedback Brings Immediate Revolutionary Change in an Organization

Very often when we as consultants of 360 Degree Feedback have taken professionals through the process, they want to know about the key deliverables that one can expect after implementing 360 Degree Feedback. And we have this to say: 360 Degree Feedback will not give any earth-shattering results. The maximum benefit that this initiative gives is to the individual who has gone through the process. If the organization gets any benefit, it may be indirect and as a by-product.

There is the case of a company where an individual participant went through the 360 Degree Feedback process and he decided that the area in which he would like to improve is in delegation. When this individual went back to the work place, he was able to successfully delegate and take on many more activities far more crucial to the organization's bottom line and was able to increase the turnover of the company substantially, besides being able to return home earlier. This example shows a change, which is immediate, visible and measurable.

However, all changes are not necessarily of this nature. 360 Degree Feedback could be a major change initiative; it aims at bringing a change at an individual behaviour level. Research in human behaviour has shown how difficult it is to change human behaviour. These changes are much harder to notice and it is even harder to measure the benefit or outcome of the change. While it might take a few months for the individual to work on the desired change, one can safely assume that it will take twice the time for people around to notice it. Hence, the process of 360 Degree Feedback focuses on individuals for the benefit of the individual and the company. Expecting that there will be a revolutionary change in motivation levels, culture, etc., is perhaps being overambitious and is likely to put undue pressure on the system and the participants.

Myth IX: 360 Degree Feedback Is a One-time Process. It Needs No Follow-up. Nor Does It Need to Be Linked with Any Other System

360 Degree Feedback marks the beginning of a significant development process. To get maximum out of the process, it needs to be institutionalized

CHAPTER 9 Myths and Realities of 360 Degree Feedback

and must be backed with a proper follow-up mechanism and interlinks. Nowadays organizations are looking at a holistic approach. Many companies are beginning with a complete and detailed 360 Degree Feedback, repeating the feedback conducted only in select sections, which have been identified as critical and later on linking it with the performance management system.

Conducting a 360 Degree Feedback periodically is like a periodic medical check-up. It identifies the strengths and the areas of improvement. A timely evaluation leads to the reinforcement of desirable behaviour and correction in the not-so-desirable areas.

360 Degree Feedback can be looked at as a top management initiative for integrated HRD, including career development initiative and management development activity. Sometimes it could be linked to succession planning too. In other words, 360 Degree Feedback can have multiple uses for an organization in addition to being a very powerful tool for individuals. Like annual appraisal, it could be an ongoing process too.

Myth X: 360 Degree Feedback Is Meant Only for Senior and Top Management. Young Managers Are Not Likely to Benefit from It

Multiple research studies have indicated that flexibility and adaptability to change take place mostly during one's childhood. As we grow up, we lose our flexibility. It is not different for the behaviours. It is more difficult to change as one advances in life. Hence, it is best to correct at source. Based on this logic, young managers are likely to benefit a lot out of 360 Degree Feedback. This can be best explained with the example of a small plant. It is much simpler to move the direction of the plant towards sunlight at the early stages of the plant's life, rather than when it becomes a full-grown tree. Investing in the beginning of a career is very beneficial.

However, to bring large-scale organizational benefit, many organizations are following a top-down approach to this initiative. They would like the change to originate from the top and would like it to later cascade down the line.

Myth XI: 360 Degree Feedback Enhances or Brings Down Shareholder Value

This myth is being perpetuated by some agencies which are either too enthusiastic or too cynical. Some of them use even the support of research. For example, Watson Wyatt's study of corporations, which is quoted repeatedly some time ago, found that shareholder value has been found to be negatively associated with the use of 360 Degree Feedback. The drop or enhancement of shareholder value changes can be associated with so many things, including monsoon failures (which selectively affect some and benefit others), inflation (which again affects positively some and negatively others), economic policies, political stability, top management changes, HR practices and market changes. To think that one practice such as 360 Degree Feedback is as powerful as to influence shareholder value of several companies is a farfetched argument which only statistics can prove. In the USA, it is possible to find a statistical association between the use of consultants and the decline in shareholder value and argue that shareholder value declined in those companies that use consultants. It would also be true that those companies which are expecting a decline in shareholder value use consultants. Which argument you will side with depends on what interest group you belong to and is not necessarily supported by truth. As someone said, statistics can be 'lies and dam lies!'

This cannot substitute common sense. A gullible reader reads a research study and picks up what suits him/her. Recently, we received an article which highlighted Watson Wyatt's study but conveniently ignored many positives about 360 Degree Feedback. The reader underlined three sentences that read negatively about 360 Degree Feedback and ignored ten others that read positively. This indicates that 'you get what you search for' and 'you see what you want to see and not necessarily what is there for you to see'.

Here are some other interesting observations made in that study. Watson Wyatt's Human Capital Index study indicated that the use of 360 Degree Feedback has a negative impact on market value (see Pfan and Kay, 2002). The study indicated that when employees have an opportunity to evaluate their managers, it is associated with the decrease in market value by 4.9 per cent and when peers evaluate, it

CHAPTER 9   Myths and Realities of 360 Degree Feedback

decreases by 5.7 per cent. The authors add both of these and conclude that together 360 Degree Feedback is linked to a 10.6 per cent decrease. First of all, these figures are not additive and do not deal as strictly with 360 Degree Feedback as defined. If an organization does such studies and piecemeal work, it can expect to get such misleading results. The readers should know that the same study indicated that if the company uses human resource development systems (HRDS) technology to improve communication, the market value declines by 7.7 per cent and if it is used to promote culture, it further declines by 6.6 per cent and the use of new HRDS technology is associated with 14.3 per cent decline in market value. Such statistical findings highly mislead the readers.

They conclude, however, that such technology, if used with fundamentals in mind, adds 6.5 per cent to the market value. The interesting part of this study is that the prudent use of resources had a 10 per cent negative impact on shareholder value. The same authors give no such figures for 360 Degree Feedback, and mere subordinate feedback or peer feedback cannot be taken as 360 Degree Feedback. The authors, however, indicate the following problems associated with 360 Degree Feedback. These are very useful observations and I agree with them.

- 360 Degree Feedback interferes with teamwork (yes, it could as it focuses on the individual, but with a carefully designed tool this can be contained).
- It takes too much time.
- It can create high stress.
- Lack of role models hampers the use of 360 Degree Feedback.
- When there are no consequences for poor performance, people show a change immediately but do not sustain it.
- Top management is often not committed.
- 360 Degree Feedback is HR-driven and not line-driven.
- Often there are abstract ratings of competencies.

To get the best of 360 Degree Feedback, they suggest the following:

- Keep it simple.
- Create an open culture.
- Train people.

They suggest the following 12 best practices to get the best out of multi-source feedback:

1. Focus on business goals and strategy.
2. Use it for development not for pay.
3. Keep it short, simple and to the point.
4. Give the line employees a voice in designing and implementing the 360 Degree Feedback.
5. Create role models.
6. Develop the art of giving and receiving feedback.
7. Enforce consequences of continued poor performance.
8. Use it to celebrate good performance.
9. Insist on an action plan after 360 Degree Feedback.
10. Make coaching by leaders a part of it.
11. Make follow-up a part.
12. Monitor, improve and make adjustments.

We would like to believe that 360 Degree Feedback is such a powerful tool that it can change the lives of people and influence shareholder value. But it is not, and we are yet to get fully convinced either way.

However, we do believe that it has the potential. In the Aditya Birla Group, quite a few senior managers attended our 360 Degree Feedback programmes. They spoke about how a top-level manager changed his styles and behaviour. We had come across instances where the top-level manager had become more participative, more informal, started communicating or delegating more and this changed the work environment in the organization. We are also told that people are happier with him now than before and presumably organizational performance has gone up. We do not rule out the possibility that in some cases such positive changes in style could mean a negative impact in terms of productivity. For example, employees may take more advantage of such a change and discipline could decline! We have come across such instances in the health and population programme of the state of Uttar Pradesh in the mid-1970s when medical officers, trained by us, reported some problems associated with a participative style they were using after attending our programmes at IIMA.

However, we have heard more positive than negative things about 360 Degree Feedback. On the negative side, there were instances where the candidate went back and shouted at his subordinates (you

CHAPTER 9 Myths and Realities of 360 Degree Feedback

cannot shout at your boss!) for rating him low on delegation, etc., and started delegating with a vengeance and criticizing every failure. It depends on how you use the feedback. 360 Degree Feedback gives you feedback but cannot ensure that the candidate has put it to proper use. Whether to use it positively to build yourself and your team or to use it to take out your anger and attribute your inadequacies to others depends on you.

Although we try our best in our feedback workshops to guide the candidate to put the 360 Degree Feedback for positive use, a lot depends on the candidate.

It is true that the tool used is important and our experience, in the last decade, with our own (Indian) tools is that they are a lot more sensitive to Indian realities and have the power to focus attention on the right things. We normally strive in our workshops to persuade people to focus on the following:

- Leverage your strengths. Work on the positives. Keep visiting and revisiting strengths.
- Start doing small things.
- Focus on roles and activities that you can easily change and have good impact.
- Focus less on qualities that cannot be easily changed (example: temperament). Start working on these as long-term goals.
- Have another person (your colleague, spouse or senior) around you whom you can trust as a sounding board.
- Keep going through your feedback profile once in a while to remind yourself the impact you created and the goals you have set.

In spite of all that we talk about in our workshops, there is no guarantee that people will implement all that they should. Almost every one leaves the workshop with good intentions and action plans. Some try, a few succeed and very few get noticed for their success. Many get noticed for not changing. This has been our experience.

We are not unhappy that people do not change after 360 Degree Feedback. It is another myth to expect that 'people should change after 360 Degree Feedback'. Just because you are asked to give feedback to your boss, or colleague or subordinate, do not expect that he/she should change from the next day of receiving feedback.

It should be remembered that the candidate is receiving feedback from multiple sources. Do not rule out the possibility that he/she got contradictory feedback and even the opposite of what you may have given.

It is our common experience that many managers get contradictory feedback. Sometimes the same behaviour by them is perceived positively by some and negatively by others. For example, we have seen several cases where 'sociability' is perceived as strength by some and as weakness by others. Similarly, the same person is rated as aggressive and dynamic by some and manipulative and selfish by others. A candidate when gets such seemingly contradictory feedback is rattled. He needs time to assimilate and find out the positive and negative sides of sociability and how his dynamism is also leading him to be perceived as manipulative. In the USA, the focus on 360 Degree Feedback is to find consistencies and make the feedback objective. On the other hand, we have been promoting the candidate to pay attention to exceptions and see if the exceptions are true with him (positive or negative). We also promote the candidate to use the past assessment to develop capabilities for the future than to take the assessment for granted.

In fact, we have been promoting 360 Degree Feedback in India as a provocative tool and as an initiation to 'self-discovery' rather than as an 'assessment tool' or as a 'prescriptive tool'. This is one significant difference between the Indian 360 Degree Feedback and the Western one. It is a self-discovery tool and the workshops lay foundation for discovery.

We also say that 360 Degree Feedback is only 'indicative' and not 'conclusive'. At best we describe 360 Degree Feedback as summated subjectivities of a group of people with whom the candidate has interacted. It is as subjective as any other assessment. In fact, in 360 Degree Feedback, the assessors are prompted to be 'subjective' by suggesting that they should assess the candidate on the basis of their experiences and as they see him/her. So the Indian 360 Degree Feedback does not claim to be an objective assessment tool. Therefore, there are dangers in using it as a potential appraisal tool for promotions. Having said this, we do want to underline the significance of the data generated.

Leadership is the game of influencing other people: your customers (internal and external), your boss, your seniors, juniors and everyone around you. They have rated you and rated anonymously and without fear. They have rated you on matters that are important to you and

CHAPTER 9 Myths and Realities of 360 Degree Feedback

to your organization. What more do you want? Is this objective not enough? We do not make a uniform impact on all. The impact we make is a consequence of who we are, what we do, what the other person is and what he/she expects. This gives you good feedback of the impact and provides you with scope to maximize your impact.

What a beautiful tool it is if you are prepared to contain the complexity of feedback and not rattled to see different *avatar*s of yourself through the eyes of others. 360 Degree Feedback enables you to look at yourself through the eyes of others.

Another myth is that, when someone rates me negatively, he/she does not know what I am doing or what I have done. It is an assessment of high ignorance rather than my incompetence.

There is some truth in this. If it is true, it is equally true that the onus of removing his/her ignorance is with you and not him/her. So, you need to do something to review it. Maybe you are not doing enough, or not doing it visibly enough or overdoing something, or you may need to communicate more. The action plan is with you.

On the other hand, it may also be true that the other person has rated you low because he/she had high expectations from you. In fact, in many of our workshops, we had suggested the participants that low ratings from their colleagues, seniors or anyone else are indicative of high expectations. They should rather be happy to see high expectations and try to cope with them than to get depressed and disappointed. A person who is rating you 6 on a 6-point scale is telling you that nothing more can be expected from you. We are happy with whatever you are doing. While a rating 4 indicates that you can do a lot more. Therefore, a lower rating, though unpalatable, is indicative of the respect the person holds for you and this is good for you.

In most of our workshops, we have seen that it is only those who get low ratings benefit the most and demonstrate changes in their behaviour.

Another myth is that 'everyone should change after 360 Degree Feedback, and if he/she does not change, it had no impact'. In our view, the following types of changes are experienced and could be expected out of 360 Degree Feedback:

1. The candidate already knows all the feedback. He/she is highly receptive and has sensed the views of people even without the feedback. The feedback just reconfirms. It is a scientific way of

telling the impact he/she made—nothing new or nothing more to be done. This is a high awareness category candidate—with very little to learn from 360 Degree Feedback. There are very few wise people who fall in this category. Our experience is that everyone has something new.
2. The candidate did not know certain things (strengths, weaknesses, etc.). He/she now knows. He/she has enhanced awareness. He/she uses this awareness in all his/her activities but shows no visible change—a high increase in awareness and no action-orientation category. In our experience, most candidates fall into this category.
3. High awareness is achieved after the feedback. The candidate discovered many strengths and weaknesses and areas to work on, and prepared action plans. Intention to change was high, but he/she failed to act—intentions high, low action category.
4. High awareness, high action but low visibility. These action plans may not be those what others expected. For example, subordinates expected him/her to be more participative, while his/her own action plan is to delegate more. His/her increased delegation is not noticed by others and they conclude that he/she has not changed. The candidate himself/herself may feel that he/she is delegating more. Action plan implemented but observable change not noticed.
5. High awareness, high action and high visibility. Here the candidate changes and is perceived by many as having changed.

A candidate may fall into any of the above categories. So do not conclude that he/she has not changed. Normally after 360 Degree Feedback, the person is not the same. At least the awareness levels go up.

Imagine a school principal who went through 360 Degree Feedback, and after she returned no one noticed any change in her for several months—same style, same behaviour—high ego, autocratic and impatient. Until one day she was being complimented in the parent–teacher meeting revamping the school transportation system, as a result of which, every child is able to save 30 minutes every day of travel time. Count the amount of time saved of children every day! Everyone was surprised when she remarked in response: 'Thank you parents for giving this feedback in the 360 Degree Feedback programme at IIMA. That is

CHAPTER 9   Myths and Realities of 360 Degree Feedback

when I decided to pay attention to the school bus system'. Thus, even if there is change, very rarely do we attribute it to 360 Degree Feedback. Thus, the following could be the results of 360 Degree Feedback:

1. Enhanced awareness of strengths, weakness, expectation, successes, failures, impact, disappointments, etc. These may deal with tasks performed, styles, traits, qualities, attitudes, values, etc., depending on the tool used.
2. The individual may plan to change or act (intentions to act) to maximize his/her influence or impact, utilize his/her strengths, reduce the impact of weaknesses, identify new areas to work, communicate more, change his/her style of doing things (manage mistakes, etc.).
3. The individual may actually act on change or show new behaviour or changed behaviours translating intentions into action. He/she attempts to try new behaviours.

Depending on the nature of change, the following are various types of impacts that 360 Degree Feedback generates:

1. If there is only awareness and intentions but no action, others may not notice this unless the candidate talks about this. The normal tendency is to write off by saying that 360 Degree Feedback was done but nothing happened. This is perhaps true in more than 50 per cent of cases.
2. If the candidate does something in a planned way, again the following are possibilities:

   (i) Such actions may get noticed by others and may have a desired impact.
   (ii) They may not be noticed and may have a desired impact.
   (iii) They may have an impact other than what the candidate expected.

Thus, it is difficult to say that 360 Degree Feedback has not had any impact. In our experience, many candidates come back to us to say that they have gained a great deal and they are now not the same as before. They are often unable to give any concrete examples of what they started doing or stopped doing. We have had a similar impact reported by candidates attending a three-week to three-month general management programme at IIMA. They say that their managerial competencies and general management skills have gone up but are unable to specifically point out how they have changed. After all, the 360 Degree Feedback workshops are, at best, of one- or two-day duration. Therefore, it is reasonable to trust the candidate and agree that it has enhanced his/her awareness and made him/her a better manager. If with a one- to two-day 360 Degree Feedback experience we can generate leaders and change the behaviour of people, overnight, the world would have been different long ago. We should have realistic expectations and learn to appreciate the report of the candidate.

In a few cases, the candidates reported that they changed but their subordinates did not see that change. In most cases (almost all), the usefulness of the 360 Degree Feedback was professed. Awareness had definitely gone up.

Awareness is the first step to growth. This should not be denied. Many candidates do not get this feedback in their day-to-day work.

Some people have argued that traditional performance appraisals are better than 360 Degree Feedback, etc., and such comparisons are not warranted. Even in the USA where almost all Fortune companies use 360 Degree Feedback, it is not seen as a substitute for traditional performance appraisals. Traditional appraisal systems are organizational requirements. They establish role clarity, enable one to plan performance, establish accountabilities and facilitate performance monitoring, assessment and rewards. 360 Degree Feedback cannot substitute the same. 360 Degree Feedback at best can sharpen and evaluate the impact you are making and identify the constituents you need to focus on. So, it is futile to make comparison of incomparable.

The 360 Degree Feedback that we have been using is an awareness-building, impact-assessing, reflective and developmental tool. It can be used by top-level people, newcomers, family members and everyone. Interest and enthusiasm are very critical for success. By itself, it quenches your thirst but may not necessarily lead to actions visible and perceived by others.

Just because the individual has not shown any visible change to you, it is not fair to conclude that it has done no good. Next time before you conclude, ask the individual who got the feedback or ask yourself, what it meant to you. Then set your expectations realistically.

CHAPTER 10

Conditions for Successful 360 Degree Feedback

A Critical Look at 360 Degree Feedback

By critical we mean having a scientific look. Science means verifiable and predictable, valid and reliable. The use of 360 Degree Feedback and assessment centres has gone up in India in the last five years. It is said that more than 90 per cent Fortune 100 companies use 360 Degree Feedback (McLean, 2002). The figures get extended from Fortune 500 to Fortune 1000 companies. Definitely in India, the number of organizations using 360 Degree Feedback has increased enormously in the last three years. So are the service providers. The CEOs and the HR managers do not differentiate or understand the significance of 360 Degree Feedback and the turmoil it can generate. Normally, the service provider is evaluated in terms of the following:

- Cost,
- Credibility,
- Proximity,
- KAS (Knowledge, Attitude and Skills) and
- Experience.

Cost

The cost quite often is the deciding factor. As Dave Ulrich observes, in the absence of any other factors, the efficiency of HR managers and HR departments is being judged on the basis of cost reduction. Hence, HR managers use their ability to get the lowest charging facilitator or consultant or the ability to bargain and bring down the costs as an indicator of effective performance. It is, therefore, understandable that anyone who can offer the services at a low cost is sometimes considered good enough to perform 360 Degree Feedback. There are no competencies required. The most important competence is the ability to collect information, analyse the data and present it in an attractive form using several graphs and bar diagrams. Instruments are easily available as it is common practice in India where copyright is interpreted as the fundamental right to copy. Several tools are available on the web, and it is not too difficult to download. Instruments published in University Associates, by Pareek (2002b) and Pareek et al. (1981), all give a number of instruments that are copyright free. Therefore, the main qualification of a 360 Degree Feedback facilitator is his/her ability to offer services at low cost by providing the tool, administering it, collecting the anonymous data and presenting the individual feedback with profiles.

Credibility

The credibility of the service provider is used as another criterion. Understandably, any HR consultant who has credibility with the company and has handled HR assignments in the past in satisfactory ways is considered credible. Nothing can be more scientific than one's own experience. On this count, the firms do not seem to err much. However, the credibility factor in 360 Degree Feedback has many dimensions. The following are its constituents:

1. **Track record:** The past record of the consultant or facilitator in terms of the deliverables (quality, time, commitments, seriousness with which the assignment is carried out, etc.).
2. **Confidentiality:** The credibility of the facilitator in 360 Degree Feedback is highly dependent on his/her ability to maintain confidentiality of the data. He or she should not, under any circumstances, part with the original assessments to the candidate or anyone. They need to be destroyed after a specific period of time. Similarly, the feedback profiles should be kept extremely confidential and made available only to the parties purported to be available from the beginning and with the candidate being a party to the understanding. In most cases, the organization desires that the feedback is given only to the individual and not

CHAPTER 10 Conditions for Successful 360 Degree Feedback

to anyone else. In some cases, the CEO would like to have them, and in a few cases, only action plans are sought.

3. **Ethics and values:** The ability of the facilitator to point out the limitations of 360 Degree Feedback and use it for the purposes for which it is meant. The ability of the facilitator to guide the client in ways that are beneficial to him/her without a bias towards the commercial benefits the facilitator may have.
4. **Knowledge credibility:** The awareness of the facilitators of the limitations of the 360 Degree Feedback and the research studies available in 360 Degree Feedback. The ability of the facilitator to have a researcher's mind and keep in touch with the growing literature in the field.
5. **Research and follow-up:** Though this is in the hands of the assessee, it is the responsibility of the facilitator to ensure that adequate follow-up mechanisms are built into the feedback process. These may include a re-administration by the candidate and discussion with the assessors where appropriate.

Normally, the credibility is judged on the basis of the track record and adequate attention may not be paid to the other aspects.

Proximity

This is a very important consideration. It is associated with costs as well as easy availability of the facilitator when facilitating various aspects. A proximate consultant is always preferable as the user could call him/her up as and when needed. This is becoming less of an issue as telephones and cell phones, video conferences, etc., have become common. For example, the authors were involved in solving the issue by using video CDs to reach remote locations all over the world and by using tele-coaching sessions. However, the proximate availability of 360 Degree Feedback coaches or facilitators helps a great deal in making the process smooth and convenient.

KAS

This is an important factor and is the most neglected at this point of time. 360 Degree Feedback is a sensitive process. The T-Group training is a similar process which is to be facilitated only by trained behavioural scientists. They go through a three-phase training programme from ISABS or National Training Laboratories or other similar bodies like the ISISD. Alternately, they should be trained counsellors or psychologists or those specially trained in the facilitation process of 360 Degree Feedback. The most important requirements are knowledge (of the purposes of 360 Degree Feedback, the process of 360 Degree Feedback, applications of 360 Degree Feedback, limitations of 360 Degree Feedback, mistakes, knowledge of feedback, leadership models, research in this area, etc.), attitudes (empathy, listening, trust, helpful attitudes, patience, flexibility, etc.) and skills (coaching, follow-up and research skills).

Experience

Experience in the field is another criterion for choosing the facilitator. An experienced facilitator always brings with him/her a lot of lessons from the good practices elsewhere and transmits the same. The experience base may bring down the cost and enhance the ROI. An experienced coach and facilitator may prevent you from making the mistakes as he/she has already discovered the wheel. He/she ensures that the entire process is smooth. He/she also knows how to deal with problems and issues. He/she anticipates them and offers you preventive medicine.

Lessons from the Past

The following are some of the lessons we have learnt from the past on 360 Degree Feedback in India.

Purposes

1. It is best suited as a development tool, and most firms are not yet ready to use it as performance measure. It could be a good tool for performance management but not for performance measurement. Do not use it to measure performance but definitely use it to develop performance.
2. We are not yet ready to link it with incentives and rewards. 360 Degree Feedback itself can be rewarding for an executive if the

firm invests on his/her development. This investment includes not mere provision of the 360 Degree Feedback or profile, but also a follow-up support. The least a corporation can do is to provide coaching help. Unless an external (external to his/her department or unit) coach is available and the candidate is required to submit development plans after a discussion with the coach, the 360 Degree Feedback may not result in leadership improvements.
3. Even if you desire to link with performance management systems, enough preparation is needed, and it is better to wait until its credibility as an objective tool is built and the process is institutionalized.
4. It is a good methodology to use for identifying potential candidates for select positions. When the author was appointed to head the HR department at BEML, in 1978, a similar method (it was not known as 360 Degree Feedback at that time) was used to identify the potential future HRD chief. The ONGC experience indicates the same.

Readiness

1. Some organizations feel that the firm should be ready to take 360 Degree Feedback. There are instruments such as 'are you ready to take 360 Degree Feedback?' among others. While it is important to assess your readiness, it is equally important to create readiness. It is true that some firms are ready to take 360 Degree Feedback and institutionalize it more than some others. The same is true with individuals. Some are more ready than others. However, experiences of organizations such as the Aditya Birla Group have indicated that a good HR manager can make the firm ready by doing the necessary preparation.
2. It is always useful to create readiness by making it in phases. The phases recommended are as follows. Phase 1: voluntary and exploring; Phase 2: purely developmental and individual focused; Phase 3: institutionalize; and Phase 4: linkages with other HR systems—open and organizational. It should be externally administered first and when the comfort level goes up, then it could be administered as one progresses to Phase 3.

3. Do not go web-based until you institutionalize the process and provide a real good experience to your employees.
4. Always prepare the employees or the assessors and assessees for the same.

Instrument

1. There are many tools and models available. There are over 100 vendors of 360 Degree Feedback tools estimated to be in the USA. They are based on the leadership models which each company deals with. It is useful to be aware of these models. However, leadership model–based 360 Degree Feedback is useful only for those firms that have fully followed the leadership competence model, institutionalized it and are committed to it. Otherwise, the tool and the feedback based on it become academic and limited to practical relevance. The choice of the tool is important. Choose the tool that suits you best and that can give you multiple results.

   a. The tool should address the objectives of the 360 Degree Feedback and not any tool. It is the heart of the 360 Degree Feedback.
   b. The tool should focus on the competencies needed by the candidate.
   c. The competencies needed by the company, the department and the culture, norms and values the firm would like to promote could be focused.
   d. It should be easily understandable and should use the language commonly used in the company.
   e. For development purposes, the tools could be changed every now and then and used as a part of the training interventions. For example, Udai Pareek's Role Efficacy Scale can be converted into a 360 Degree Feedback tool, or any other tools can be converted and used as 360 Degree Feedback tools but they are for one-time administration and not regular use.
   f. Reliability and validity are always issues and one cannot wait. If you understand the concept and limitations of 360 Degree Feedback, they become lesser issues. Face validity and content validity are suggested at best. Test–retest reliability with a

CHAPTER 10 Conditions for Successful 360 Degree Feedback

gap of about a week to two preceding feedback may be useful to aim at. Internal homogeneity could be used (item total correlations, etc.).
2. It is recommended to use tailor-made tools for each firm. Some organizations are developing tools for each role with some common items and a few specific items.
3. The tool can be lengthier in the first administration. This gives a comprehensive assessment. Then it can be shortened. In any case it should not take too much time. Around more than an hour is considered as bringing down the efficiency and effectiveness of that tool. Thirty to forty minutes will be ideal.
4. Open-ended item seeking open-ended feedback are the most useful parts.
5. The best tool is the one that takes into account the expectations and views and opinions of the assessees and assessors.

Process

1. The administration should be preceded by firm-wide education, explaining the purpose and other details. Without education of assessees and assessors, the quality of feedback may become questionable.
2. The feedback should always be given after explaining the scope and limitations of feedback. Prepare the candidate in terms of creating readiness and receptivity to feedback.
3. Always provide scope for the candidate to have a dialogue with the coach or facilitators to help him/her understand and interpret the feedback appropriately.
4. Insist that the 360 Degree Feedback could be as biased as any other feedback and give enough scope for reflections about the feedback.
5. Identify common issues and provide for the participants to debate and discuss as well as come up with organizationally acceptable and managed action plans.
6. Appoint mentors wherever possible.
7. Provide benchmarks but treat them with caution.
8. Warn the individuals not to attempt to identify the assessee on the basis of the language. TVRLS research indicates that

only 18 per cent of the guesses on the basis of the language and individual ratings are correct. There is 80 per cent chance of a mistaken identity. Hence, it should be used to reflect and prove to oneself that the feedback is true or false most of the time. The feedback giver and his/her views should be respected but not blindly taken for granted; the onus is always on the candidate to prove to himself/herself that he/she possesses the strengths and does not have the weaknesses.

Follow-up

1. Most 360 Degree Feedback experiences do not give the ROI because, like Performance Management System (PMS), the organization thinks that its job is over once the 360 Degree Feedback is provided. Very little is done to follow up or to provide the needed follow-up support. The follow-up support may take the following forms:

   a. Insisting or asking the candidate to give his/her development plans or insights or lessons drawn and sharing with others (boss, juniors, etc.) what he/she desires to share.
   b. Asking the consultant to give suggestions on development in the form of training needs, etc., and offering the same. These are not to be asked by name but for the entire organization with frequencies and without names (see Mishra and Chawla, 2003).
   c. Conducting follow-up workshops after a period of three months or six months or an year.
   d. Re-administration and seeing the profile changes.
   e. Offering online coaching.
   f. Making mentors and coaches available.
   g. Encouraging the candidates to create their own tools and seek feedback on their own.
   h. Integrating it into PMS through KPAs, etc.

2. The HR department should be able to play an active role and task-forces may be used.
3. Documenting the success experience and sharing the same to inspire each other.

CHAPTER 10 Conditions for Successful 360 Degree Feedback

Building internal competencies

360 Degree Feedback is a great tool. Its potential and limitations need to be understood. There is no substitute for developing internal competencies of line managers and HR facilitators for administering and using the same. Those who are in this will not only contribute to developing leaders but may also themselves improve their leadership competencies. They are facilitating the building of intellectual capital.

PART 3
Lessons from Experience and Research

CHAPTER 11

360 Degree Feedback: Indian Experience

In the last one decade or so, there have been a number of research attempts to study the impact of 360 Degree Feedback. A few of them are summarized here. 360 Degree Feedback has emerged as one of the most used interventions of recent years for leadership development (as indicated by the number of organizations conducting 360 Degree Feedback-based interventions by Nair et al., 2009, Rao et al., 2000, 2002; Rao and Chawla, 2005; Vohra and Singh, 2005). 360 Degree Feedback has been linked to several positive outcomes such as improved performance, better interpersonal communication and smoother work relationships (Rai and Singh, 2005). In a recent study, Rai and Singh (2005) empirically examined the mediating effects in the relationship between 360 Degree Feedback and employee performance with a sample of executives ($N = 198$) working in four organizations in Western India. The results showed that interpersonal communication and quality of work life had a complete mediating effect. Leader–member exchange, quality and perceived organizational support were found to have a partial but significant mediating effect.

Studies, in general, on the impact of 360 Degree Feedback are limited. Raju Rao (see Rao et al., 2000) reports a follow-up study of 32 candidates who underwent 360 Degree Feedback a few months after the feedback. Interviews were used to get feedback. The survey revealed that the participants were still in the process of implementing their action plans. Some of them had shared their data with their juniors and seniors and were making efforts to validate the data from 360 Degree Feedback. In another study conducted by the same author, the questionnaire methodology was used as a follow-up, to ascertain the changes experienced after a 360 Degree Feedback implementation. (Number of candidates is not mentioned.) The survey indicated that a number of changes were reported by the assessors, including articulating vision, enhancing internal customer orientation and change in leadership styles. However, this study did not offer any conclusive evidence of change.

In another study reported by Rao and Annapurna (2005), 18 participants were re-assessed using the same tool one year after the first assessment. The 360 Degree Feedback tool used was based on the RSDQ model of leadership. When a comparison was made between the two assessments, changes in multiple areas were observed. For example, 8 of the 18 participations (45 per cent) showed improvements in all areas of the RSDQ model. Vision, customer focus, encouragement of juniors, communication, motivation, increased activity level and marketing activities were some of the frequently observed changes after 360 Degree Feedback, as reported by the participants' juniors, colleagues and bosses. While it must be mentioned that both positive and negative changes were observed, the changes were more in the positive direction. Changes in the leadership style were also observed, though only in a few cases.

Rao and Chawla (2010) conducted a follow-up study of 43 participants from four organizations, who underwent a 360 Degree Feedback programme. A self-assessment by the participants indicated the following:

The survey indicated that 88 per cent of the participants had visited their report at least twice, in the last one year.

- Ninety-one per cent of the participants were of the opinion that there was certainly a positive improvement in their professional life, after having undergone a 360 Degree Feedback process.
- Seventy per cent of the sample surveyed expressed that the 360 Degree Feedback process had made a positive impact in their personal life.

The survey indicated very positive results (93 per cent of the participants having accomplished at least 50 per cent of the action plans set) on the success that the participants had in implementing the action plans that they have set at the end of the 360 Degree Feedback process. When asked to list down the top three changes that the participants

CHAPTER 11 360 Degree Feedback: Indian Experience **145**

had observed in themselves after the 360 Degree Feedback, the findings were as follows:

1. Better communication (better interactions, enhanced listening skills, greater frequency of communication with peers/management, sharing knowledge) (about 20 per cent reported this);
2. Improved interpersonal skills (being more even tempered, improved dealings with others, better understanding of others, greater consciousness of one's own behaviour, being less critical, etc.) (about 46 per cent reported this);
3. Subordinate development and delegation (making conscious effort to develop team members, spending more time with team, enhanced sensitivity, empowerment, etc.) (about 30 per cent reported this);
4. Better time management, being more organized, prioritization and work–life balance (about 12 per cent reported this);
5. Articulating the vision and being more involved in company level plans, values, etc. (about 12 per cent reported this);
6. Enhanced self-awareness (weaknesses, receptivity to feedback, leveraging strengths, etc.) (about 17 per cent reported this);
7. Others (greater confidence, cost consciousness, customer orientation, systems orientation, out-of-the-box thinking, result orientation, etc.) (about 23 per cent reported this).

It is very interesting to note that the areas in which the participants have been successful in bringing about change are exactly those which have been listed under the 'High ease of development' in the book *Grow Your Own Leaders* by William Byham, Audrey Smith and Matthew Paese, with interpersonal skills, communication, empowerment, delegation being the easiest areas to build on/develop further (Byham et al., 2002).

With respect to the top three areas where the participants were not able to improve and see the changes as expected or desired, the key areas identified were as follows (the items have been clubbed under broad categories based on the nature/similarity):

1. The ability to motivate team members more effectively (by creating development opportunities for all, encouraging independent decisions, highlighting good work, etc.);

2. Ability to influence top management (liaisoning with them, rapport building, etc.);
3. Bring about changes in personal attributes (being more diplomatic, less irritable, more positive outlook, accountability, etc.);
4. Being more flexible and open minded;
5. Better conflict management;
6. Business-related skills (hands-on approach/understanding of ground realities, execution skills, presentation skills, IT/computer skills, technical knowledge).

The most significant changes observed at the organizational level were as follows:

- Better interpersonal sensitivity and improvement in relations at the workplace (better networking, free sharing or expectations and experiences between departments, enhanced understanding between people, healthy interactions, greater communication, cross-functional synergy);
- Increased receptivity towards feedback (openness to criticism, feedback, etc.);
- Better change management (positive outlook to change, acceptance of change, encouragement for change);
- Overall improvement in the culture of the organization (enhanced transparency, HR focusing on more people-orientated activities, people-driven culture);
- Change in leadership styles of individuals (higher consciousness and seriousness to bring about improvements, more professional style of leadership);
- Focus on innovation.

It was interesting to note that the comments on the negative changes observed in the organization after 360 Degree Feedback were very few compared to the positive ones.

- Tendency to go into a shell immediately after the feedback is received;
- Barriers in functioning and coordination amongst people at the workplace (due to self-defensiveness) leading to process & system deviations;

CHAPTER 11 360 Degree Feedback: Indian Experience **147**

- Individuals taking the feedback personally;
- Using 360 Degree Feedback as an opportunity to settle old scores;
- Increased suspicion amongst people—specially at a peer level;
- Slow pace of change due to daily work pressures (in some cases the ability to sustain the momentum of bringing about the required changes was low).

Ramnarayan (2010) analysed 360 Degree Feedback data from 11,761 assessors of 1288 candidates at the Indian School of Business to identify factors in a 35-item 360 Degree Feedback tool. The analysis indicated six factors as underlying the 35 items. These include emotional intelligence, personal leadership, adaptability, persuasive communication, networking, and motivating and influencing for improvements. Analysis of 16 courses taken by the students across the one-year period has indicated three clusters of these courses. The 360 Degree Feedback data of the candidates were correlated with the admission scores, course performance and placement performance. Placement performance was measured on the basis of the number of offers received as well as salary and nature of jobs. The 360 Degree Feedback data correlated with the course performance and placement data indicating some of the factors to have predictive validity on course performance and placement performance. However, it did not correlate with the admission scores.

Raju Rao (2010) compared the 360 Degree Feedback assessments of 51 star performers and 26 average performers drawn from six organizations. Star and average performances were identified from among a number of senior managers with the help of the assessments made by the CEO and the HR directors. The 360 Degree Feedback tool assessed the effective performance of nine roles and 55 activities under these roles, the leadership styles, delegation and other qualities of the candidates. All the 360 Degree Feedback assessments were done by 447 assessors for the 51 star performers and 289 for the 26 average performers. The data revealed that the star performers tend to show significantly higher scores in 360 Degree Feedback on the roles and activities part of the questionnaire. Star performers have been rated as performing various managerial and leadership activities significantly more effectively than the average performers. The leadership styles did not differentiate. Some of the qualities differentiated star performers from the average performers. Star performers seem to have created a higher level of learning culture and job satisfaction amongst their juniors. Raju Rao (2010) concluded on the basis of his study that 360 Degree Feedback is effective in differentiating individuals based on performance and can clearly indicate high flyers or fast-track individuals from the rest of the group. The differences are clearly brought out through the role assessment questionnaire of the RSDQ model. The study recommends focusing on activities and roles in developing leadership capabilities through 360 Degree Feedback.

Bhide (2010) describes a success experience in J.K. Organization using a combination of competence mapping, assessment centres and 360 Degree Feedback. According to Bhide, J.K. Organization connected them all to preparation of leadership pipeline and integrated systems framework. Bhide (2010) reports that the success is due to the following factors: top management 'buy-in' by no other way than linking competence to business results, making the various interventions a business initiative rather than an HR initiative, starting from the top, continuous communications, simplicity of the process, adaptation, empathy and credibility of the process owner through walking the talk.

The 360 Degree Feedback-based Leadership Development Programme (LDP) was initiated at Bharat Electronics Ltd. (BEL), with the primary intention of enhancing the *leadership effectiveness of the senior executives at BEL*. TVRLS designed the LDPs and conducted a total of 14 of them over a five-year period, covering around 240 DGMs, AGMs and GMs. A follow-up study was undertaken through a series of workshops and a questionnaire study. The study indicated the following strengths of the programmes:

- More than 38 per cent of the participants visited their 360 Degree Feedback data every quarter and 34 per cent of the participants visited 360 Degree Feedback data every six months.
- At least 50 per cent of the action plans were achieved by 95 out of 142 participants.
- The 360 Degree Feedback tool by TVRLS was seen to be a very effective tool in providing a detailed insight into the various parameters of one's role.
- 137 out of the 142 participants (96 per cent) felt that there was certainly an improvement in a positive way after having undergone the 360 Degree Feedback process.

CHAPTER 11 360 Degree Feedback: Indian Experience 149

- 5 out of the 142 participants (a mere 4 per cent) felt that there was no visible change in their professional life after having undergone the 360 Degree Feedback process.
- A total of 115 participants (81 per cent) felt that 360 Degree Feedback had made a positive impact on their personal life.
- Only 2 participants (less than 1 per cent) felt that there was deterioration in their personal life after 360 Degree Feedback.
- A total of 25 participants (18 per cent) felt that there was no visible change in their personal life as an impact of 360 Degree Feedback.

The participants also reported the change in the following areas as a result of the 360 Degree Feedback programme:

- Better communication/interaction with others,
- Better receptivity/openness to feedback,
- Better self-awareness among people,
- Improvement in listening to others,
- Better delegation of tasks,
- Leveraging on strengths is on an increase and
- Overall improvement in behaviour towards others was seen in the participants.

The common areas where participants were not able to observe the change after 360 Degree Feedback are as follows:

- Time management,
- Technological upgradation,
- Being more assertive/delegating more and
- Improvement in culture/liaisoning with the boss and top management and subordinate development.

The study also indicated the following areas that need improvement:

- Need for a mechanism for periodic follow-up: Feedback review sessions should be conducted every quarter/half yearly/yearly and can be anchored by internal HR with help from consultants.
- Better time management and a more open attitude towards delegation required in the organization.

- Internal resistance to change can be further improved upon to ensure better implementation of the action plans set by participants.

Gati Limited is a pioneer and leader in Express Distribution and Supply Chain Solutions in India. It was the revolutionary approach adopted by Gati that helped it launch many path-breaking initiatives in the logistics segment and many were the first for the Indian market. In a span of 20 years, Gati has consistently explored various ways to bring premium value to the customer, always setting benchmarks in quality of service and customer satisfaction. Mahendra Agarwal, the managing director (MD) of Gati, himself narrated in a paper the implementation and use of 360 Degree Feedback across a 12-year period. The MD participated in the first ever leadership development and organizational effectiveness workshop conducted at the Indian Institute of Management Ahmedabad in the year 1987. Subsequently, he sent some of his top-level executives to the public programmes organized by TVRLS and finally exposed his top management team to 360 Degree Feedback. This experience indicated gradual changes in the design of follow-up activities after the team was exposed to 360 Degree Feedback. The most important follow-up activities included sharing of action plans by the teams, sharing of the implementation success by the team, individual coaching and role negotiation exercises conducted immediately after the feedback between the candidate and his seniors or juniors. The result of all these is a gradual change in the culture and more professionalization of organizational processes (Agarwal, 2010).

Agarwal reports:

> We had about six rounds of 360 Degree Feedback in the last twelve years. In the first round feedback was given to the top 20 individually in a workshop and they prepared and presented action plans. The second round was a group review of the implementation of action plans with a follow-up feedback on a short questionnaire. The third round was devoted to team building wherein after the feedback was given on the TVRLS questionnaire, as Managing Director of the corporation, I expressed my surprise at some of the feedback I got and voluntarily read out the feedback. This led to other members sharing their feedback and surprises in a group. This has taken place in a two-day workshop at Bangkok where all of us went for

CHAPTER 11 360 Degree Feedback: Indian Experience

a business review. The sharing and team-building work took place prior to the business development workshop. In the next round of the 360 Degree Feedback, the next levels of managers were covered and the feedback workshops included three levels of managers including the MD. In two of these rounds the feedback and coaching was followed by role negotiation exercises between the candidate and his role set members. The role negotiation exercises were based on the action plans prepared by the candidate which were shared with his role set members (boss, juniors and colleagues in separate groups) and expectations were set. The role set-based meetings also included discussions about expectations from each other besides giving feedback. For example, if someone got low ratings on the meeting internal customers' expectations, he sat with his colleagues and explored more and prepared action plans. These meetings were held in Ramoji Film city. I also participated in the discussions and shared my expectations with some of them.

As we started growing the numbers were becoming large. In the two rounds we exposed to 360 Degree Feedback almost all our top 100 managers to 360 Degree Feedback and also modified the tools to suit our requirements. In all these I went through the 360 degree feedback at least four times more since the time I got my first 360 DF at IIMA in 1987. At that time I understand it was not even called 360 Degree Feedback and we were only trying to assess the impact we made on others. Looking back I feel that this intervention combined with the Assessment and development centres is one of the best we have done for enhancing our managerial and leadership effectiveness. In all these interventions I never insisted on discussing the feedback of any individual. Our managers shared their feedback voluntarily with me. All feedback sessions were outside the location and in my view the location and combination of the workshop timing with discussion of business plans is an important matter in the success of the Feedback. The most important contribution it makes is enhancing self awareness and enabling you to examine the impact you are making on others. This is critical for success. (Agarwal, 2010, p. 352)

The most visible of the changes observed in the beginning were as follows:

- Reduction in gap between the heads and bottom line staff. The employees became more comfortable with their heads of the departments and were able to communicate with them from time to time.

- Enhancement in the importance of information flow from top to bottom line, which helped in quick implementation of the decisions taken by the top management.
- Improvement in the effectiveness of managers in roles, styles, delegation and qualities aspects. A manager plays both transformational role (leadership role) and transactional role (managerial). It helped in articulating vision and values too.
- Change in the approach of leaders towards their subordinates from the old-fashioned style of dictating/commanding to being friendlier. The leaders not only assigned the tasks, but also could give advice from time to time. They also understood the importance of delegation, which led to the development of their subordinates and made them future managers.

The implementation of this programme surely brought in several changes in the minds of the employees at Gati, such as follows:

- They began to feel how they were perceived in the eyes of others. Gaps are identified in one's self-perception versus the perception of the manager, peer or direct reports.
- Increased awareness among senior management that they too have development needs. Increasing self-awareness of people managers of how they personally impact upon others—positively and negatively.
- Gaining acceptance of the principle of multiple stakeholders as a measure of performance. A rounded view of the individual's/team's/organization's performance and what the strengths and weaknesses are.
- Encouraging more open feedback—new insights.
- Identifying strengths that can be used to the best advantage of the business.
- Perception of feedback as more valid and objective, leading to acceptance of results and actions required.

Maruti Suzuki India Limited (MSIL) conducted 360 Degree Feedback for managers a few years ago. The initial process covered 580 managers and included a first exposure, followed by generating a list of assessors for each candidate. The consulting company made the choice of assessors, profiled and finalized the feedback. The feedback

CHAPTER 11 360 Degree Feedback: Indian Experience 153

seminars were conducted internally. The process ensured confidentiality and established credibility. The process has been established and matured. Follow-up is now planned (Sinha, 2010).

Sinha (2010) reports the following results: The individual feedback report has been an eye opener for many of the managers as shared by the incumbents. There has been significant transformation of the leadership style of many individuals.

Some of the respondents have quoted: "The style of handling of my superiors has changed and it is being reflected in day today intention with the team members".

Some of the incumbents (feedback seeker) have quoted: "I never thought my people perceive me this way, although my intention was good but it might not have reflected in my behaviour".

> We have also noticed managers appreciating their juniors and peers in a greater way even for their small contributions. Celebrating success even for their achievement along with the team has been a part of our culture. People have started interacting much more with their internal customers over a cup of tea to strength their networking and partnership skill and understand them in a better way.

Overall 360 Degree Feedback in MSIL is further strengthening the leadership style of managers by collaborating, participating, developing and appreciating the people and becoming a role model for others (Sinha, 2010).

Dixit (2010) reports the 360 Degree Feedback experience in a fast growing business group Adani in Ahmedabad. This business group started as a trading company and now is an established infrastructure business giant in Gujarat and perhaps in the entire country. Out of the 34 of the top-level managers exposed to an introductory session of 360 Degree Feedback, 21 opted to undergo the 360 Degree Feedback process in the year 2005. The 360 Degree Feedback profiles were made using the TVRLS leadership models. The feedback profiles were prepared by the consultant and shared in a workshop on a one-to-one basis. One round of coaching was conducted after the feedback was shared. No follow-up was done subsequently. Action plans were prepared by the candidates and shared with the HR department. However, in the absence of the feedback, nothing could be ascertained for the next three years. A quick review was undertaken. A resurvey indicated positive changes in terms of self-assessment. There was a positive recall of the programme though concrete actions could be claimed to have been undertaken by the candidates. The exercise however resulted in strengthening the internal process and establishing a knowledge centre for the group and various other interventions. With more systematic follow-ups, perhaps a lot more could have been achieved.

Besides these, many other organizations report using 360 Degree Feedback very productively. In a book that lists the HR innovations for excellence, Nair et al. (2009) report the following experiences by some of the organizations in the manufacturing sector:

Companies also engage in 360 Degree Feedback for the development of their employees. This is usually done for a select group of generally senior level employees. Using the multi-rater feedback which provides both self-assessment and assessment by important stakeholders such as superiors, team members/colleagues, subordinates and customers, a holistic picture of individual's performance and developmental needs is identified through the process.

It has been observed at Philips that managers getting exposed to 360 Degree Feedback assessments have improved their performance levels in the organization. The assessment at Philips is done for the management team of the unit as well as for the high potentials. At SKF India, 360 Degree Feedback is conducted using the CUBIKS tool designed on the basis of SKF competence clusters. The clusters include competencies relating to understanding, analysing and making sound use of the strategic and business environment, competencies for influencing, leading and interacting with others, competencies required to constantly improve own performance and behaviour, and competencies specific to individuals' jobs and positions. Employees at all levels are part of this tool that is optional and purely used for self-development. The feedback is used for working on areas of development and the same is converted into action plans for improvement.

The 360 Degree Feedback process at Moser Baer is employed for general manager and above levels, as these levels are thought to decide the future growth of the organization in the short and long term. In order to identify possible stars and provide inputs for their career plans in terms of development, movement and succession planning, the 360 Degree Feedback process is used. Since the feedback holds a mirror to how seniors, peers, customers or subordinates perceive

CHAPTER 11 360 Degree Feedback: Indian Experience

the assessed at work, it helps them be more self-aware as well on the requisite competencies.

As part of the LEAD initiative at NTPC, 360 Degree Feedback is conducted once in three years for senior grade employees. An IT-enabled system called LEAD Circle for positions at the level of AGMs and GMs has been used for assessing and developing 88 AGMs and GMs in the past.

Castrol runs 360 Degree Feedback for all team leaders at least once a year. A standard online tool called *Novations* is used for the purpose. Feedback collected is shared with the concerned manager through a facilitation process by HR and any gaps are incorporated in the individuals' development plans.

CHAPTER 12

Life after 360 Degree Feedback: Lessons for the Future

Many companies are now conducting 360 Degree Feedback along with Assessment and Development Centres (ADCs). The ADCs are conducted normally to assess the potential of managers to occupy roles they have not occupied so far and test competencies that have not been tested before. While the ADCs have come as a tool to build future managerial and leadership pipeline, there are many variations in the way they are used. Both ADCs and 360 Degree Feedback have become very popular new era HR tools. With human resources gaining strategic importance combined with raising costs of talented managers, and their scarce availability, organizations are left with no better alternatives than identifying and grooming talent from within. This has led to the increased use of ADCs and 360 Degree Feedback tools for developing leadership competencies. Sometimes 360 Degree Feedback is used as a tool for career development and succession planning purposes. Sometimes ADCs are used as predictors of fast-track managers. However, research on the predictive ability of ADCs or 360 Degree Feedback is scant. A detailed study was conducted by the author based on data gathered from three organizations that have conducted assessment centres as well as 360 Degree Feedback (Rao, 2010). In all the three organizations, the ADCs and 360 Degree Feedback were used as development tools. In these organizations, competence mapping was done and the common competencies were identified using behaviour indicators. Tools were developed to assess the competencies. The competencies were assessed for each candidate by external assessors in an assessment centre setting. They were also assessed by their seniors, juniors and colleagues on the same competence model on specially designed tools to measure the very competencies measured by the assessment centres. Results indicated no definite patterns.

CHAPTER 12 Life after 360 Degree Feedback

The results lead to the conclusion that past performance as assessed by 360 DF is not necessarily a good predictor of future potential as assessed by the Assessment centres. The findings seem to be valid irrespective of the nature of competencies assessed and across various categories of employee. The results suggest that each should be treated as separate development tool and be given the place that is due to them. Given the lack of correlation caution should be taken in using the data for promotion and succession planning purposes. (Rao, 2010, p. 104, Rao, Ramnarayan and Chawla, editors)

"We have conducted 360 Degree Feedback and covered 586 executives. The experience has been great".

"We started from the top. It started a good trend. The Credibility is established and now we can go ahead".

"There is total involvement from the top and it has been a great experience".

"Our Individual Development Plans (IDPs) were of excellent quality".

"We appointed executive coaches for our top management team after the exercise".

These were the most common responses that we got when we tried to collect data on the experiences on life after 360 Degree Feedback and ADCs. Life after 360 Degree Feedback when combined with ADCs was seen to revolve more around excitement, sponsorship to training, foreign visits, executive coaching, etc. However, in those organizations that have merely done 360 Degree Feedback, understandably not so much of fanfare has been observed. The success of these initiatives was being evaluated largely in terms of the targets met, number of executives covered, amount of money spent, top management time used, assessors efforts, etc.

There are some organizations that do undertake a lot of silent work on 360 Degree Feedback and ADCs and make numerous efforts for integrating them into the employees' life, without any great fanfare or huge investments. After all, 360 Degree Feedback and ADCs are important milestones in an individual's, team's and organization's journey of leadership. Treating them as target-fulfilling tools is akin to treating patients in a hospital using a target-centred approach, i.e. ensuring use of various pieces of hospital equipment such as X-ray,

CAT scan and other machines to fulfil only the targets of the particular department rather than fulfilling/serving the need of the patient. Unfortunately, commercialization and over-professionalization do seem to have done this damage. At times HR managers seem to focus more on numbers covered and budgets spent rather than on the actual benefits and growth of employees.

It was with the intention of ascertaining the deeper impact that these two initiatives had, that TVRLS chooses its theme as 'Life after 360 Degree Feedback and ADCs' for its fourth conference. The main purpose was to find deeper answers to questions such as follows:

> *What exactly did those who went through these powerful initiatives do?*
> *What results were they able to produce?*
> *What changes have they initiated?*
> *What difficulties did they face?*
> *How did they overcome these difficulties or challenges?*
> *What suggestions would they have to make these two initiatives more powerful?*

While one must acknowledge that there is difficulty in measuring or ascertaining the impact of such initiatives on leadership and managerial effectiveness, 360 Degree Feedback and ADCs must be used at best as starting points. Organizations should appreciate the nature of these interventions and the nature of output that can be expected of them. It is sad to see that in some organizations, senior HR professionals are not even aware of the similarities or differences between these two initiatives. It therefore came as no surprise when one of the directors asked our consulting company to implement a 360 Degree Feedback tool and thereafter validate the findings by conducting an ADC for the same set of participants.

360 Degree Feedback versus Assessment Development Centres (ADCs)

- 360 Degree Feedback is an assessment of the employees by known people, while ADCs are an assessment made by less known or totally unknown people. Even when internal assessors are used, the common practice is that the candidate should not

be assessed by those who know her/him and the assessor should be at least two levels above the organizational positioning of the candidate.
- 360 Degree Feedback is an assessment of the past performance or feedback of the chemistry that the individual has generated in the past, whereas ADCs are an assessment of the potential of the individual. 360 Degree Feedback is based on what is seen or demonstrated on the job, while ADCs are based on what is demonstrated in simulation games and exercises. Hence, if a job does not have any element of strategic thinking and it is one of the factors in a 360 Degree Feedback tool, the participant may get low scores on this parameter in a 360 Degree Feedback tool simply because the role does not require her/him to demonstrate the same and hence the respondents have not seen this behaviour. However, the same individual assessed on the same competence using an ADC may get high scores simply because the simulation requires her/him to demonstrate his/her inherent strategic thinking, which (s)he did so, to a good extent.
- Another important difference between the two initiatives is that a 360 Degree Feedback tool uses self-assessment and compares ratings of others with self. However, an ADC does not take into account or does not focus on self-assessment.
- A 360 Degree Feedback tool accepts emotions and treats all assessments as subjective. ADCs, however, are more objective as they rely on multiple exercises and multiple assessors.

While these differences exist between the two initiatives, what unites them is the fact that both are powerful tools for development—360 Degree Feedback lends itself well for development in the current job and ADCs can be used very effectively to prepare for future jobs. Both are based on competence models of organizations, but both have limitations, imposed by competence models. An ideal 360 Degree Feedback tool should use the current job profile, and the ideal ADC should use the expected future job profile.

Whether an organization implements a 360 Degree Feedback tool or an ADC, organizations should chart out a powerful road map to ensure that individuals benefit from it and are able to live a changed life after these initiatives. The results of our survey and the papers presented indicate that there is still a long way to go for organizations to ensure this. While few organizations such as Gati and JK Group seem to have used these interventions well, in the JK Group the most important finding was the constant effort and search for appropriate experiences and adaptation of the consultant models.

While presenting in the conference, the author of this paper stated that the HR department should always do more work than the consultants and should be one step ahead of the consultants so that they can direct their effort rather than assigning the project and forgetting all about it (Bhide, 2010).

Our past work in these two areas over the last decade and a half has helped us conclude that 100 per cent consultant-dependent interventions do not do as much good to a corporation as HR department designed and initiated interventions. The excellent experience of Aditya Birla Group, Tata Group and JK Group illustrates this point well. On the whole, it is our finding that very few organizations seem to go beyond conducting the 360 Degree Feedback and ADCs on a target-centred approach. The stability of an HR team seems to be an important factor in this. As HR directors change their jobs, they seem to change consultants and along with them the competence models of companies. Along with HR's credibility, the credibility of such initiatives also gets adversely affected.

While this is our finding at an organization level, it is refreshing to find that a lot seems to be happening at an individual level, based on feedback received after a 360 Degree Feedback tool or an ADC. Though not well followed up, the experience of Bharat Electronics Limited as well as the Adani Group has indicated that even without any follow-up, the 360 Degree Feedback has proved to be a useful tool, as many candidates seem to be motivated by feedback.

In this chapter, we share some of the ways in which one can proactively facilitate a better life after 360 Degree Feedback and ADCs.

At a Process and Implementation Level

Starting right

In order to make the entire initiative a milestone in an individual's life, it is very important to begin right. Organizing a proper launch of 360 Degree Feedback, by orienting participants about what they should

CHAPTER 12 Life after 360 Degree Feedback

expect, their role/contribution in the initiative and likely outcomes etc. is the first step in making the entire initiative successful. Our experience has indicated that when sufficient time is not invested in this, participants do not take it seriously; they do not participate with the right mental framework and hence this impacts life after 360 Degree Feedback adversely.

Starting right is the first step towards ensuring that life after 360 Degree Feedback moves in the right direction. One of the organizations that we consulted for scheduled a daylong workshop to launch their ADC- and 360 Degree Feedback–based leadership initiative. They invited guests from other leadership institutes and industry stalwarts to share their experiences and set the tone for leadership development. The entire leadership initiative was designed internally and key role holders had spent more than a year ideating, designing and getting the necessary inputs, before a roll-out. This is the kind of effort that is required to help initiatives like these make a difference. Another client went a step ahead and had half-day sessions for participants and their seniors on what the participants have done after 360 Degree Feedback and the plans for future and support required. This enhanced the seriousness and accountability of the managers. The HRD head and the managing director of the company participated actively in such reviews.

Inclusive approach

Involving key family members (spouse, older children, etc.) as a part of the process is a very important step in ensuring the long-lasting impact of the process—this is especially true of the 360 Degree Feedback process. This is very beneficial, in our opinion, as family gives feedback with a lot of genuineness and, more importantly, they become an integral part of the change process. Involving family in the feedback process begins the journey of involving them in the change process that follows. Key behavioural changes that need to be worked on, such as temper management, being more patient and giving more appreciation, are easy to practice and change in one's personal life. This is true especially when areas that need to be improved are temper control, being more appreciative of others, patience, etc. Carrying forward these changes to one's professional life is then relatively easy.

Focus on strengths

One of the key takeaways from these initiatives is that it is very important to focus on leveraging strengths rather than chasing areas of improvement or focusing on things that are not our natural talent or areas that we have not consciously developed. Some of the effort reviews that we have conducted in the past seem to indicate that many of the participants have improved on their overall 360 Degree Feedback scores by simply focusing more on their strengths.

Increased touch points

Very often, participants are overwhelmed with the actual 360 Degree Feedback data. They believe that once the workshops are over and the feedback is in their hands, most of their task is over. However, the workshops only mark the beginning of a long journey that needs to be punctuated with effort reviews and checks on progress made. Instead of assessing whether the individual has managed to change or not, the focus should be on assessing the input or the effort put in by the individuals—the results will surely follow.

To make life after 360 Degree Feedback more impactful, having more talk points to helping participants remain connected with the outcomes of this initiative is very important. The daily grind of work life and fire fighting that typically line managers face results in individuals gradually forgetting about the key purpose of these powerful initiatives. Hence, sponsors of the initiative can ensure a long-lasting impact by providing enough opportunities for the individual to visit and move forward on the action plans that have been set during the course of the initiatives. In one of the organizations where we were implementing a 360 Degree Feedback tool, the entire initiative began with feedback but, thereafter, there were a series of one-day workshops conducted every month on different inputs identified based on the outcomes of the feedback. Organizing experience-sharing workshops, using this data for other training workshops, etc. are ways to increase touch points.

At a Stakeholder Level

We believe that to get a good ROI 360 Degree Feedback and such other initiatives, multiple role holders from the organization have to play an active role. The top management, the participant her/himself, the HR team and the consultants are the four critical parties that have a significant role to play, as given below.

A. List of activities that could be undertaken and the role to be played by the candidate after 360 Degree Feedback

- The candidate should make efforts to understand the feedback in its context. Sufficient time should be spent (after receiving feedback through either of the initiatives), introspecting and exploring the deeper meaning behind the feedback received. One needs time to go beyond the obvious and read between the lines.
- The candidate should also be aware of the limitations of the 360 Degree Feedback. To give an illustration of the limitations:

> a. All assessments of people by other people are subjective. Hence, 360 Degree Feedback can be as subjective as any other assessment. However, it is the aggregate feedback and consistency in feedback that tends to make it more objective.
> b. 360 Degree Feedback should be used as indicative and reflected upon.
> c. 360 Degree Feedback could also be provocative. The candidate should use this for review, reflection and action.
> d. The action plans worked out as an outcome of the feedback should primarily be directed at empowering self and changing oneself where necessary.
> e. Even if one has to change others, it requires change in oneself: one's approach, attitude, communication, etc.
> f. 360 Degree Feedback should be used to empower the person through enhanced self-awareness.
>
> *As given in the manual for leadership development through 360 Degree Feedback by TVRLS.*

- It is a very good idea for the candidate to make a summary of the feedback received, key strengths, areas of improvement, etc. and send it all those who gave feedback, along with a thank you note. Our past experience has indicated that those who share their feedback are likely to have a much more effective life after 360 Degree Feedback. Those who do not share it and do not discuss freely about it are not likely to do much about it. In fact, the example set by Vineet Nayar of HCL technologies is worth emulating. He posted his 360 Degree Feedback's both the strong and weak points on an Intranet website for all his assessors to see. He even encouraged all other senior employees to do the same (Cappelli et al., 2010, p. 53).

- Participants who actually want to have a changed life after 360 Degree Feedback or ADCs should build the courage to make a public commitment to the change they want to be, by sharing their feedback. Another advantage of sharing feedback is that people get to know one's intention and may also offer suggestions on how one can bring about the changes that one would like. We have known of other great leaders and CEOs who have actually posted key aspects of their feedback on the Intranet for all to see. What an example to set and what positive role modelling! There was one particular CEO who actually shared his entire 360 Degree Feedback with his team, and though others were embarrassed to hear it, he was perfectly comfortable sharing every aspect. This is the perfect way to consciously choose a different life after 360 Degree Feedback. If this CEO were to ever forget which aspects he needed to work on, he would have multiple people all around him to serve as perfect reminders.
- It is a good idea to share the feedback in detail with a colleague (in/outside the organization) and use him/her as a mentor or sounding board. Similarly, sharing the data with one's spouse would also help.
- Similarly, conscious effort should be made to share relevant aspects of the data with one's juniors.
- It is a good idea to keep revisiting the open-ended data periodically (at least one a month, or once a quarter) and saving areas of focus as 'screen savers' in one's computer.
- Finally, the candidate can opt for a reassessment done on a shorter version of the questionnaire after one year—provided the individual has worked hard on her/his action plans and can expect movement in the scores.

CHAPTER 12   Life after 360 Degree Feedback   165

B. List of activities that could be undertaken and the role to be played by the candidate's boss or seniors after 360 Degree Feedback

- Seniors can play an important role in encouraging candidates after such initiatives by offering to act as a sounding board to help them reconcile feedback that is not very clear or feedback that the participant is not sure how to take.
- A group meeting can be organized, where each participant from the particular department gives a summary of his/her learning's and take away from the 360 Degree Feedback. (In case the 360 Degree Feedback is a part of a larger leadership development initiative, the participant can give a summary of the workshop proceedings and later focus on specific feedback (s)he received.)
- The participant can also be requested to present a summary of the feedback received and action plans. The group can thereafter give additional suggestions, keeping their knowledge of the individual as well as the culture of the organization in mind.
- Seniors can also encourage the participant to move one or two significant action plans into the individual PMS by adding it in the KPAs section.
- Finally, seniors can focus much more on the individual's areas of strength and consciously explore ways and means by which they can be actively used for the good of the department or the role that the candidate is playing.

C. List of activities that could be undertaken and the role to be played by the top management/HR after 360 Degree Feedback

- Ensure that consultants give their recommendations, on the basis of their findings, that may have organization-wide implications. For example, most 360 Degree Feedback tools do indicate to a limited extent the organization-wide competence strengths and areas of improvement. Top management can ensure that along with facilitating individual action planning, organization-wide strengths are utilized more effectively and sessions are held to overcome some of the areas of improvement.

166 THE POWER OF 360 DEGREE FEEDBACK

- Organize and ensure frequent counselling or coaching sessions (at least one every four to six months) to ensure that good progress is made by individuals. Treat 360 Degree Feedback as an initiative and not an activity.
- Facilitate effort reviews and ensure that the team of participants assembles a few days after the feedback.
- Invite speakers from other organizations who have been participants in such initiatives, to share how they approached these initiatives, what feedback they received and how did they benefit from it.
- Explore ways and means by which the data generated from 360 Degree Feedback can be linked with other initiatives in the organization. For example, individual 360 Degree Feedback data can be linked with a climate survey or engagement survey at the department level. Similarly, ensure that other development initiatives use the data generated from these initiatives so that it gives individuals an opportunity to keep revisiting their feedback. Similarly organization-wide training programmes can be organized based on the group trends and data.

D. List of activities that could be undertaken and the roles to be played by the consultant after 360 Degree Feedback

- It helps immensely if consultants have a yearlong calendar for each of these initiatives. The organization and the consultants should have a mutual understanding that such initiatives are not overnight result providers and are still largely dependent on external help and frequent follow-up. Hence, resources should be budgeted keeping a one- or two-year perspective in mind and time should be allocated accordingly.
- The entire gamut of follow-up activities, coaching, etc. should be factored into the budget.
- Key milestones such as launch, actual process, feedback workshops, counselling and effort reviews should be tabled right in the beginning of the assignment, and consultants should insist on launch of the same, with the CEO or the MD having an active participation in the launch—this sends out the right signals on the importance given to this initiative by the leadership team as well as it gives the candidate enough time to be prepared mentally and psychologically.

CHAPTER 12 Life after 360 Degree Feedback

- Once the feedback has been given to the participants, a summary of the key observations, findings, experiences and a short report of organizational interventions that are possible should be given by the consultants.

To summarize, in order to ensure a strong ROI and high effectiveness after 360 Degree Feedback, given below is a list of follow-up activities that can be undertaken by the organization:

LIST OF FOLLOW-UP ACTIVITIES

Coaching:

- Organize individual coaching sessions immediately after giving feedback in 360 Degree Feedback.
- Have one to three rounds of coaching by internal/external coaches to ensure internalization of the focus on development and enhanced action orientation.

Action planning:

- Ensure that final IDPs are prepared by the candidates (with help from the coaches) and sent to the HR department.
- Organize for the action plans to be read out by the respective candidates in public, as a way of public commitment.
- Make the action plans available for all by making them available on the organization Intranet.
- Finally, incorporate the action plans in the PMS as developmental KPAs/KRAs.

Effort reviews:

- Incorporate an effort review to review the effort/progress/inputs by the candidate after 8–12 months of the feedback through 360 Degree Feedback.
- Identify any further development needs and arrange for self-study.
- Review implementation and give weightage as a part of the KPAs.

(Contd.)

(Contd.)

Integrating into the PMS:

- Ask the individual to identify one key strength to be leveraged and one area of improvement and action plans for the same.
- Add this on in the PMS as a development KRA/KPA with some weightage given to it.
- Integrate the findings on change observed into the Human Resource Information System (HRIS) of the individual. Please take care not to use the 360 Degree Feedback data itself but rather the change observed after 360 Degree Feedback.
- In case any development-oriented workshops have to be attended by the candidate, add it as a part of the training budget.

Other steps to strengthen the impact:

- Develop internal coaches.
- Ensure that internal research is conducted from time to time on the effectiveness of such initiatives, suggestions, etc. Publish the trends, results and action plans.
- Encourage individuals to introspect and share how these initiatives have made a difference. Publish such articles or personal experiences for all to read.
- Arrange experience sharing by guest faculty from other organizations to get different insights on how others have benefited from such initiatives.
- Organize for a reassessment (specially of the 360 Degree Feedback) after a year.

CHAPTER 13

Getting ROI on 360 Degree Feedback*

Estimating Returns on Investments for HR Interventions

In an earlier book entitled *Hurconomics*, a formula for estimating the returns on investments made in HR interventions is presented. In this book the concept of real cost to company (R-COT) and opportunity cost (O-COT) has been explained. The R-COT is what is usually known as Cost to Company (CTC) divided by the number of hours a person is expected to work (for example, with a CTC of ₹1.2 million, the R-COT is ₹600 an hour or ₹10 a minute counting 2000 hours of work in year). The O-COT is the work output expected to be delivered by the individual in financial terms. This is normally about four to ten times depending on the industry. This factor is arrived at by dividing the annual financial turnover of the company by its people costs. Thus, in an IT or financial services company, the O-COT is four times the R-COT as the people costs are around one-fourth of the turnover or top line (see Rao, 2011, for details). Using the formula suggested, let us look at various costs and benefits of 360 Degree Feedback.

The Cost of a Smile

Take the case of Varun discussed in the Introduction. To recapitulate, Varun is a serious, sincere and hard-working SVP. The average tenure of his junior staff was about six months, and every year at least 50 per cent requested transfers or left the department. Most of the time,

---

*Modified shorter version of Chapter 6 from *Hurconomics* by T.V. Rao (New Delhi: Pearson Education, 2011).

these departures were explained away as resulting from a high demand for chartered accountants and commerce graduates from outside the department. Only a few people internally knew the truth of the matter.

Through the 360 Degree Feedback process, he understood his strengths and weaknesses for the first time. While he was happy to see that his strengths were noticed and acknowledged by everyone, the discovery that his interpersonal competence was rated as extremely poor, and that team work within the department was bad and his juniors' morale low, shook him. First, he found it very difficult to reconcile his department's high regard for his abilities and the results he helped bring about, with the assertion that he was very poor at team work and at maintaining interpersonal relations. The question he asked during the workshop was: 'How is it that I am delivering results year after year and getting promoted faster than anyone else, if my team work is poor and interpersonal competence low?'

Within a few days of the 360 Degree Feedback workshop, the SVP initiated a number of changes. Everyone noticed the change in him and he no longer behaved as formally as before. He stopped insisting that people come early or leave late, as long as they completed their work on time. Gradually, he also cultivated the practice of holding informal departmental meetings. In three months, the SVP had changed visibly. According to some of the juniors, 'He smiles now, which he rarely ever did before, and we are no longer afraid to approach him'. A couple of years later he was adjudged one of the best presidents of the company.

What is the cost of his smile? What are the benefits of smiling? If 360 Degree Feedback can help you to become more aware of your strengths and weaknesses, what is the ROI?

Some answers

A 360 Degree Feedback conducted with a proper tool costs about ₹5000. Combined with a feedback workshop of two days (normally, 360 Degree Feedback workshops are two to three days long and focus on leadership development), the exercise costs another ₹30,000 to ₹1 lakh for the top management, depending upon the institution that offers the workshop. Positing the cost of the SVP's 360 Degree Feedback at ₹50,000, including the CTC for the two days of his attendance, travel costs, profiling costs and faculty fee, getting him to smile cost the company ₹50,000. The cost of his new-found humaneness is only ₹50,000.

The benefits

Now, let us estimate the benefits of his smile. The following is the list of benefits:

1. Retention has gone up. Ever since the SVP changed his behaviour, employees have begun to feel more comfortable working with him. Earlier, employees in the department could be retained for only six months or so. Now the average period of retention has risen to two years. Every employee who left cost the company three months of adjustment time (for the new employee) and also transfer and other HR costs of at least 10 man days per employee. These 70 days of wages lost without productivity (60 days + 10 days of HR time) meant ₹2.1 lakh per person seeking change. If in a department of 30 people, 50 per cent change jobs every now and then, and even if five of the changes are attributable to the behaviour of the SVP, the annual savings due to his changed behaviour are 5 × ₹2.1 lakh = ₹10.5 lakh.
2. Productivity has risen as there is now less tension. Employee morale has been boosted too. These are difficult to cost. Assuming a gain of half an hour per person per day due to the SVP's friendly and supportive attitude (studies have shown that productivity is higher when the day begins on a positive rather than a negative note) and assuming that on an average about six people interact with the SVP, there is a gain of three hours of productive time per day. Annually this works out to about 750 hours.
3. Satisfied employees tend to satisfy their customers too. The improved morale and enthusiasm of the commercial department has had some positive effects on internal and external customers. Assuming that every employee reduces half an hour of transaction costs for internal customers per day and 20 internal customers and vendors are served by the employees with a smile, there is a 10-hour saving per day, and the resultant goodwill.

Thus, with a ₹50,000 smile, you can win ₹10 lakh in return annually. These returns only keep multiplying.

Consider the benefits to a company if its CEO (whose strategic thinking is appreciated by the employees but whose communication skills are an issue) works hard to improve her/his communication skills and spreads the benefits of her/his strategic thinking to the rest of the company. Can we put a figure to the consequent development of five of her/his general managers as powerful strategic thinkers?

Similarly, another top-level manager of a company finds that contrary to her/his perception of herself/himself as a great delegator, her/his juniors do not think that she/he delegates adequately. On discovering this through 360 Degree Feedback, she/he begins to delegate more; as a result, a year later there is a saving of at least two hours of her/his time per day. This saved time can be utilized to help set up a new plant.

The need

You are a manager and you are doing a good job of your assignments. Year after year, you are receiving your promotions on time, and are being appreciated for your work. Your organization, like many others, is recruiting newcomers, changing its systems and beginning to use new technology. Sometimes you feel that the younger generation is smarter, more hard-working and career-minded, and has little loyalty to the organization. You also feel that with a little support—which you are not getting—you can do a lot more work. You think you are a leader in your own way but you do not know what others think of you. You share good relations with others and mind your job. But is that all you should be doing? How can you help take your organization into the future? Do people think that you have the ability to lead them? You know what your strengths are but you are not sure if your seniors, juniors and colleagues see your strengths the same way as you do. You are wondering how to find out. A 360 Degree Feedback exercise gives you the answers.

Hurconomics: ROI on 360 Degree Feedback

360 Degree Feedback is one of the least expensive HRD interventions or growth tools that have been developed in recent times. Though the term 360 Degree Feedback came from the USA, the practice has been

CHAPTER 13 Getting ROI on 360 Degree Feedback

followed in India since antiquity. Kings used to go about in disguise to find out what their subjects or people thought of them, and adjusted their leadership styles according to the feedback they got. Sometimes they used *Gudachari* or spies to collect the impressions they were creating in the minds of their public. For example, in the Ramayana, Rama sends his wife Sita away, based on a spy report of a *dhobi*'s impressions of Rama. In the mid-1980s, a programme that I designed at IIMA attempted to systematically capture the perceptions of managerial staff. This went on to become a very popular methodology, and is now known as 360 Degree Feedback.

At TVRLS, a 360 Degree Feedback profile is done for a teacher or a headmaster for as little as ₹2000. For managers it costs a maximum of ₹5000 per profiling. This includes the cost of the questionnaires, and so on. On the Internet, there are sites that offer free tools. Any interested manager can get herself/himself assessed even without involving a consultant. The real costs of 360 Degree Feedback are not the consultancy costs but the time required by assessors to assess the candidate. Each person seeking feedback is to be assessed on an average by 10 people—the R-COT will be the equivalent of about 10 hours' time. If this is done as a part of an in-house workshop, add to this another eight hours. The total costs are as follows:

Profiling cost = ₹5000
Workshop cost = ₹5000 (normally, feedback is given after the first workshop on how to use or not use 360 Degree Feedback)
Travel and workshop cost if the feedback is outside the city = ₹10,000
Time investment by assessors (R-COT) = 10 hours
R-COT of the assessee who has to mail the questionnaires, attend a workshop to receive her/his feedback data and gain insights = 10 hours
R-COT for 20 hours = ₹20,000 (at a CTC of ₹20 lakh and 200 work hours)
Total cost per head = ₹20,000 direct costs + ₹20,000
R-COT = ₹40,000

This is a one-time cost and normally a lifetime cost, as once you go through a 360 Degree Feedback workshop, a second one is not required.

The O-COT for the time spent by the candidate ranges between ₹80,000 for the IT sector and ₹200,000 (₹2 lakh) for the manufacturing sector. The ROI expected from 360 Degree Feedback for each candidate = ₹20,000 direct or fixed cost + ₹80,000 O-COT = ₹1 lakh in an IT company and more in others.

Table 13.1 illustrates the benefits of 360 Degree Feedback.

TABLE 13.1 Benefits of 360 Degree Feedback

Issue	Possible Benefits
What is the benefit of discovering your new talent?	You will apply it more and benefit the company and also build your career. Perhaps, your income will double in the next five years. Only 1 per cent of this is the expense you have incurred on your 360 Degree Feedback.
What is the benefit of finding out that you do not fully understand the expectations of your internal customers or your juniors, and that your wavelength is different from that of the company?	You meet your internal customers and get to know more about them. There is more communication with colleagues and therefore more respect. There is more integration, team work and respect from your internal customers.
What is the benefit of discovering that you are not delegating work?	You start delegating more. This may release a lot of your time from routine work and lift up your level of operations in the company. You will have more competent and well-rounded juniors who admire you more.
What is the benefit of discovering that you are a good leader, your juniors and seniors are happy with you, and that your leadership style is appropriate?	There is more self-confidence and more dynamism, and at least a 10 per cent increase in your efficiency, motivation and morale.

(Table 13.1 Contd.)

(Table 13.1 Contd.)

Issue	Possible Benefits
What is the benefit of discovering that your style becomes coercive when your juniors make mistakes and you lose your cool, and that this creates low morale and motivation problems in the company?	You alter your style as you become more sensitive. Subordinates are more adjusting. There is better management of mistakes in the department and higher learning from them.
What is the benefit of discovering that you are not perceived as benchmarking with the best and that you need to be better-informed and get more world-class manufacturing practices into the company?	You study other practices, get wiser and introduce new practices. You come to be known as a leader and initiative taker. The company gains from your interventions in terms of cost reduction, greater efficiency and better quality of products and services.

One of the managers to whom we happened to provide 360 Degree Feedback could have avoided hospitalization if only he had taken the feedback seriously. He is a hard-working, loyal, sincere and dynamic person. He takes his job seriously, plans his work well, monitors his juniors and their work, and is always available to them. However, he was considered a very serious and introverted person. He rarely interacted with his juniors at the informal level or even smiled at them. He received feedback that while he was admired by his juniors and everyone else for his work and sincerity, he would be better liked if he became a little more informal, had lunch with them, joked around and appeared to enjoy his work more. His family also concurred with this feedback. The manager showed some change for a few days, but soon reverted to his earlier ways. A year after the feedback, he had to be hospitalized for stress and was off work for several months because of his stress-related ailments. So do get your 360 Degree Feedback profiling, but act on it too in order to reap the benefits.

On the other hand, 360 Degree Feedback also may have an emotional cost. Sometimes when people do not receive positive feedback or if someone is ultra-sensitive to negative feedback, the cost of the feedback is likely to be high, in terms of the candidate developing negativity and a vengeful attitude. Though such cases are rare, they cannot be ruled out. Beware of the costs if the seeker of the feedback is excessively defensive or is not ready to learn. 360 Degree Feedback is useful for learners. Hence, it should not be used indiscriminately. The workshops prepare candidates for receiving the feedback and this is an important step.

CHAPTER 14

Lessons from 100 Impact-making Managers*

TVRLS has been conducting 360 Degree Feedback programmes since 1996 and has a large database of their profiles. From the database we have at TVRLS in Ahmedabad and Bangalore, we have profiled over 8000 Indian managers between 1996 and 2010. These were assessed by over 80,000 managers who constituted their seniors (bosses), juniors (subordinates) and peers. These were drawn from over 200 Indian organizations from different sectors. These were largely senior managers as most Indian companies invest on the 360 Degree Feedback of their senior managers, which included the heads of SBUs, departments, sections and functions. There may also be a few middle-level and junior managers.

We used a reasonably standardized tool using the RSDQ models of TVRLS. The tool or instrument used is referred to as the 360 Degree Feedback tool and the RSDQ model is developed by TVRLS. The instrument by itself is scientifically developed and includes areas which are critical for successful performance of the individual(s) and the organization.

We selected from our database all those who had crossed a certain cut-off point (above 70 per cent score on the managerial roles tool) and emerged as mangers that made an impact on the people with whom they work. They were the ones who demonstrated leadership qualities. On an average in the 360 Degree Feedback scheme of TVRLS, each candidate would have been assessed by at least 10 and in most case as much as 15 to 20.

---

* Modified version of Chapter 11 from the book *100 Managers in Action* by T.V. Rao and Charu Sharma (New Delhi: Tata McGraw-Hill, 2012), pp. 380–387.

The 100 managers, who were studied in-depth, were selected from our database of over 8000 senior and top-level managers on whom 360 Degree Feedback assessments were available at TVRLS. Only high scoring managers in terms of the assessments were considered. Their own self-assessments were not taken into consideration. These managers were contacted by mail and their profiles generated. Their 360 Degree Feedback was used only in selecting them, and no attempt has been made to give their 360 Degree Feedback data here. These managers have undoubtedly made a high impact on the following dimensions:

1. They develop and articulate a vision for their sphere of work. Even if it is small department or section or function, they are known to create a vision for the department or function. There could be HR vision, quality-related vision, cost-centric vision, customer-related vision, technology-related or value-driven vision, culture-dominated vision or some form of a dream or long-term goal or state they would like to achieve. They also pass on this vision to their juniors and colleagues by talking about it. Some of them are bold dreamers and a few of them are very articulate and communicative. Some of them are not as aggressive in their approach and are silent workers. Those who are not aggressive communicators usually take some time to make an impact. However, even if they do not aggressively communicate either due to their introverted nature or due to their personal belief system, they do get noticed eventually and are seen as vision-driven individuals.
2. They are driven by technology. They are open to innovations and constantly search for new technologies, systems and improvements in their work sphere. They also build the technological competencies of their juniors. They are good at attending seminars and conferences, reading journals, visiting other organizations to benchmark and look for innovations in technologies and systems. They are also quick and, at the same time, calculative in introducing new technologies and systems.
3. While they think long term, they do not neglect short-term results and targets. They have a knack of balancing both immediate goals and short-term results with the long-term

CHAPTER 14 Lessons from 100 Impact-making Managers

goals and intellectual capital building. They strive to build intellectual capital by including brand image, internal culture and capabilities, customer loyalty and such other characteristics required for a sustainable organization.

4. They are also conscious of the need for and the importance of building an appropriate organizational culture. They articulate the culture for their units and departments and pay a lot of attention to culture and values of the organization.
5. They are good motivators and developers of people. They inspire their juniors by setting clear-cut goals, listening to the problems and solving them, coaching them, empowering them and recognizing constantly their good work and encouraging innovativeness among their juniors. They are good people managers. They are willing to accept negative feedback and rework on their relationships in managing their juniors. They are open to feedback and are reasonably HR driven.
6. They are also good in understanding the needs and requirements of their colleagues and internal customers. They are quick to identify their internal customers, develop respect for them, interact with them, share their own work and attempt to learn from their colleagues and manage their relationships.
7. They are good team workers. They work well as members of the teams acknowledging the contributions of others and volunteering help to others whenever required. They tend to put the team above their individual interests.
8. They are good 'boss managers'. We found that almost all managers in India are good at managing their bosses. In a few cases, where they were unable to make an impact on their bosses, they also have difficulty managing other stake holders and do not make it to our list. These managers understand the expectation of their seniors, take their help and support in managing their activities and in the process generate data, feed it to their bosses and influence their thinking.
9. They also strive to understand their customers, listen to them, understand their expectations and problems, and solve their problems proactively.
10. They have a personal philosophy of faith and belief in their juniors and consequently exhibit a developmental and empowering

style. As a result of their empowering style, their juniors become capable of independent action and work with a good morale and team spirit.

These 10 differentiating areas of impact by the managers were the starting point of our study rather than the conclusions from the study. The managers we chose had already demonstrated these qualities in our 360 Degree Feedback. The case studies of these managers revealed further competencies of the high-impact-making managers.

In this study, there are 19 young managers who are 40 years and below. About 40 per cent of the managers are in the age bracket of 40 to 50 years, while another 40 per cent are above 50 years of age. Very few are over 60. A few of the retired continue working as advisors to their organizations post-retirement. The study also highlights that most of these managers are highly qualified. Also some of them are only graduates and yet reached the heights and done commendable work.

How are these managers able to make a high impact? What is it that they do or what other qualities do they exhibit. These are the lessons we like to draw in this chapter.

Lessons from 100 Managers

Our descriptions of the 100 managers have indicated the following lessons about what makes a good impact-making manager:

- **They are hard-core networkers:** They are spread all across on the Internet communities such as linkedin.com, facebook.com, etc. They could be seen on the boards of organizations, in social functions, conferences, quality meets, etc. They are spread all over the Internet. People write to them often. This ability to network leverages their performance.
- **They are great learners:** Carrying forth from the above point, these managers learn from each experience. They keep a mental note or write it in a diary of what they find interesting. Also, they apply these learnings elsewhere. They can replicate the learnings in a different scenario. They take a head on in certain situations which apparently lead to an abyss.

CHAPTER 14 Lessons from 100 Impact-making Managers

- **They are achievement driven and focus on building achievement and problem-solving culture:** For example, one of the candidates played a critical role to maintain industrial peace in the difficult conditions. To put forth a view, which is primarily with an intention of improving the prevailing conditions which is completely opposite to the thinking of the audience, is a mammoth task. Culture building is a challenging task and takes a long time and involves numerous communications.
- **They want to live many lives:** These leaders want to share their own experience with others. They are teachers, mentors and role models. They want to expand their aura continuously. They are the moving training inventories. In the process of energy exchange with them, both the parties come out with greater abilities.
- **They are perseverant:** They implement systems and keep coming back to them for monitoring. They are process drivers and process owners. This trait forms an integral part of their leadership. They understand that things have their own incubation time to take up shape and become cash cows—not only in financial terms, but otherwise too.
- **Early exhibition of leadership skills:** One can see that the people mentioned in the study had leadership qualities right from their childhood days. Most of them were either holding leadership roles as a school monitor/prefect or as a sports captain leading the team. They were known to guide, delegate and monitor responsibilities.
- **They are self-motivated:** As James Allen has put it in his book *As a Man Thinketh*, "You are the master of your thought, you mould your own character, the maker and shaker of your condition, environment and destiny". Man is buffeted by circumstances as long as he believes himself to be the creative power and that he may command the hidden soil and seeds of his being out of which circumstances grow; he then becomes the rightful master of himself.
- **They are aware about self:** They are deliberately conscious about themselves. Not only they know about their strengths, but also they know about their weaknesses. They have awareness about self, admit their qualities, and take first few steps

for self-improvements. Knowing the low points may also be an advantage. They teach you the art of doing things differently.
- **They are open:** They like to talk about themselves and that is how they contribute to documentation of their case studies. It is intentional, as they want to increase the first quadrant of the Johari window. Leaving their egos behind, they talk about themselves and accept criticism. Such a manager keeps asking himself/herself, 'Will adopting this trait be fruitful to me others around?'
- **They build on strengths:** In the open-ended feedback section of the 360 Degree Feedback report, there are three sections: area of strengths, area of weakness and suggestions. All the managers covered here have focused the most on their strengths. They have taken care of the weaknesses also. This particular attitude has made them even more successful. A general attitude of a person is to pay attention to only the weak areas. In this process, he/she attempts to see a magnified picture of his/her mistakes which definitely hampers high achievement and motivation. A more intelligent step is to utilize strengths to be even more effective.
- **They follow up with the outside world:** Ideas on the Asian leadership have been captured in the cases. The fact that they have opinions explains that they know the pulse of the market. The actions reflect long-sightedness.
- **They have family support:** Their families have been with them throughout. Many a times, they have kept the organization before families. Their wives and children have not been as complaining about this fact.

In this section, we would like to put emphasis on a larger perspective of using the 360 Degree Feedback and such other tools keeping the organizational and the societal good in consideration.

- **Develop leaders:** Organizations should try to find out the few triggering factors for the leaders. There is no one rule which can be applied. It is for the organization to find out the suitable support factors. The leaders need their own space of function where they can bloom and pass on the effects to others down the

CHAPTER 14 Lessons from 100 Impact-making Managers

line. Also, they should be made aware of the high expectations of the company.

- **Retain leaders:** Leaders are not available for ever. In this competitive world, a person lives four to five careers. Poaching good performers is considered as the KRA of the recruitment team. Leaders have become a rare element. Wisdom suggests to retain them for as long as possible.
- **Develop the next line:** Leadership is the legacy to be passed on to the next line to make the success sustainable. Generally, high achievers are pre-occupied with their domain area. It becomes imperative for the HR department to assist in succession planning.
- **Keep the long-term approach on priority:** Companies which have focused merely on the profit figures of here and now have faced issues in the long term. It is important to balance both short- and long-term goals.
- **Develop a culture of dialogue:** In our experience of 360 Degree Feedback surveys, we have come across cases where the role set members—peers, boss, subordinates, external customers—do not know the work the role holder is doing. The outcomes are fatal. The role-set members live in the darkness of not appreciating the work being done by the role holder. This kind of perception can be overcome by building a culture of open and free dialogue.

Our analysis proves the core competence theory. It lends support to the observations made by Zenger and Folkman that one can be a leader by impacting others. For that purpose you should have domain knowledge, deliver results and maintain good interpersonal competence and team work. With good interpersonal relations and team work you can manage yourself, boss, juniors, seniors and customers. With domain knowledge and some or the other superior qualities like systems thinking, technical knowhow or ability to learn continuously one can deliver results. Vision, values and foresight take you to higher level positions, while execution and delivery of results make you an influential and impacting individual.

Even though the managers belong to different industries and age groups, and have different experiences, leadership styles and outlooks, they all share a common pursuit for excellence. And they are relentless in this. As they rose in experience and designation, they found higher responsibilities to shoulder, thereby acquiring higher skills in the process.

Here we do not have data to support the impact these managers have created on the financial front of the company. But going by the fact of the exceptionally high ratings received in the 360 Degree Format, we would like to believe that the overall impact would be significant.

CHAPTER 15

Experiences from Other Countries

There have been a number of books, articles and other literature on 360 Degree Feedback from the West. This chapter makes an attempt to summarize some of the prominent articles and books on 360 Degree Feedback. The intention is to give the reader a flavour of what is happening in this field.

Novack (1993) in his article on 360 Degree Feedback talked about the increasing use of 360 Degree Feedback primarily due to the cost-effective mode of operation, and the increasing urge for job-related feedback for employees affected by career plateauing among other reasons for initiating the 360 Degree Feedback process.

Further, Novack questioned the accuracy of self-reports when compared to the reports by others, and validated through studies that self-reports are less accurate than the reports from others. The feedback received from others may tend to put the employee on the defensive, especially if it is a critical feedback and at that point of time the initial step would be in getting employees to accept this feedback from others. Novack suggests that in 360 Degree Feedback the number of feedback providers is more important than who gives the feedback.

In an attempt to design a 360 Degree Feedback assessment to meet organizational needs, Novack provided five models which are as follows:

1. **Job analysis:** Here the knowledge–skills–attitudes based on the traditional job-analysis procedures are measured through focus group discussions, interviews and a job–task information questionnaire.
2. **Competence based:** In this model, competencies are measured rather than knowledge, skills and attitudes, through comparisons

between the behaviours of high performers to form a set of best competencies.
3. **Strategic planning:** This model is based on the organization's strategic plans. The strategic knowledge–skills–attitudes are identified through interviews and focus group discussions with key senior executives.
4. **Developmental theory:** This model identifies critical knowledge–skills–attitudes for various developmental stages of employee growth and development.
5. **Personality theory:** This model is based on personality-based knowledge–skills–attitudes, including qualities, traits, temperaments and styles in communication, leadership, interpersonal relations and cognition.

Later, while discussing the subject, Novack (1993) identified two distinct scoring patterns normally used for 360 Degree Feedback assessments. They are as follows:

1. **Ispative scoring:** In this pattern, the employees benchmark against themselves by tracking their own job performances over a certain period of time.
2. **Normative scoring:** Here, the employees compare their scores with the scores of a representative group of similar employees.

First Rate Multi-rater Feedback

Church (1995) has discussed the steps that need to be taken to ensure the validity, confidentiality, usefulness and effectiveness of the multi-rater feedback system before linking it to the formal performance appraisal system.

Church begins by talking about the relevant evaluation at every stage of managerial life and the various devices or instruments used by the organizations to evaluate the performances of their employees especially with the usage of the 360 Degree Feedback and 450 Degree Feedback system.

He outlines the basic hurdle in implementing the 360 Degree Feedback as a part of the formal appraisal process and gives the following concurrent suggestions.

Winning support

The organizations should seek the visible and enthusiastic support of the top management before penetrating 360 Degree Feedback among the lower ranks. This can be done in two ways:

1. The top managers should be the first to undergo the 360 Degree Feedback process.
2. They should link the participation of managers to a bonus system.

Some common implications and fears associated with 360 Degree Feedback include co-workers and direct reports worrying about confidentiality since they fear dismissal.

Peers mistrust

Peers mistrust the 360 Degree Feedback process since they want to preserve their working relationship with their co-workers. Some suggestions for maintaining confidentiality include the following:

- Feedback to be distributed in sealed packets,
- Usage of optimal scan codes to identify individual rater's roles,
- Inclusion of addressed envelope to facilitate the raters to send their completed questionnaires directly to the person who organizes the data,
- Combining feedback collected from the same type of source,
- Feedback responses not to be included unless their representatives of the group have responded and
- Participant assesses not to be provided with individual responses.

Choose instruments carefully

The following checklist should be maintained to check the accuracy of the instrument:

- Specificity of the questions,
- Objectivity of the questions,
- Clarity of questions and
- The instrument should be customized for the organization.

Making feedback meaningful

To integrate the feedback into performance plans, the following elements should be included:

- **Self-evaluation:** The comparison between self and others' rating enables the individual to integrate feedback into his/her self-usage.
- **Integrating feedback:** The organization must provide managers with enough time and structure for reflecting on the feedback and development plans.

Follow-up

Once the assessment is completed, the assessee should meet the various constituencies in different groups to discuss the positive and difficult aspects of the feedback.

Thus, in this way Church sums up that the effectiveness of the instrument determines the role of multi-rater assessment in enhancing the PMS.

Vinson (1996) outlined the need for 360 Degree Feedback in business and the positive and negative implications of its usage. She outlines some individual specific behaviours as an outcome of having undergone 360 Degree Feedback based on personal, as well as others' illustrations:

- Choosing the best candidates for assessment,
- More importance given to boss's rating as it is assumed to be linked to promotions and salary and
- Feeling of hatred on receiving critical feedback with people the individual has not worked with.

Further she pointed out some of the advantages of 360 Degree Feedback, such as follows:

- Multi-rater feedback has the potential to promote team cohesiveness.
- Employees want to meet the expectations of their peers as well as their bosses when they know that their peers will be rating them.

CHAPTER 15 Experiences from Other Countries 189

- Lessening of discrimination and bias because responsibility for feedback involves more people.

However, looking at some of the negative implications, Vinson pointed out the following:

- Feedback seen as an opportunity for criticism.
- Conflicting opinions: Who decides who is right?
- Choosing friends to provide feedback: How valuable is the process?
- Survey fatigue: How accurate and reliable is the feedback?
- How truthful is the feedback?

After discussing all the positive and negative implications, Vinson attempted to answer the most important question: *Does the 360 Degree Feedback improve performance?* According to Vinson, people may tend to act on their feedback, but being busy they make no efforts to improve or change their behaviour. She supports the argument through a live illustration wherein a company launched the 360 Degree Feedback programme to assess its senior executives. The feedback surveys required them to distribute 'two direct' reports and 'two indirect' reports to complete, apart from the self-assessment. It had been a long time since the senior executives had been appraised by their subordinates and the executives were quite apprehensive. Also, the subordinates felt that it was dangerous to be truthful. Once the data was compiled and tabulated, some called an external consultant to provide feedback, some did not, but all of them admitted that in due course of time they all reverted to their old behaviour patterns.

Taking into consideration the results of her studies, Vinson (1996) recommends the following:

1. Anonymous and confidential feedback is a must for success.
2. Considering the length of time in the position, valid feedback should be sought from people who have long working relations with the assessees and know them well.
3. A feedback expert/consultant should interpret the feedback.
4. Feedback should be followed by a follow-up survey about six months later to know the progress in action plans on low scoring areas.

5. Feedback providers should give written description as well as numerical rating to make it more meaningful.
6. Ensure reliability and validity of the instruments based on the statistical methods.
7. Avoid survey fatigue through staggering the distribution of the forms in a work group.

Mistakes in 360 Degree Feedback: How to Make It Effective?

Haworth (1998) points out the dangers associated with using multi-rater feedback injudiciously and ineffectively leading to dramatic and life-changing results. She has pointed out 10 ways in which the 360 Degree Feedback assessments can be misused:

Mistake # 10: Buying low

Haworth warns people of using invalid and unprofessionally developed questionnaires due to low cost of administration. Such exercises according to her become a waste of time and energy. Haworth suggests the following ways of validating the questionnaire to make it more effective:

- Each skill should be defined by concrete behaviour.
- Double-barrelled items should be avoided.
- The skill sets or competencies should be clearly determined for evaluation.
- Ensuring that the competencies are related to the job and reinforced through performance appraisals or other HR initiatives.
- An external consultant should be hired to deliver assessments to ensure the consistent quality of the feedback.
- Employees should have the opportunity to engage in dialogue, evaluate the report and discover its merits over time.

Mistake # 9: Selling high

Haworth clarifies the myth associated with the 360 Degree Feedback assessment that it is a panacea for individual deficiencies or organizational woes. The author declines the high opinions held for 360 Degree Feedback as being very imaginative and inventive. According to her, 360 Degree Feedback is an instrument which improves someone's ability to work with others. She suggests the following:

- Multi-rater assessments linked to development plans, concrete methods for improving skills and reinforcement for making progress.
- Testing and fine-tuning the feedback with organizational support through annual usage of multi-rater assessments can institutionalize the process and encourage people to take actions on their feedback.

Mistake # 8: Keep them guessing

Another mistake sighted by Haworth is the perception of multi-rater feedback as multi-problem due to bad experiences or bad press. Hence, the author suggests the following ways for dispelling such myths:

- Inform employees of how the tools were developed, how they will be used, how raters would be selected and who will have access to the results. At least a letter attached to the materials should clearly define the purpose and use of the tool.
- Selecting a liberal number of evaluations (three to five raters per category) per employee should avoid biased results.
- Privacy of the feedback needs to be communicated to the employee in the form of a discussion.
- The development plan and results can be part of an HR resource file.

Mistake # 7: Change the rules midstream

Another mistake commonly committed by organizations while using the 360 Degree Feedback is when the multi-rater assessment is introduced as a developmental tool to performance appraisal and promotions. Haworth suggests that the conditions under which the feedback will be used be stated right from the beginning.

Mistake # 6: Parade the losers

At times the 360 Degree Feedback is only administered for a select group, i.e. the slow learners or star performers, and is then attached to fear, resentment and/or overblown expectations. The best way to combat such problems is to introduce 360 Degree Feedback for the entire work group. A top-down approach is ideal for building rapport and support for 360 Degree Feedback.

Mistake # 5: Bury the survivors

Due to the large number of evaluators, the multi-rater assessments require efficient administration. Managers with a high number of direct reports may not be aware of the time commitment involved in a multi-rater assessment. Also, the questionnaires should be comprehensive yet not lengthy. The items should be easy to understand and free of technical jargon or complex phrases.

Mistake # 4: Hurry up and wait

Once the 360 Degree Feedback initiative is implemented, timetables for distribution, collection and debriefing should be established. The way is to provide feedback four to six weeks after questionnaires have been completed.

Mistake # 3: Giving marching orders without maps

Once the feedback reaches the employee with respect to his/her strengths and weaknesses, he/she gets confused and directionless. At this point of time, providing a course of action or a map, otherwise known as a developmental plan, is necessary.

Mistake # 2: Do as we say, not as we do

The 360 Degree Feedback should not be treated as an academic process which would make it frustrating and demoralizing, i.e. when the assessment tools fail to address the organizational culture, like any other initiative the organization must endorse, practice and reinforce the criteria by which it measures its managers.

Mistake # 1: Take no prisoners

The 360 Degree Feedback should not be treated as a substitute for coaching or direct communication. These assessment tools should not be used punitively. Hence, the 360 Degree Feedback should be administered sensitively, and patiently introduced.

High Tech 360 Degree Feedback

Bracken et al. (1998) have thrown an alternative solution to conducting 360 Degree Feedback with the use of latest technology to make it more effective and accurate. They talk of an Internet-based 360 Degree Feedback process consisting of a survey loaded at a website. The process can be summarized as follows:

Step 1:	Service providers build many of the administrative steps involved in conducting a 360 Degree Feedback programme, into the engine that runs the website.
Step 2:	An administrator (HR personnel) within an organization for setting up and maintaining the Internet-based process.
Step 3:	Personal 360 Degree Feedback working:
	1. Service provider giving instructions and time frames for assessment.
	2. Using PC's standard browser, access to service provider's website in the Internet and key in your personal ID and password.
	3. Create a list of raters asked to provide a feedback about you.
	4. Rater sent e-mail message requesting to go to the website and complete the assessment.
	5. At the end of the time window, feedback collected, collated and assembled into feedback reports.
Step 4:	The administrator sets all the parameters such as time frame, deadlines, content, e-mail wording, identification of rater group and provisions for anonymity such as how and to whom feedback reports will be routed.

Bracken et al. argue that Internet-based solutions can improve the 360 Degree Feedback process in the following ways.

Logistics

In an Internet-based process, e-mails replace paper communication and hence the following implications:

- The administrator does not have to initiate each communication because the distribution and collection are automatic.
- Information is collated and one mail is sent to each rater regardless of the number of assessments that the rater has been requested to do.
- Request can be made online via e-mail from the service provider as part of the administrative automation.
- It reduces chances of someone being overrated by bogus raters without valid IDs and passwords from gaining access to the website.

Rater overload

The rater overload can be reduced by putting a cap on a limited number of assessments and by displaying a notice on screen saying that the rater is 'booked up' as soon as an additional assessment comes.

Rater reliability

Some technical steps can improve the quality of rater-provided data. Some systems can also prevent invalid inputs from being submitted.

Insulating layer of comfort

To increase rater accountability with technology-based systems is to give raters feedback reports on how closely they agree with others' ratings of the same participant.

Creating behaviour change

The online training module devised to prepare the participant to accept the feedback when used as a prerequisite to working with a feedback coach.

Cost

Internet applications are designed to handle large volumes of work and much of the administrative labour is automated. As a result the price per participant is considerably less and the administrative work is minimized.

Bracken et al. talk of the factors necessary to evaluate organizational readiness for 360 Degree Feedback. They are as follows:

- **Prior 360 Degree Feedback experience:** The users felt more comfortable with the Internet-based 360 Degree Feedback rather than the traditional 360 Degree Feedback mainly because it is a confidential, secure medium and it alleviates administrative burdens.
- **Accessibility:** Access to the Internet facility also serves as a determining factor for technology-based 360 Degree Feedback as it can raise costs and logistical complexities to a considerable degree.
- **Familiarity:** If the organization already uses Internet facilities, then the employees are very comfortable online, thus making the addition of 360 Degree Feedback a minor step.
- **A technology-supportive outline:** Companies which are technologically competitive generally are very open to Internet-based 360 Degree Feedback.
- **Adequate IT resources:** The amount of internal IT support in the form of providing accurate e-mail addresses of all feedback recipients is very essential, and hence the IT group should work with a service provider on fire wall issues and security interference.
- **Geography:** Companies with global sites will see a substantial advantage in getting transnational data access in the Internet.

- **HRIS database:** The company should have a reliable, up-to-date HRIS database which helps to identify participants for 360 Degree Feedback.

Internet-based 360 Degree Feedback assessment thus seems to be a very attractive proposition for technically competent organizations.

How to Benefit from the 360 Degree Feedback

Wimer and Novack (1998) highlighted the effectiveness of the 360 Degree Feedback as a powerful stimulator for change, especially in the area of 'Emotional intelligence'. Managers with low EQ are not likely to be sensitive to the five components of emotional intelligence, namely:

1. Persistence in the face of failure,
2. Emotional control in dealing with interpersonal stress and conflict,
3. Humility or lack of arrogance in dealing with others,
4. Interpersonal sensitivity and empathy and
5. Self-awareness and insight.

Hence for these managers the 360 Degree Feedback can be an effective tool to improve his/her performance. Some guidelines they offered for designing 360 Degree Feedback effectively include the following:

1. **Have a clear purpose:** It is very essential to outline the purpose of the feedback and agree on it at the outset and eventually communicate it clearly.
2. **Start at the top:** To acquire the support of the top management it is pertinent to conduct the 360 Degree Feedback for the top management.
3. **Have an open mind and the willingness to change:** The feedback should be looked as an eye-opener and should be incorporated in professional development, rather than be shunned off with ignorance.

CHAPTER 15 Experiences from Other Countries 197

4. **Communicate, communicate, communicate:** The people should be communicated clearly with regard to the treatment of their data and report preparation.
5. **Safeguard confidentiality at all times:** Ensuring confidentiality of the feedback is a very important aspect of the feedback which makes the feedback very authentic and reliable.
6. **Evaluate and fine-tune the system:** Constant evaluation of the effectiveness of the feedback needs to be done to ensure its reliability and validity.

Gebelian (1996) suggested a definite strategy for implementing multi-rater feedback in the organization. According to her, the strategic implementation of 360 Degree Feedback runs into four phases, namely:

1. The Groundwork,
2. The Competency Model,
3. The Implementation Plans and
4. Full Implementation.

Phase 1: The groundwork

During the first and initial phase, i.e. the groundwork phase, the organization needs to be prepared for the multi-rater feedback, and hence it is a preparatory phase. The main steps involved during this phase include the following:

- Clarifying the company's strategies and goals,
- Defining the scope of the multi-rater process and
- Planning the process with regard to the following issues:
    a. Initiation of the multi-rater feedback—Who will be the first to use the multi-rater feedback?
    b. Using the multi-rater form in-house, or use of the consultant's instruments.
    c. The frequency of evaluation of employees through the multi-rater feedback.

According to Gebelian, the multi-rater feedback should be initiated from the top to gain thin support and gradually precipitate downward.

Phase 2: Competency model

In the second phase, possible linkage should be established between the multi-rater feedback and the competencies, skills and behaviours required for achieving organizational goals. This would provide a base for further systematic change in HR. A competency model would help the organization to streamline its systems and synergize it with the organizational goals.

Phase 3: Implementation plans

During this phase, with support from the top management, the following issues need to be addressed:

- **Educating key players:** The multi-rater feedback should not be based on prior assumptions of the understanding of line managers on the feedback. They should be thoroughly brief on the nature, purpose and process of the multi-rater feedback.
- **Determine your feedback strategy:** The mode of imparting feedback should be given considerable attention and decisions should be made for providing feedback, either through one-to-one sessions or group training programmes.

Phase 4: Full implementation

In this final phase, the following steps need to be taken:

- Holding kick-off meetings. In this an executive from each group would meet with employees and discuss the use of the feedback in development plans.
- After the first round of feedback, the process needs to be rolled out to other teams and departments, or level by level. Once everyone in the team or department has undergone the experiences one can plan for group feedback sessions.
- The feedback should focus on the development of the employees.
- Finally, the multi-rater feedback instrument needs to be evaluated constantly.

Thus, Gebelian seeks to provide an overview of the strategic linkage of the 360 Degree Feedback assessments with the organizational goals.

Flannigon (1997) presented a case study of Nalco's success in using 360 Degree Feedback for developing their sales personnel. The case study stemmed from Nalco's attempts to reduce the annual turnover of its sales through the initiative of its Quality Action Team. The team had identified the main reasons for the considerable decrease of its high turnover, but they also found that the one primary issue that commanded attention was the problems with the boss.

To address this grave issue, the 360 Degree Feedback assessment process was initiated by Nalco along with the North Brook, a consulting firm and a pioneer in the 360 Degree Feedback assessment process.

The 360 Degree Feedback assessment was essentially aimed at the district sales managers. The managers assessed themselves and were assessed by their own sales managers and sales representatives who reported to them. The data was analysed and a profile of each individual was shared confidentially with the concerned person. Eventually, the action plans were drawn out and the group recommendations initiated.

Each manager was aided in identifying those milestones that indicated s(he) had undergone a significant change. The Nalco experience of implementing 360 Degree Feedback for the district sales managers was a success.

Evaluating 360 degree feedback efforts

Novack et al. (1999) have presented some suggestions on how to evaluate 360 Degree Feedback in an organization, the most efficient way of which is to administer a post-programme, multi-rater, 360 Degree Feedback survey. The major steps involved in this process are as follows:

Step 1: Defining what to evaluate and measure

The business needs and objectives should be tied directly to your evaluation approach. The areas on which the evaluation could be made are whether the participants have increased awareness about strengths and development areas, whether participants are more proficient in one or more competencies, whether the multi-rater feedback was cost-effective and the key changes in specific and measurable individual and organizational outcomes.

Step 2: Designing the survey

In designing the survey, a target audience which includes participants and their managers, staff, team members and other peers, and internal and external customers as part of the rating process must be identified. Once this is done, you need to define what level of evaluation is to be done in terms of reaction, awareness or insight, transfer or cost-effectiveness. For example, participant reaction to the multi-rater intervention process, as well as specific behaviour modified on the job, can be measured. After this survey questions specific to the evaluation level being assessed should be written. The more specific the question the more accurate the result would be. Thereafter, one has to determine what actually has to be measured—frequency of behaviour practised back on the job, level of satisfaction, commitment or confidence. Before the actual survey begins it is important to pilot test the survey which would provide feedback about the clarity of instructions given, survey questions and administration procedures. The revised survey should look graphically appealing and easy to complete.

Step 3: Gathering data

This is the next step of the survey. This could be administered online through the Intranet or Internet. Feedback should be provided to all respondents through appropriate means. The anonymity and confidentiality of the process must be maximized and there should be minimum use of multiple, open-ended questions to ensure that the survey is brief yet comprehensive.

Step 4: Analysing the data and summarizing the results

With the use of commercially available statistical software (SPSS) or spreadsheet software (Excel), basic data analysis useful for evaluation study, including item frequencies, chi-square analyses, correlations and t-tests, could be carried out.

Thus, a multi-rater feedback evaluation survey helps to understand what can be done to ensure that an organization is implementing best practices in these types of training and development interventions.

Visual 360 Degree Feedback: A Performance Appraisal System That Is Fun

Meade (1999) presented a visual 360 Degree Feedback which automates 360 Degree Feedback assessments, thus saving a lot of time on the administrative front and making it interesting and simple to rate people. The author explains in detail how to use the technology, right from logging on to rating the assessee through visual 360 Degree Feedback assessments. It is also easy to use and the raters have reported to be enjoying the process. The visual 360 Degree Feedback also carries out the task of completing and compiling performance ratings. The programme is connected to various other relevant databases which can verify data and allow analysis. The people receive and return their assessments quickly through e-mail. The report can also be prepared in different formats. The heart of the system basically is developing meaningful competencies that truly reflect the company's mission.

On the whole, visual 360 Degree Feedback assessment is useful for reasonably large companies. It helps employees complete their rating forms easily, helps administrators track what is happening and provides everyone in the process with meaningful reports.

The Acceptability of 360 Degree Feedback Appraisals: A Customer–Supplier Relationship Perspective

Waldman and Bowen (1998) argue that 'acceptability' is a key issue relevant to the success of the 360 Degree Feedback appraisal processes. They present conceptual arguments to show how a customer–supplier relationship (CSR) perspective provides a useful means of depicting possible 360 Degree Feedback linkages, as well as discussing the types of raters and ratees for whom acceptance of the process is important. A categorization scheme then provides the primary factors relevant to the acceptance of the process. These factors include: (i) organizational characteristics and (ii) CSR characteristics and appraisals content. Comparisons are made between customers and suppliers in terms of their probable acceptance of 360 Degree Feedback appraisals.

Waldman and Bowen try to sensitize HR practitioners to some of the key issues of potentially affecting acceptability, while at the same time outline a framework for researchers seeking to investigate acceptability phenomena. They present a typology of 360 Degree Feedback appraisals based on different customers–suppliers relationships in which the suppliers are the participants themselves and the raters could be: (i) external customers; (ii) internal customers of other work groups; (iii) co-workers within a work group and (iv) subordinates.

The broad organizational characteristics that influence the overall acceptability of 360 Degree Feedback appraisal are the following: (i) in an organization with total quality management (TQM) cultural orientation acceptance should be strong and (ii) organizational cultures where a common learned belief exists that potentially fixable problems will not be resolved due to variables that individuals cannot control which is called 'organizational cynicism', which also negatively affects acceptability. Acceptability is also strongly a function of characteristics associated with CSRs and the appraisal context. A number of procedural conditions heighten the acceptance of 360 Degree Feedback appraisals. There is continuing debate whether 360 Degree Feedback must be used for evaluative purposes or developmental purposes. Using it for developmental purposes may increase the acceptability of 360 Degree Feedback appraisals. Also, the anonymity of ratings may serve the same purpose. An acceptability factor that is specifically relevant to co-workers involves the extent to which work has been designed based on teams. It has also been found that 360 Degree Feedback appraisals are more acceptable if applied at the group level. 360 Degree Feedback appraisal will be more accepted and indeed more valid if employees have the autonomy, training and organizational resources necessary to satisfy customers. Another point of worry for the assessee may be the lack of competence of customers. It can either be that the customer may not be familiar enough with their work, or it is less likely that assessee may accept ratings from customers who they perceive are not able to adequately perform the rating task and/or are not willing to do so. The supplier's acceptance of 360 Degree Feedback appraisals could be enhanced if the participation rate on the part of raters or customers is high. Also, 360 Degree Feedback appraisals should be more readily accepted when coupled with traditional appraisals.

Thus, on the whole, Waldman's and Bowen's article is beneficial in two ways. First, it can set in motion a more comprehensive research agenda on acceptability. Second, it identifies specific organizational, CSR and appraisal context factors that managers can influence to enhance acceptability.

The 10 Reasons Why You Should Be Using 360 Degree Feedback

Hoffman's (1997) article on the 10 reasons why we should use 360 Degree Feedback makes an interesting argument for 360 Degree Feedback users. It presents 10 rational facts for initiating 360 Degree Feedback in the organization. The reasons are outlined here.

Defines corporate competencies through 360 degree feedback

When the 360 Degree Feedback is used, through comparison between self-evaluations with organizational norms, areas requiring attention are brought to the forefront. Once the competencies are known, the top management can work to synergize the individual goals with the overall corporate strategy.

Increases the focus on customer service

Since the 360 Degree Feedback involves both external and internal customers, it serves as a tool for evaluating the validity of the TQM programme through the extent of positive feedback received in customer orientation.

Supports team initiatives

The multi-rater feedback promotes team building since it incorporates feedback from subordinates, peers and the boss, and fosters the transition to teams. In this way the employee's actions are not exclusively governed by the boss's expectations, but also by the working group.

Creates a high involvement workforce

Since the 360 Degree Feedback ensures the involvement of the entire team and generates a feeling that their views, opinions and evaluation are being valued by the organization, it stimulates an environment that accentuates involvement and can speed up voluntary collaboration.

Decreases hierarchies, promotes streamlining

Through the 360 Degree Feedback the rating responsibilities move to a mixed group of employees which reinforce the new corporate structure that shifts accountability to many. Consequently multi-level feedback promotes the streamlining initiatives.

Detects barriers to success

360 Degree Feedback on a department basis is an effective method that determines how we can be better as individuals and as an organization. The feedback results can be used for planning the departmental training needs.

Assesses the developmental needs

Most of the 360 Degree Feedback programmes emphasize employee development. Unlike traditional development tools the process focuses on skills across the organizational boundaries. A development plan is then created and improvements are measured during subsequent feedback evaluations.

Avoids discrimination and bias

In 360 Degree Feedback, the role of evaluation is shared. Shifting the responsibilities from one individual reduces the severity of any one person's shortcomings as an evaluator, including errors of leniency, personal bias and subjectivity. Using rater feedback reduces the potential for personal bias and thus legal exposure.

Identifies performance threshold

The predictive ability of 360 Degree Feedback highlights long-term success factors. Potential defects and attributes are used as baseline performance measures. The final analysis identifies behaviours connected with high growth potential and those associated with career derailment.

Easy to implement

Introducing a 360 Degree Feedback programme to an organization can be accomplished with relative administrative ease by the human resource staff or an outside consultant.

One of the earliest books to appear on 360 Degree Feedback was by Edwards and Ewen (1996). In this book, the authors have presented, in detail, a conceptual framework of the 360 Degree Feedback and discussed its evolution and variations, and design, implementation and evaluation.

The 360 Degree Feedback assessments are known as multi-rater assessments since the number of evaluations increased to include peers, the boss and subordinates to offer a more balanced and comprehensive view and improve the quality of performance measures. Through the assessments, not only do organizations gain access to credible, quantitative information, the stakeholders, including the managers, customers, employees, team members, leaders and managers, also enjoy reasonable benefits. 360 Degree Feedback is being increasingly adopted by both the public and private sector companies, and more than 90 per cent of the Fortune 500 companies use some form of the multi-source assessment system as at least developmental feedback. Organizations are basically adopting these systems to improvise on structural changes, changes in organizational culture and employee relations. A formalized 360 Degree Feedback system provides safeguards to ensure data integrity which is lost when 360 Degree Feedback assessments are approached through informal systems.

The 360 Degree Feedback systems evolved from organizational surveys, TQM, development feedback and performance appraisals. The main reasons for the slow adoption of 360 Degree Feedback systems as observed by Edwards and Ewen include:

- Multi-source assessments are considered as counterculture,
- Organizational inertia to change,

- Little research data available and
- Technological jargon.

Also, there are a variety of feedback providers such as 1 Degree Feedback (self/manager assessment), 90 Degree Feedback (colleague assessment), 180 Degree Feedback (upward review) and 360 Degree Feedback.

The applications of 360 Degree Feedback vary from developmental feedback to performance feedback. Both are collected in exactly the same way as performance feedback. The difference between the two rests on who actually sees the resulting information. Each type has its own set of pros and cons. While the latter loses the developmental impact and user manipulation is high, it is considered to be credible and valid, and can be used to make pay/policy decisions. The Team Evaluation and Management System (TEAMS) model offers a competency-based pay structure which considers how the work gets done and what gets done. The TEAMS model provides a structure for making pay policy decisions where the component weights may be a function of the trust in each part. Such models are used for special cases, for example, when many people report to one manager or a group works together as a self-directed team. However, the 360 Degree Feedback process works best as a two-step implementation, starting from developmental feedback and then migrating to performance management.

Edwards and Ewen offer the following guidelines for moving 360 Degree Feedback from development to pay and appraisal:

1. Surveying user satisfaction,
2. Guaranteeing anonymity,
3. Differentiating performance or spread of scores,
4. Examining scores for valid difference,
5. Ensuring the meaning of response rates,
6. Keeping administrative overheads low,
7. Dealing with invalid respondents,
8. Adding to diversity fairness,
9. Providing training and
10. Developing safeguards.

Before an organization begins to implement a 360 Degree Feedback process, its leaders or key change agents need to commit to the

CHAPTER 15 Experiences from Other Countries 207

process, select a design team and create a communication plan to inform employees about the new process. The design team assesses the organizational readiness for 360 Degree Feedback by determining whether the organization's culture and environment support such a process. After assessment of the readiness, the design team is ready to develop a vision statement identifying the desired outcomes for the 360 Degree Feedback project. A number of objectives may be identified for the new process which must be clearly stated and communicated to all employees. After testing the project on a pilot basis other features can be added in which the design team members should involve themselves to see, first-hand, how their proposed process works. *Survey development*, also called *instrument development*, is often the most difficult and lengthiest task of the 360 Degree Feedback project because of the importance in achieving content validity and user support. Targeting the specific application and developing the core competencies are logical first steps in this process.

In initiating the implementation phase the design team needs to select the evaluation team, which ideally should be more than six to allow more reliable and comprehensive evaluation. The 360 Degree Feedback cannot be conducted without a thorough understanding of the process, which calls for training people on the benefits and administration of this process in order to avoid unnecessary fears. The evaluations should be conducted fairly, quickly and simply, and the survey response time should be less than 15 minutes. Data collection can be accomplished through paper survey forms, optical scan forms or automated data capture such as e-mail, computer disk or online modes. In scoring the results of the data, informal scoring in the form of a spreadsheet, a calculator or a database management programme for a small group is appropriate, while for a large group, formal scoring patterns need to be developed through software development. The feedback reports should be simple and statistically sound, and should use the best available methods for presenting the information. Training on interpreting the feedback by the participants once they receive their reports is also very important which is followed by preparing action plans.

The third and final phase of implementation consists of analysing safeguards, gaining insights from participants and developing recommendations to improve the process for the next round of evaluations.

208 THE POWER OF 360 DEGREE FEEDBACK

Some of the common pitfalls that undermine the implementation of 360 Degree Feedback, as discussed by Edwards and Ewen, are as follows:

- Misapplying old learning: forcing the multi-source model to comply with the traditional survey research,
- Lack of safeguards,
- Substituting labour for technology,
- Home-grown technology,
- Administrative overhead,
- Culture shock,
- Autocracy,
- Cronyism: Political favourites in the organization are threatened by 360 Degree Feedback and hence discourage the process,
- Nepotism and
- Coasters.

These obstacles to the 360 Degree Feedback occur consistently and must be addressed in earnest. The verdict on 360 Degree Feedback remains to be decided. Organizations and researchers will continue to study the impact of 360 Degree Feedback. It seems to offer an equitable and useful development and assessment process for all the organization members.

PART 4
360 Degree Feedback Tools for Other Sectors

CHAPTER 16

360 Degree Feedback Tools for School Principals

A lot of learning and formation of personality takes place in children during the school years. The school provides the milieu for this and the principal is a significant role player in creating the milieu. In order to create the right culture that influences teachers who, in turn, influence and build the student personality and achievement, the principal has a complex set of leadership roles to play. The principal should be a leader, visionary, pace-setter, developer, resource provider, faculty team builder, educationist, manager, administrator, etc.

How effective are school principals as educationists, leaders, personality developers of students, networkers, etc.? How do the teachers, parents, students, management, non-academic staff, etc. perceive them? The tool developed by TVRLS assesses the principal on the following roles:

- Providing a vision for the school,
- Educationist,
- Culture builder,
- Resource provider,
- Image builder,
- Solution provider for students' problems and growth,
- Linkage builder with parents,
- Developer of teachers,
- Manager of staff,
- Administrator,
- Networker with other schools and
- Manager of the management.

Students, teachers, parents, administrative staff and management committee members assess the principal on a number of items. In addition, it has a leadership quality assessment on 30 qualities.

LEADERSHIP ROLES AND ACTIVITIES

The principal may be assessed using a 5-point scale where 5 represents that the principal or headmaster performs that activity extraordinarily well, 4 represents that the principal performs this activity very well, 3 represents average performance or somewhat well, 2 represents that he/she performs the activity only to a little extent and 1 represents that this activity is not being done by the principal or done to a negligible extent.

Vision and Values

1. Initiates changes in the school on the basis of changes in the educational scenario.
2. Shares and emphasizes the vision and change at all occasions.
3. Initiates innovations in the school.
4. Encourages teacher and student participation in the school activities.

Educationist

5. Shares ideas and philosophy about education of children.
6. Integrates extracurricular activities with academic activities.
7. Adopts creative methods in teaching.
8. Gives adequate attention to the growth of students at every stage (pre-primary to higher secondary).

Culture Building

9. Communicates the values which are important to the school in various internal meetings and gatherings.
10. Encourages an atmosphere of openness among students and teachers.
11. Stresses on cleanliness and sanitation in the school premises.
12. Emphasizes discipline.
13. Sets personal example in terms of values to be followed.
14. Promotes cooperation and helpfulness (empathy and sensitivity) among teachers and staff.

(Contd.)

(Contd.)

Resource Management

15. Allocates adequate number of *ayahs* and peons on duty to ensure smooth running.
16. Ensures smooth running of the school transportation system.

Image Building

17. Participates in public forums, seminars and conferences held by educational institutes/universities.
18. Approaches and interacts with the media (through interviews, articles and press notes) to propagate new things being done in the school.
19. Ensures that the school is known not only in academic areas but all areas as well.
20. Goes out of the way to ensure that the school students and teachers participate in inter-institutes/state/national-level events.
21. Talks about the achievements of the school, teachers and students in public forums.

Sensitivity to Students' Growth and Problems

22. Makes the student development as the centre of the school's goal.
23. Organizes various competitions and activities giving opportunity for individual students to develop their potential.
24. Tries to solve the problems being faced by the students.
25. Is available to the students whenever required.
26. Collects periodic feedback from students about various issues in the school.
27. Discusses decisions made with the students or their representatives instead of simply communicating the same to them.
28. Facilitates learning by sharing personal experiences and readings with students.
29. Ensures good health of students through proper counselling and regular medical check-ups.

(Contd.)

(Contd.)

> 30. Relates to students on a one-to-one basis. Develops personal rapport.
> 31. Encourages students to take up talent exams conducted by educational bodies.
>
> **Management of Parents**
>
> 32. Is approachable to parents. Listens patiently to their grievances.
> 33. Handles complaints of parents with a view to resolve the issue rather than making it an ego issue in itself.
> 34. Discusses the problems and issues faced by the school with people.
> 35. Involves the parents and community in improving the school and its activities.
> 36. Shares information with parents and community to inculcate a sense of pride in them about their school.
> 37. Elicits feedback and suggestions from parents to bring about improvements in the school.
> 38. Discusses and sorts out the problems of children with respective parents instead of merely communicating the same.
> 39. Implements parents' suggestions and ideas.
> 40. Promotes openness and transparency.
> 41. Encourages parent participation and cooperation in school activities.
> 42. Treats parents with respect and commands respect.
> 43. Conducts regular meetings with parent body.
> 44. Encourages parent participation in teaching and other academic activities.
> 45. Keeps parents regularly informed of the changes (staff, teaching methodology, etc.) taking place in the school.
>
> **Management and Development of Teachers**
>
> 46. Is personally involved in the selection of competent and suitable teachers.
> 47. Clearly states the responsibilities to be handled by each teacher.
> 48. Helps teachers plan their work (academic as well as extra-curricular) well in advance.

(Contd.)

(Contd.)

49. Is open to views and suggestions being given by teachers.
50. Encourages creativity in teachers in terms of teaching methods and other activities.
51. Handles conflicts between different teachers with a view to resolve the issue rather than taking sides.
52. Holds regular meetings with teachers to discuss various issues and plan activities.
53. Works closely with the teachers instead of being very autocratic or directive.
54. Establishes a strong rapport with the teachers.
55. Communicates directly with the teachers without being too lenient or too strict.
56. Empathizes with the problems being faced by the teachers.
57. Shares all relevant information with the teachers and involves them in decision-making.
58. Is perceived as a friend and mentor by teachers.
59. Encourages responsibility sharing and collaboration among teachers.
60. Encourages teachers to take initiative and provide full support.
61. Counsels teachers to ensure fair dealing of the students.
62. Sponsors teachers for training and other development activities.

Management of Staff

63. Handles conflicts between staff members.
64. Is sensitive to the problems and difficulties faced by the staff.
65. Ensures proper work allocation among staff.
66. Involves staff in school activities wherever possible.

Administrative

67. Takes administrative decisions promptly on time.
68. Delegates and develops senior staff to handle routine administrative responsibilities.
69. Explains rules, regulations and culture of the school to new teachers.
70. Prepares a comprehensive outline of the school activities well in advance.

(Contd.)

(Contd.)

71. Implements the plan and ensures that all activities are brought to their logical conclusion.
72. Conducts a regular review of academics and other activities.
73. Monitors to ensure that all administrative systems are followed.
74. Ensures that staff payments are made on time.
75. Ensures proper availability and management of finances.

Liaison with School Management Bodies

76. Communicates the expectations and requirements of the teachers, staff and students to the school management.
77. Influences the thinking of the school management for trying out new activities.
78. Ensures that all compliances are adhered to.
79. Ensures that all forms and records are sent to various regulatory bodies on time.

Collaborating with Other Schools

80. Studies and benchmarks with the good practices being followed in the other schools.
81. Collaborates with other schools through joint projects and activities.
82. Encourages inter-school competitions.
83. Forms symbiotic relationship with neighbouring schools—mutual use of each other's facilities.
84. Speaks to the governing board in one voice to bring about changes required.

BEHAVIOURAL QUALITIES

Please rate the principal or headmaster on a 5-point scale where 5 represents highly characteristic of the principal, 4 characteristic mostly, 3 somewhat characteristic, 2 a little characteristic and 1 represents that it is rarely or never a characteristic of this principal.

(Contd.)

(Contd.)

1. Achievement-driven,
2. Innovative,
3. Proactive (initiative taking),
4. Value-driven,
5. Organized,
6. Delegating and empowering teachers,
7. Interpersonally sensitive,
8. Patient rather than impatient and short-tempered,
9. Maintains dignity—the way the principal conducts self,
10. Shows respect for others,
11. Approachable,
12. Participative rather than authoritarian,
13. Good listener—has listening skills,
14. All-rounder,
15. Collaborative,
16. Commanding respect from teachers and students,
17. Guiding,
18. Flexible,
19. Putting the other person at ease,
20. Dynamic,
21. Motivates others,
22. Empathetic (understands and appreciates others' point of view),
23. Ethical,
24. Humane,
25. Inspiring,
26. Nurturing,
27. Open-minded,
28. Assertive,
29. Modest and
30. Disciplinarian.

CHAPTER 17

360 Degree Feedback Tools for Teachers, Students and Parents

360 Degree Feedback for Teachers

Normally, a student spends about 50 per cent of his/her waking life in the school and more than 70 per cent of it in school-related activities in the first 12 formative years of life. Studies have indicated that the behaviour of the teacher in the classroom significantly impacts on the student. In a project sponsored by the Indian Council of Medical Research (ICMR) at the National Institute of Health Administration and Education in New Delhi, in the early 1970s, studies by Udai Pareek and T.V. Rao have revealed that the patterns of classroom interaction (classified as directive and nondirective behaviour) of the teacher impacts the initiative, adjustment, learning, etc. of the child. The nondirective style was found to produce initiative, adjustment, independence and also the ability to cope with frustration, while the directive patterns were found to contribute to academic learning. Some of the teachers did not know the teaching styles they were using until they were given feedback by observers.

A lot of learning and personality formation takes place during these first 12 years of learning. It is therefore important for the teacher to be competent, understanding and effective. It is the teachers who shape the destiny of the child, and thus, in turn, the destiny of nations. David McClelland of Harvard University found that the early socialization offered by the family and the school determines and shapes the personality of the individual subsequently and also impacts the economic development of nations, through the inculcation of achievement and other motivational patterns and values. Hence, it is important that teachers provide appropriate learning experiences to children.

Every teacher thinks that (s)he is trying her/his best and doing a wonderful job. What do others think? What is the impact (s)he is having on young minds? What do other significant individuals such as the parents, colleagues, headmaster and the students themselves think about the teacher? Is (s)he attending to various dimensions of her/his role as a teacher and enhancing her/his teaching effectiveness? Is (s)he performing various roles with equal effectiveness? To know answers to these questions it is important and useful to get feedback from others.

It is our experience that school inspection reports and external evaluations by casual or official visitors do not do full justice and provide full and appropriate feedback to the teachers. Also, the schools as well as the teachers are known to take extra care at the time of inspection to project an image that may not exist. Such casual evaluations also suffer from biases and sampling errors. Hence, it is important to ask the people who matter for feedback. These people include (as mentioned earlier) the students, parents, colleagues and the teacher herself/himself.

Self-assessment

First, the teacher should evaluate herself/himself in terms of how well (s)he is doing as a teacher. Self-assessment is an important starting point of growth and development. The tools given in the following are intended to facilitate such self-evaluation of the teacher.

Student assessment

The students are also the best sources of feedback and evaluation for the teacher. In educational institutions such as the IIMs, the students not only evaluate their faculty, but also publicize the results of their evaluation so that it has public accountability and control value. This also provides motivational value for the teacher. Student feedback is the most important part of the growth and development of the teacher. The tool for this is also developed with the help of a student.

Principal's assessment

The principal or the headmaster is in continuous touch with the teachers. (S)he sees the results, gets feedback from students, and also from the other teachers, parents, etc. So the headmaster/headmistress, as a manager and an information collector of the school, is an important source of feedback for the teacher.

Fellow teachers

The co-teachers get information and evaluation from their own observations, interactions with each other and interactions with students and parents. Hence, the assessment of some of the co-teachers may also provide significant inputs to the feedback. However, the feedback of the co-teachers should be interpreted with caution as they may reflect their own selective perceptions. All feedback in a way is based on perceptions and biases. The instrument for assessment should be given only to those teachers who have had some experience of observing and interacting with the teacher being assessed.

Parents

The parents keep hearing about the teacher from the child. Some parents who take an active interest in the school also meet the teacher periodically, and form their own views about her/him. The school notebooks that carry the corrections of the teacher, the child's feedback and parent–teacher association (PTA) meetings, all of these give the parents some idea about the teacher. It is therefore appropriate to ask some of the parents who know the teacher intimately to provide feedback. This feedback should be anonymous as parents might feel that their feedback might affect the teacher's attitude towards their child, and thus affect their child's performance in class. Only select parents must, therefore, be used to collect feedback.

How to Collect Feedback

A third party should collect the feedback. The questionnaire should be distributed after explaining to the respondent (assessor including students, parents, fellow teachers and principal) the purpose of the questionnaire, and assuring anonymity. While collecting the feedback forms the respondent may be asked to drop it in a collection box where all those who fill the questionnaire may deposit the same. Alternately an external consultant could be used to collect the same.

CHAPTER 17 360 Degree Feedback Tools

The following are sample items and they may be used to construct a questionnaire to suit each institution's requirements (see Box 17.1).

BOX 17.1 TEACHER EFFECTIVENESS QUESTIONNAIRE: SOME ITEMS

1. Comes well prepared for classes.
2. Reads many books and other material for keeping updated in subject matter knowledge.
3. Shares knowledge freely with others.
4. Shows openness to new ideas from students.
5. Shows openness to new ideas from colleagues.
6. Shows respect for institutional norms and discipline.
7. Articulates his/her point of view and communicates clearly.
8. Shows respect for fellow teachers.
9. Maintains good relations with other non-teaching staff.
10. Takes pains to help weak students.
11. Patiently teaches slow learners.
12. Makes effort to improve classroom teaching continuously.
13. Uses various aids in teaching to make it interesting and experiential.
14. Patiently answers questions by students.
15. Acknowledges if he/she does not have answers or solutions and later takes pains to find the same.
16. Shows interest in facilitating learning as contrasted with rote memory.
17. Takes pains to set quizzes and other forms of evaluation to monitor the progress of students.
18. Shows sensitivity to the moods of students.
19. Takes time to assess his/her impact and make midcourse corrections.
20. Builds on the ideas of the students.
21. Consults a variety of sources and prepares well for the class.
22. Experiments with new methods of teaching and makes classroom learning interesting.
23. Attempts different methods of evaluation to make learning exhaustive.
24. Conducts research.

(Box 17.1 Contd.)

(Box 17.1 Contd.)

---

25. Publishes papers.
26. Encourages other working with him/her to publish.
27. Undertakes to assist the school or institutional authorities with administration.
28. Manages classroom activities well.
29. Manages time in the class effectively.
30. Makes sure to be available outside the class for students.
31. Teaches well.
32. Works hard to get good results for the students.
33. Does not show favouritism to some students and treats all equally well.
34. Maintains warm relations with others in the school/institution.
35. Takes initiative to participate in other co-curricular activities.
36. Interacts freely with students outside the class.
37. Anticipates difficulties of others and plans to solve them.
38. Manages conflicts among various parties.
39. Sets personal example by honouring his/her commitments and always speaking the truth.
40. Promotes values among various constituents in the institution.

---

360 Degree Feedback for Parents

Parents play a very important role in the development of children. Children's personalities, including their attitudes and values, are formed at an early stage by the way their parents behave with them. In the Indian culture, children are not allowed to question, argue or share their feelings and opinions. Children often do not get the space to express themselves. Parents also may not be aware of the impact they have on their own children. There may, in fact, be drawbacks in the way the children are brought up. It is therefore important for parents to know the impact they have on the way they influence their children. Hence 360 Degree Feedback would be helpful.

The following tool is meant for parents to seek feedback from each other, their children, and also from their own parents. The person interested could get him/her self-assessed by the generations below, or the generations above the parents of other families for 360 Degree Feedback. The feedback could be collected by one of the children or by the parents themselves. The feedback could also be discussed in the family at the dinner table, or in exclusive meetings with an outside facilitator (see Box 17.2).

BOX 17.2 QUESTIONNAIRE FOR PARENTS

Name of the parent:

Please rate yourself using the following scale:

5 points = this is most characteristic of you. You perform this activity extremely well. This exceeds your expectations (exceptional performance nearly 100 per cent).

4 points = This is quite characteristic of you. You perform this activity well and to a level more than what is expected (75 per cent).

3 points = This is somewhat characteristic of you. You just about meet the expectations (50 per cent).

2 points = You are low on this activity as you exhibit the same only occasionally. You perform this role activity somewhat inadequately and somewhat below expectations (25 per cent).

1 point = This is not at all characteristic of you. You perform this activity far below expectations, amounting to practically either extremely poor performance or non-performance of this role (almost 0 per cent).

How well do you perform the following activities?

5 = extremely well; 4 = very well; 3 = somewhat well; 2 = somewhat poorly; 1 = very weak or do not perform this at all. NA = Not Applicable, Don't Know, Can't Say.

1. Gives freedom to children at the same time ensuring that they use it properly.
2. Does not keep poking his/her nose in unnecessary situations.
3. Does not keep taunting children, but instead keeps encouraging them.

(Box 17.2 Contd.)

(Box 17.2 Contd.)

---

4. Gives attention to their whereabouts and the company they keep.
5. Encourages them to take decisions on their own.
6. Encourages them to think in an independent manner.
7. Encourages and makes sure that they meet everyone with an open mind (not reserved) and talk in the same way.
8. Gives attention to their studies.
9. During hard times gives advice to children, which leads them on to the correct path.
10. Gives them a feeling that he/she is more a friend than a parent.
11. Allows the children to be on their own so that they learn to handle hard situations easily.
12. Exposes them to the harder side of life so that they tackle future problems if any.
13. Encourages children to participate in co-curricular activities (non-academic activities that build their personality).
14. Allows children to go on tours so that they get a taste of freedom.
15. Ensures that the child never feels lonely or gets depressed by any problem at a young age.
16. Shouts when angry but apologizes quickly and in a cool manner sorts out the problems with the child.
17. Keeps away all the work and pays attention to what the child says when the child is sharing a problem.
18. Takes good care of the child by fulfilling her/his daily needs, at the same time not allowing her/him to get pampered by buying whatever s/he wants.
19. Attempts to bring out the child's hidden talents by sending her/him to classes and encouraging the talent to be used in the future.
20. Gives enough time for the child to realize her/his mistakes and helps her/him to repair them accordingly.
21. Supports the child to develop her/his own judgement of right and wrong.
22. Imbibes good manners and etiquette in the child.
23. Attempts to remove the child's shyness.
24. Makes the child responsible.

Peer Feedback for Students

Assessment takes many forms. Assessment is a tool. It paves the way for growth; it is not an end. As a student, one goes through numerous tests and assessments. Each helps the individual know where he/she stands in relation to certain standards, as well as in relation to others.

360 Degree Feedback has become quite familiar to the corporate world today. A lot has been written on how it has helped individuals as well as organizations in the process of change and leadership. However, the flexibility of this tool has not been explored beyond the corporate world. The tool presented here was originally developed a group of students from the Indian School of Business (ISB) a decade ago and administered on them. Since then the authors of this book have been working with students. Normally, the postgraduate students in any institution and also the undergraduate students in professional institutions such as Medicine, Teacher training, Management, etc. work in groups. By the time they come to their senior classes or final year, they may have already interacted with each other in large numbers for their project work and other ways. They would have made an impact on those with whom they worked. Similarly if they go for summer training or internships, they would have interacted with their seniors or prospective employers and made an impact on them. Their parents and relatives as well as friends from their home towns or villages will have useful feedback to offer. A feedback of their behaviour and characteristics could go a long way to promote introspection, enhance sensitivity and help prepare plans for future development and cultivation of some desirable qualities. The tool below has been used with modifications by the authors at the Indian Institute of Management, Ahmedabad, Ranchi and various other places besides the ISB (see Box 17.3). TVRLS also has started a 360 Degree Feedback service for students (www.tvrls.com).

BOX 17.3 360 TOOL FOR POSTGRADUATE STUDENTS

1. Takes initiative to organize groups and ensures that uncertainties are clarified and contributions are understood.
2. Is reliable and trustworthy. Keeps up his/her promises.

(Box 17.3 Contd.)

(Box 17.3 Contd.)

> 3. Has clear understanding of the strengths and weaknesses of team members in the context of group tasks assigned. Willing to spend time to pull up the weaker members of the team.
> 4. Has the capacity to put aside self-interest for the good of the team.
> 5. Seeks to learn from everybody, whether junior or senior, in the team.
> 6. Actively listens and paraphrases to enhance understanding and appreciation of each other's point of view.
> 7. Is open to ideas from all quarters to find new ways of solving problems.
> 8. Is a person with whom I would rather express myself freely without the risk of being castigated or labelled as incompetent?
> 9. Strives to create an environment of collaboration, team spirit and trust.
> 10. Is always willing to share experiences, which enhance his/her learning.
> 11. A team with diverse backgrounds does not hinder the quality and quantity of his/her interactions.
> 12. Respects every individual for his/her inane qualities.
> 13. Sets personal example for team members to follow.
> 14. Seeks feedback and learns from it. Uses feedback to improve his/her performance.
> 15. Provides feedback to others to help them improve.
> 16. Manages different views in the team to foster a collaborative environment.
> 17. Acknowledges contribution of all members.
> 18. Displays continued enthusiasm and interest in group goals.
> 19. Communicates effectively.
> 20. Handles pressures, stress and crisis effectively and calmly.
> 21. Develops and maintains smooth and effective interpersonal relationships.
> 22. Is achievement and excellence driven in his/her work. Consistently looks for better way of doing things.
> 23. Recognizes people for doing a good job and gives them credit.
> 24. Is creative and flexible in his/her thinking. Out-of-the-box thinker.

(Box 17.3 Contd.)

(Box 17.3 Contd.)

25. Takes initiative and does not look for having to be told all the time.
26. Is empathetic, helpful and supportive as a person to others.
27. Exhibits high level of self-confidence.
28. When faced with difficult situations in studies or with friends shows maturity, both emotionally and mentally, to overcome the situation.
29. Is decisive in taking action whenever needed.
30. Takes calculated risks.
31. What are the five main strong points of this individual?
32. What are the areas where the candidates need to work more (his/her weak areas or areas he/she needs improvements)?

CHAPTER 18

360 Degree Feedback Tools for Non-governmental Organizations*

Non-governmental organizations (NGOs) play a very crucial role in the development sector. They are into education, health, old age homes, orphanages, environmental concerns, legal support for the disadvantaged, agriculture, social forestry, women and girl child, and other social causes as well as development initiatives. As they play a crucial role and sometimes even the government agencies look for guidance from them, it is important that they are managed well. The founders and trustees of these NGOs and their styles of functioning matter a lot in their effectiveness. Sometimes due to the respect for the founders, who are individuals that have made a lot of sacrifices in setting up and managing the NGO, the employees and others hesitate to give them feedback. The employees as well as beneficiaries tend to tell them more of good things and suppress the negatives. Hence it is important that the trustees and other leaders in NGOs become sensitive to the impact they have made or are making on their employees, donors, beneficiaries and other stakeholders.

By virtue of their nature, separate tools are needed to suit the NGOs. This chapter presents one such tool developed by TVRLS. The tool reproduced below has four parts. The first part deals with the leadership and managerial roles to be performed by the trustees. The second part deals with their leadership styles. This uses the same framework of leadership styles presented earlier in Chapter 5. The delegation (D) in RSDQ is substituted by 'empowerment' (E) that is both a need and a value for NGOs. The model can, therefore, be called the 'RSEQ' model, instead of RSDQ, for NGOs.

*© TV Rao Learning Systems Pvt. Ltd. TVRLS will be happy to permit select NGOs to use this tool free provided certain conditions are fulfilled. Please write for a free use of this tool to: tvrls@tvrao.com. or rajurao@hotmail.com or tvrao@tvrao.com.

CHAPTER 18 360 Degree Feedback Tools for NGOs

The format reproduced in this section is meant for assessment by others (called version O), and can also be used for self-assessment by the candidate.

HOW EFFECTIVELY IS THE PERSON PERFORMING VARIOUS ROLES?

(Form NGO-O)

Name of the Assessee:

Please assess the person on how effectively (s)he is performing each of the following roles or activities. Please use the following scale:

4 = *(S)he is performing this role/activity extraordinarily well. There cannot be anything better than this. Performance is far above what is expected of him/her.*
3 = *(S)he is performing this role very well. His/her performance is somewhat above what is expected and there is only a little scope for doing this any better.*
2 = *(S)he is performing this role just adequately. Just meets expectations and there is some scope to do this even better to be called extraordinary.*
1 = *(S)he is performing this role slightly below what is expected of her/him. Some improvement in this is desirable.*
0 = *(S)he is performing this role far below what is expected of her/him. (S)he should improve performance on this substantially.*
NA = *Not applicable. This role is not applicable to her/him. (S)he need not perform this. Or I do not have information or knowledge on this.*

(Please read the term *staff* to mean all employees or volunteers or all other social workers who work for the beneficiaries on behalf of the NGO. *Beneficiaries* mean those people whom the NGO and its activities are set up to serve, e.g. women, old people, orphans, the disabled, farmers, children, etc.)

Vision, Values and Culture

1. Articulating and developing a vision for the future of the organization or the programme.

(Contd.)

(Contd.)

2. Inspiring the staff (those who work for the NGO) with the vision of the organization or institution or programme (communicating and reminding the staff periodically and following the vision and values by personal example, etc.).
3. Clearly stating the values and desired culture of the organization (e.g. selfless service, empowerment, nonprofits orientation, etc.).
4. Paying attention towards the values and desired culture of the organization (honesty, trustworthiness, integrity, etc.).

Capacity Building and Inspiring Staff

5. Investing time and effort in the capacity building of the members of the organization (staff).
6. Mentoring and providing proper guidance and counselling to all staff members to enable them to perform their tasks well.
7. Acting as a role model for the staff and setting high standards.
8. Providing a sense of ownership and significance to employees through recognition of their work, etc.
9. Setting and communicating clear-cut norms, values, discipline and other standards of excellence to be followed by staff.
10. Providing information and other resources necessary for the staff to perform their tasks well.
11. Providing periodic feedback to the staff and helping them to review their performance and learn from the past.
12. Encouraging innovativeness among the staff.
13. Listening to the problems and difficulties of the staff and resolving conflicts amongst them.

Networking with Others: Agencies and People (GOs, NGOs, Media, etc.)

14. Development of good working relationships with the government and other local agencies that are involved in serving the beneficiaries.
15. Influencing the thinking of the government for policy-making on various related issues.

(Contd.)

CHAPTER 18 360 Degree Feedback Tools for NGOs

(Contd.)

16. Maintaining good relations with public and other agencies *(panchayats,* municipal corporations, political parties (where needed), etc.).
17. Maintaining good public relations with the media, both newspapers and other agencies, to create a good image and mobilize goodwill.
18. Keeping in touch with other NGOs doing similar work, and learning from them.
19. Understanding the needs, expectations and requirements of the beneficiaries by visiting them, interacting with them and learning from them.
20. Learning from other trustees and staff, and benefiting from their experience.

Donor Management

21. Maintaining linkages with the donor agencies and keeping them informed about the work of the NGO.
22. Influencing the thinking of the donor agencies.
23. Supplying information and documentation on time and with required details to the donor agencies.
24. Inviting donor agencies to the field and communicating with them the work being done and experiences of the agency.
25. Learning from the experiences of the donors and others by visiting them, participating in seminars, conferences, etc.
26. Seeking new donors and mobilizing resources for the beneficiaries.

Liaison with Management (Seniors and Other Trustees)

27. Communicating and liaisoning with the seniors and other trustees, and keeping them informed of various developments, decisions, events, etc.
28. Understanding the expectations of the seniors (other trustees/management committee members, etc.).
29. Influencing the thinking of the donors and getting their support and resources.
30. Taking guidance and learning from the experiences of seniors and experienced donors and specialists.

(Contd.)

(Contd.)

Beneficiary Management (Service and Learning)

31. Evolving strategies to improve the services to beneficiaries.
32. Communicating to other staff about the beneficiaries and their concerns and needs.
33. Understanding the difficulties faced by the beneficiaries and solving their problems.
34. Visiting the field, interacting with the beneficiaries and understanding their environment and conditions.
35. Seeking suggestions from the beneficiaries in order to improve services and interventions provided by the organization.

Strategy Formulation and Goal Setting

36. Securing the critical information required for intervention planning and strategy formulation in the areas of work done by the organization.
37. Formulating schemes and programmes that are effective and timely, and beneficial for others in the community.
38. Planning performance improvements of the organization/projects and programmes.
39. Setting long-term goals for the organization/programme/projects.
40. Setting short-term tasks and targets for the organization/programme/projects.

Intervention Planning and Systems Management

41. Introducing new interventions and methodologies for making development faster and more cost-effective, and helping them reach those people they are meant for.
42. Keeping in touch with developments in the areas of work—locally, nationally and globally.
43. Introducing new systems of management to manage various activities and processes, effectively.
44. Supplying information and other documentation to donor agencies and others promptly.
45. Monitoring the effective implementation and utilization of various systems (performance appraisal, periodic meetings, performance reviews, data management, information and documentation, etc.).

LEADERSHIP AND MANAGEMENT STYLES

(Form O)

Name of the Assessee:

Given below are statements describing different leadership and managerial styles of any manager/trustee. Please assess the candidate using a five-point scale where

    4 = The statement is most (nearly 100 per cent) characteristic of the individual. (S)he behaves that way almost all the time.

    3 = The statement is more true of him/her and (s)he behaves that way more often than not (about 75 per cent of the time).

    2 = The statement is somewhat characteristic of him/her and (s)he behaves that way about 50 per cent of the time.

    1 = The statement is a little characteristic of him/her. (S)he uses that style about 25 per cent of the time.

    0 = The statement is not at all characteristic of him/her and (s)he does not behave that way and it is least characteristic of him/her (more or less 0 per cent).

Decision-making

1. Takes all decisions by him/herself. Does not consult others.
2. Takes decisions by consulting a few closer to him/her and ignores others.
3. Takes decisions by consulting as many as possible. Gives everyone the opportunity to participate in decision-making.

Problem-solving

4. Gets personally involved in problem-solving in the field whenever problems occur. Good problem-solver and staff look to his/her interventions as and when problems arise.
5. Gets impatient when problems occur. Loses balance and tends to get angry and reprimand others when problem arises.
6. Encourages staff and beneficiaries to solve their problems and learn from them. Invests in the development of the problem-solving capabilities of the staff.

Mistake Management

7. Treats the mistakes of a favourite few with understanding and protects them.

(Contd.)

(Contd.)

8. Cannot tolerate mistakes. Loses temper and tends to reprimand or sulk.
9. Helps people to learn from their mistakes by coolly analysing and diagnosing as a team, or individually through introspection.

Information Sharing and Communications

10. Shares information with a few members who are close to him/her.
11. Does not share any information normally. Secretive and treats information as power.
12. Shares information freely with all and keeps explaining things to build people and their competencies.

Recognition and Rewards

13. Recognizes and rewards a few who are close to him/her.
14. Does not reward anyone or recognize anyone. Feels that recognition and reward spoil people.
15. Rewards objectively to build competencies and motivation of people. Tries his/her best to be objective in rewards.

Training and Development

16. Sponsors a few whom he/she relies on for training and other development interventions.
17. Does not sponsor anyone for development activities. Uses all opportunities for self. Seems to be afraid of building the competencies of others. May fear that others may surpass him/her.
18. Tries his/her best to build the competencies of all staff. Believes in empowerment and development of staff.

Expression of Emotions

19. Expresses emotions selectively with a few. Warm and affectionate. Relationship-oriented person.
20. Does not express any positive emotions. Expresses anger and annoyance freely. Has no qualms in pulling others down.

(Contd.)

(Contd.)

21. Controls emotions and is expressive only when necessary. Expresses largely empowering emotions such as warmth, happiness, etc.

Task Assignment and Work Allocation

22. Favours a few whom (s)he likes in assigning tasks and goal setting.
23. Goes strictly according to rules and norms without consideration for individual interest and competence.
24. Sets goals through a dialogue with a definite view of challenging the staff to grow.

Support and Resources

25. Provides support and resources selectively to a few of those who are close to him/her.
26. Does not provide adequate support and resources, or provides it grudgingly when asked.
27. Expects staff to develop competencies to working through problems and issues, and provides support readily whenever needed.

Impact of His/Her Styles on the Staff and Juniors

(4 = Very true, nearly 100 per cent. 3 = True about 75 per cent of the time. 2 = Sometimes true (50 per cent). 1 = Only a little (25 per cent of the time) true. 0 = Not at all true, 0 per cent of the time.)

28. His/her staff can be characterized as loyal and dependent on him/her.
29. Her/his staff can be characterized as resenting his/her style and feeling incompetent and demotivated at times.
30. His/her staff can be characterized as becoming independent in thinking, empowered and good at teamwork.
31. Those who work with him/her tend to learn a lot.
32. The staff working with him/her exhibits a high degree of morality and satisfaction.

LEADERSHIP QUALITIES QUESTIONNAIRE

(Form NGO-O)

Name of the Assessee:

Please assess the person on the following qualities. Use the following scale for assessment:

4 = This quality is highly characteristic of him/her. S(he) exhibits this quality almost all the time (90–100 per cent of the time).
3 = This quality is most characteristic of him/her. S(he) exhibits this most of the time (about 75 per cent of the time).
2 = This is somewhat characteristic of him/her. S(he) exhibits this sometimes (about 50 per cent of the time).
1 = This quality is very little of his/her characteristic. S(he) exhibits this only a few times (about 25 per cent of the time).
0 = This quality is not at all characteristic of him/her. S(he) does not exhibit this except once in a while (0–10 per cent of the time).
NA = Not applicable, don't know.

1. Takes initiative.
2. Takes risks when required.
3. Is transparent—shares true feelings and opinions.
4. Is highly committed to the organization.
5. Listens to others. Values other people and their viewpoint. Takes decision quickly.
6. Takes quick and quality decisions.
7. Connects with people easily and establishes a good rapport.
8. Anticipates the needs and requirements of others and tries to help them.
9. Is receptive to feedback and tries to benefit from it.
10. Trusts others.
11. Is a constant learner. Always looks for opportunities to learn and grow.
12. Sets an example for others to follow.
13. Creates development opportunities for others.
14. Is change-oriented rather than status-quo-oriented.
15. Walks the talk.
16. Is fair in dealings with people.
17. Is active and dynamic rather than passive and laid back.
18. Is proactive rather than reactive.

(Contd.)

(Contd.)

19. Is trustworthy and reliable.
20. Is flexible.
21. Has high integrity.
22. Is open-minded.
23. Is honest and candid.
24. Is gender sensitive.
25. Has high ethical standards.
26. Is calm and composed rather than irritable and short-tempered.
27. Is proactive rather than authoritarian.
28. Is innovative rather than being conformist.
29. Is receptive rather than defensive.
30. Is approachable.

EMPOWERMENT QUESTIONNAIRE

(Form O)

Name of the Assessee:

Please put a tick mark on the items that are characteristic of the person concerned.

1. Encourages team members to identify various projects independently and develop action plans for the execution of the same.
2. Encourages team members to interact/build relations independently with donors, government, other NGOs, etc.
3. Encourages independent decision-making at individual and team levels in work methodology.
4. Prefers his/her staff/volunteers to check with him/her whenever a problem arises in an ongoing project/assignment or in the field.
5. Creates opportunities for staff to get noticed and make an impact.
6. Encourages members to set some of their own goals independently and review them from time to time.

(Contd.)

(Contd.)

7. Allows members to review and bring about necessary changes in project implementation and other interventions.
8. Allows members to interact with the media independently on various issues.
9. Invests time and effort to develop a second line of leadership.
10. Does not insist on taking permission or seeking approval for everything the staff/volunteers undertake.

Strengths, Weak Areas and Suggestions

Please mention below his/her strengths and weaknesses as a leader and your suggestions for improvement.

Strong points or the things that the person should continue to do.

1. _____
2. _____
3. _____
4. _____
5. _____

Areas that he/she needs to improve to be more effective as a leader.

1. _____
2. _____
3. _____
4. _____
5. _____

Your specific suggestions for improving on the aforementioned areas.

1. _____
2. _____
3. _____
4. _____
5. _____

(Contd.)

(Contd.)

> Please indicate if you are his/her staff, colleague, senior, boss or beneficiary, or donor. This is for our analysis purposes.
>
> am his/her staff
> am his/her boss/senior
> am a donor
>
> The rater is a user of the services of the person being assessed.
> I am his/her client or user of his/her services.

Appendix: Organizations Using 360 Degree Feedback

TVRLS has profiled over 10,000 top-level managers through 360 Degree Feedback over the last 17 years. Over 80,000 respondents have given them feedback. TVRLS has conducted around 300 leadership development workshops using 360 Degree Feedback. This has also been followed up with individual counselling sessions post the feedback workshop to come up with Individual Development Plans (IDPs).

Some of the organizations that have used 360 Degree Feedback and RSDQ Model of TVRLS are listed below:

1. Adani Group
2. Aditya Birla Group (a multinational with presence in Malaysia, Indonesia, Philippines, Thailand, Canada and Egypt)
3. Aditya Birla Minacs
4. Advanta
5. Akshaya Patra Foundation
6. Alexandria Carbon Black, Egypt
7. Altair Engineering
8. AMP India (Tyco International, an American multinational)
9. Amway
10. Apeejay Group
11. Astrazeneca
12. ATE Marketing Pvt. Ltd.
13. ATUL
14. Bajaj Auto
15. BGGTS
16. Bharat Electronics Limited (BEL—total of 31 leadership workshops)
17. Bharati Enterprises
18. Bhoruka
19. Birla Grasim
20. Bosch Rexroth

Appendix: Organizations Using 360 Degree Feedback **241**

21. BPL Limited
22. BSI
23. CP Ships
24. Catsglobal
25. Chinmaya Vidhalaya
26. Clariant (formerly known as Colorchem)
27. Commercial Bank, Sri Lanka
28. Dominos
29. Dr Reddy's Laboratories
30. ECIL Rapiscan
31. Elitecore
32. Ferromatic Milacron
33. Flextronics
34. Fortis Healthcare Ltd.
35. Fulford
36. Gati Cargo Management Services
37. Geometric
38. Godfrey Phillips
39. Gujarat Venture Finance Limited
40. Hemas Holdings Ltd.
41. Himalaya Drug Company
42. Hindalco Industries
43. Hinduja Group
44. HP-Digital
45. Idea Cellular
46. IL&FS (a financial service company)
47. Indian Group of Hotels
48. Indian School of Business
49. Indogulf
50. Interglobe Enterprises Ltd.
51. Interra Software
52. Intervet
53. Ion Exchange
54. ISABS
55. Jindal Steel and Power Limited
56. Jindal Steel Works
57. Kewalram Chanrai Group (Nigeria)
58. KHS Machinery Pvt. Ltd.
59. KYONI

60. Larsen & Toubro
61. Linde Engineering
62. LMGF
63. Mafatlal Group
64. Micro Devices Metrohm (Chennai)
65. MRPL (Mangalore)
66. Nestle
67. Neterwala Group of Companies
68. Novartis
69. Novell Software
70. NTPC
71. Oracle
72. Power Finance Corporation
73. Qwest India
74. Raymond Ltd.
75. RED Retail
76. Reliance Power Ltd.
77. Reserve Bank of India
78. Rubamin Ltd
79. SAIL
80. Satyam
81. SCB
82. Seagram Manufacturing
83. Shreyas Relay Systems Pvt. Ltd.
84. Spheris (formerly known as Healthscribe)
85. State Bank of India
86. Sterlite Industries (Vedanta Group)
87. Taj Group (India Hotels)
88. Tata Coffee
89. Tata Cummins
90. Tata Finance
91. Tata Interactive Systems
92. Tata Tea
93. Titan Industries Limited
94. Torrent Pharma
95. Torry Harris
96. Transasia Biomedicals
97. Transcorp Int. Ltd.
98. Transport Corporation of India

99. TSPL
100. Valvoline Cummins Ltd.
101. Watanmal
102. Wockhardt
103. Wyeth
104. XIndia Steels Pvt. Ltd.
105. You Telecom
106. Zydus Cadila Healthcare Ltd.

References and Select Bibliography

Agarwal, M. (2010) Self-revelation in Leadership Style: Gati Experience, in Rao, T.V., Ramnarayan, S. and Chawla, N. (eds) *Life after 360 Degree Feedback and Assessment Development Centers*. New Delhi: Excel Publications, pp. 344–352.

Anthony deMello, S.J. (1987) *The Prayer of the Frog*. Anand, India: Gujarat Sahitya Prakash.

Anthony deMello, S.J. (1987a) *One Minute Wisdom*. Anand, India: Gujarat Sahitya Prakash.

Anthony deMello, S.J. (1987b) *The Song of the Bird*. Anand, India: Gujarat Sahitya Prakash.

BEL Corporate HR. (2010) Learning from 360º Feedback & Leadership: BEL Experience, in Rao, T.V., Ramnarayan, S. and Chawla, N. (eds) *Life after 360 Degree Feedback and Assessment Development Centers*. New Delhi: Excel Publications, pp. 278–295.

Bennis, W. and Nonus, B. (1985) *Leaders: The Strategies for Taking Charge*. New York: Harper & Row.

Bhide, P.V. (2010) Life after 360 Degree Feedback & Assessment Development Centers—JK Organization Experience, in Rao, T.V., Ramnarayan, S. and Chawla, N. (eds) *Life after 360 Degree Feedback and Assessment Development Centers*. New Delhi: Excel Publications, pp. 245–277.

Blanchard, K. (1985) *Leadership and the One Minute Manager*. Morrow, NY: Blanchard Management Corporation.

Blanchard, K. (1985) *Putting the One Minute Manager to Work*. Morrow, NY: Blanchard Management Corporation.

Bracken, D.W., Summers, L. and Fleenor, J. (1998) High Tech 360. *Training and Development*, 52, August, pp. 42–45.

Byham, W.C., Smith, A.B. and Paese, M.J. (2002) *Grow Your Own Leaders: How to Identify, Develop, and Retain Leadership Talent*. Upper Saddle River, NJ: Prentice-Hall.

Cappelli, P., Singh, H., Singh, J. and Useem, M. (2010) *The India Way: How India's Top Business Leaders Are Revolutionalising Management*. Boston, MA: Harvard Business Press.

Chappelow, C. (2003) News Flash: 360-Degree Feedback Is Alive and Well. *Leadership in Action*, 23(2), pp. 22–23.

Chary, S.N. (2002) *Business Guru's Speak*. New Delhi: Macmillan India.

References and Select Bibliography 245

Chawla, N. (2004) 360 Degree Feedback: Miles to Go before We Sleep. Unpublished report. Bangalore: TVRLS.
Chawla, N. and Rao, T.V. (2010) Life after 360 Degree feedback and ADCs: Lessons for the Future, in Rao, T.V., Ramnarayan, S. and Chawla, N. (eds) *Life after 360 Degree Feedback and Assessment Development Centers.* New Delhi: Excel Publications, pp. 381–395.
Church, A.H. (1995) First-rate Multi-rater Feedback. *Training and Development*, 49, August, pp. 42–43.
Dixit, S. (2010), Adani Groups Experience of 360 Degree Feedback for Top and Senior Management, in Rao, T.V., Ramnarayan, S. and Chawla, N. (eds) *Life after 360 Degree Feedback and Assessment Development Centers.* New Delhi: Excel Publications, pp. 328–336.
Edwards, M.R. and Ewen, A.J. (1996) *360 Degree Feedback: The Powerful New Model for Employee Assessment and Performance Improvement.* New York: Amacom, American Management Association.
Flannigon, B. (1997) Turnaround from Feedback. *HR Focus*, October, p. 3.
Fournies, F.F. (2003) *Coaching for Improved Work Performance.* New Delhi: Tata McGraw-Hill.
Gardener, J.W. (1990) *On Leadership.* New York: Free Press, p. 49.
Gebelian, S.H. (1996) Multi-rater Feedback Goes Strategic. *HR Focus*, January, pp. 1–6.
Ghoshal, S. and Bartlett, C.A. (1997) *The Individualized Corporation.* New York: Harper Business Book.
Glacel, B.P. (2002) The Role of the Executive Coach. *The 2002 Annual: Volume 2, Consulting.* San Francisco: CA John Wiley and Sons.
Glacel, B.P. (2003). Coaching the Super Stars: Learning the Lessons of Hardship. *The 2003 Annual: Volume 1, Training.* San Francisco: CA John Wiley and Sons.
Goleman, D. (1998) *Working with Emotional Intelligence.* New York: Bantam Books.
Goleman, D. (2002) *The New Leaders: Transforming the Art of Leadership into the Science of Results.* London: Little, Brown.
Haworth, S. (1998) The Dark Side of Multi-rater Assessment. *HR Magazine*, pp. 106–114.
Hesselbein, F. and Paul, M.C. (1999) *Leader to Leader.* San Francisco: Jossy Bass.
Hoffman, R. (1995) Ten Reasons You Should Be Using 360 Degree Feedback. *HR Magazine*, April.
Hoffman, R. (1997) Ten Reasons You Should Be Using 360 Degree Feedback. *Training and Development*, April.
Khandwalla, P.N. (1995) *Management Styles.* New Delhi: Tata McGraw-Hill.
Khera, S. (1998) *You Can Win.* New Delhi: Macmillan India.
Lala, R.M. (1986) *In Search of Leadership.* New Delhi: Vision Books.
Lee, B. (1997) *The Power Principle: Influence with Honour.* Fireside, NY: Franklin Covey Co.

McCauley, C. (2003) Should Managers Be Able to Review the Ratings Their Subordinates Receive from 360-Degree Feedback Instruments? *Leadership in Action*, 23(2), p. 13.
McClelland, D.C. and Burnham, D.H. (1995) Power Is the Great Motivator. *Harvard Business Review*, January, 54(2), 100–110.
McLean, G. (2002) Multi-rater Feedback. Presentation made at the *First Asian Conference on HRD*, Bangalore, IIM, October.
Meade, J. (1999) Visual 360: A Performance Appraisal System That's Fun. *HR Magazine*, July, pp. 119–122.
Mishra, S. and Chawla, N. (2003) *Deriving Training Needs from 360 Degree Feedback*. Ahmedabad: TVRLS.
Nair, N., Vohra, N., Rao, T.V. and Srivastava, A. (2009) *HR Best Practices: Manufacturing Sector in India*. New Delhi: Steel Authority of India.
Novack, K.M. (1993) 360 Degree Feedback: The Whole Story. *Training and Development*, January, pp. 69–72.
Novack, K.M., Hartley, J. and Bradley, W. (1999) How to Evaluate Your 360 Feedback Efforts. *Training and Development*, April, pp. 48–53.
Nulty, P. (1994) The National Business Hall of Fame. *Fortune Magazine*, 29(7), April, p. 118.
Pandit, S. (2001) *Thought Leaders*. New Delhi: Tata McGraw-Hill.
Pareek, U. (1990) Task Analysis for Human Resources Development. *Annual Handbook for Group Facilitators*. University Associates.
Pareek, U. (1994) *Beyond Management*. 2nd edition. New Delhi: Oxford & IBH.
Pareek, U. (2002a) *Effective Organizations: Beyond Management to Institution Building*. New Delhi: Oxford & IBH.
Pareek, U. (2002b) *Handbook of HRD Instruments*. New Delhi: Tata McGraw-Hill.
Pareek, U., Rao, T.V. and Pestonjee, D.M. (1981) *Behavior Processes in Organizations*. New Delhi: Oxford & IBH.
Pareek, U. and Rao, T.V. (1981/2003) *Designing and Managing Human Resource System*. 3rd edition. New Delhi: Oxford & IBH.
Pareek, U. and Rao, T.V (1990) Performance Coaching. *Annual Handbook for Group Facilitators*. La Jola, CA: University Associates, pp. 249–263.
Pareek, U. and Rao, T.V. (1997) Pioneering Human Resource System in L&T. Consulting report of 1975 and 1976. Ahmedabad: Academy of Human Resources Development.
Parul, R. (2002) Leading JFM through Nurturance: An Indian Scenario. *International Forestry Review*, 4(2), pp. 143–147.
Peters, T. (1997) *The Circle of Innovation: You Can't Shirk Your Way to Greatness*. London: Hodder & Stoughton,.
Pfan, R.N. and Kay, I.T. (2002) *The Human Capital Edge*. New York, NY: McGraw-Hill.
Pfeffer, J. (1998) *The Human Equation*. Harvard Business School Press.
Piramal, G. (1996) *Business Maharajas*. New Delhi: Viking, Penguin Books.

References and Select Bibliography 247

Rai, H. and Singh, M. (2005) Mediating Effects in the Relationship between 360-Degree Feedback and Employee Performance. Working Papers, 2005 (W.P. No. 2005-04-06). Ahmedabad: Indian Institute of Management.

Ramnarayan, S. (2010) Not just for Individual Development: Gaining Organizational Insights from 360-Degree Assessment, in Rao, T.V., Ramnarayan, S. and Chawla, N. (eds) *Life after 360 Degree Feedback and Assessment Development Centers*. New Delhi: Excel Publications, pp. 3–51.

Rao, R. (2010) A Study of Differences in the 360 Degree Feedback of Star and Average Performers Using RSDQ Model in Rao, T. V., Ramnarayan, S. and Chawla, N. (eds), *Life after 360 Degree Feedback and Assessment and Development Centers*. New Delhi: Excel Publications, pp. 70–90.

Rao, T.V. (1986) The Supervisory and Leadership Beliefs Questionnaire, in Pfeiffer, J.W. and Goodstein, L.D. (eds) *The 1986 Annual: Developing Human Resources*. San Diego, CA: University Associates, pp. 111–116.

Rao, T.V. (1999) Making 360 Degree Feedback Work. *Human Capital*, August.

Rao, T.V. (2010) A Study of the Relationships between Competency Assessment through Assessment Centers and 360 Degree Tools, in Rao, T.V., Ramnarayan, S. and Chawla, N. (eds) *Life after 360 Degree Feedback and Assessment Development Centers*. New Delhi: Excel Publications, pp. 103–135.

Rao, T.V. and Annapurna, J. (2005) An Exploratory Study of Changes in the Roles and Competencies of Top-level Managers due to 360-Degree Feedback. Unpublished research paper. Ahmedabad: TV Rao Learning Systems Pvt. Ltd.

Rao, T.V. and Chawla, N. (2005) *360 Degree Feedback and Assessment and Development Centres*. New Delhi: Excel Publications.

Rao, T.V. and Chawla, N. (2010) Impact of 360 Degree Feedback: A Follow-up Study of Four Organizations, in Rao, T.V., Ramnarayan, S. and Chawla, N. (eds) *Life after 360 Degree Feedback and Assessment Development Centers*. New Delhi: Excel Publications, pp. 52–69.

Rao, T.V., Mahapatra, G., Rao, R. and Chawla, N. (2002). *360 Degree Feedback and Performance Management Systems*. New Delhi: Excel Publications.

Rao, T.V. and Rao, R. (2001) *360 Degree Feedback and Performance Management Systems*. New Delhi: Excel Publications.

Rao, T.V. and Rao, R. (2002) A Study of Leadership Roles, Styles, Delegation and Qualities in Indian CEOs. Paper presented at the *First Asian Conference on HRD in Asia*, Academy of HRD, Bangalore, pp. 661–668.

Rao, T.V. and Rao, R. (2003) *The Power of 360 Degree Feedback*. New Delhi: SAGE Response Books.

Rao, T.V. and Selvan, T. (1992) Strengths and Weaknesses of Senior Executives, *Productivity*, 33(3), October–December, pp. 443–451.

Rao, T.V. and Stewart, A. (1975) *Stewart Maturity Scale: Indian Adaptation*. New Delhi: Manasayan.

Rao, T.V. and Vijayalakshmi, M. (2000) RSDQ Model of 360 Degree Feedback, in Rao, T.V., Vijayalakshmi, M. and Rao, R. (eds) *360 Degree Feedback and Performance Management Systems*. New Delhi: Excel Publications.

Rao, T.V., Vijayalakshmi, M. and Rao, R. (2000) *360 Degree Feedback and Performance Management Systems*. New Delhi: Excel Publications.
Robins, S.P. (2002) *The Truth about Managing People: And Nothing but the Truth*. Singapore: Pearson Education.
Singh, M. and Vohra, N. (2005) Multi-faceted Feedback for Organisational Heads for Self and Organisational Development: Experiences, *International Journal of Training and Development*, 9(3), September.
Singh, P. and Bhandarkar, A. (1990) *Corporate Success and Transformational Leadership*. New Delhi: Wiley Eastern Limited.
Sinha, J.B.P. (1980) *The Nurturant Task Leader*. New Delhi: Concept Publishing.
Sinha, J.B.P. (1984) A Model for Effective Leadership Styles in India. *International Studies of Management and Organization*, 14(2–3), pp. 86–98.
Sinha, J.B.P. (1995) *The Cultural Context of Leadership and Power*. New Delhi: SAGE.
Sinha, S.K. (2010) 360 Degree Feedback at MSIL, in Rao, T.V., Ramnarayan, S. and Chawla, N. (eds) *Life after 360 Degree Feedback and Assessment Development Centers*. New Delhi: Excel Publications, pp. 296–300.
Smart, B.D. (1999) *Top Grading: How Leading Companies Win by Hiring, Coaching and Keeping the Best People*. New York: Prentice-Hall.
Spencer, L.M. and Spencer, S.M. (1993) *Competencies at Work*. New York: John Wiley & Sons.
Srivastava, M.K. (2003) *Transformational Leadership*. New Delhi: Macmillan India.
Sukhabodhananda, S. (2002) *Oh, Mind Relax Please! Roots of Yoga Winds of Management*. Bangalore: Prasanna Trust.
Tichy, N.M. and Cohen, E. (1997) *The Leadership Engine: How Winning Companies Build Leaders at Every Level*. New York: Harper Business.
Tornow, W.W., London, M. and CCL Associates. (1998) *Maximizing the Value of 360 Degree Feedback*. San Francisco: CA Jossy Bass.
Vinson, M.N. (1996) The Pros and Cons of 360 Degree Feedback: Making It Work. *Training and Development*, April, pp. 11–12.
Vohra, N. and Singh, M. (2005) Mental Traps to Avoid while Interpreting Feedback: Insights from Administering Feedback to School Principals. *Human Resources Development Quarterly*, 16(1), pp. 139–147.
Waldman, D.A. and Bowen, D.E. (1998) The Acceptability of 360 Degree Appraisals: A Customer–Supplier relationship perspective. *Human Resource Management*, 37(2), Summer.
Wimer, S. and Novack, K.M. (1998) How to Benefit from the 360 Degree Feedback. *Executive Excellence*, 15(10), October.
Zenger, J.H. and Folkman, J. (2003) *The Extraordinary Leader: Turning Good Managers into Great Leaders*. New Delhi: Tata McGraw-Hill.

Index

action-oriented explorer, 10
action plans, xxii
ADCs. *See* Assessment and
 Development Centres (ADCs)
Annapurna, J., 144
appraisal, 72, 201, 206
Assessment and Development
 Centres (ADCs), 156–160
authoritarian styles, 46
awareness-building tool, xxiv–xxv. *See
 also* 360 Degree Feedback

Bartlett, C.A., 20
behavioural qualities, 86
behaviour change, 195
benevolent style, 50–51
Bennis, Warren, 23
Bhide, P.V., 148
blind spots, 19
boss managers, 179
Bower, Marwin, 26, 27, 28
Bracken, D.W., 193, 194
building achievement, 181
building internal competencies, 139
building leadership competencies,
 30–31
business competence, 16
business-related feedback, 75
Byham, William, 145

CEO, 107–109
Chary, S.N., 22
Chawla, N., 144
childhood problems, 114–115
Church, A.H., 186, 188
The Circle of Innovation (Peters,
 Tom), 26, 31

coach(ing)
 case studies, 103–111
 competencies, 101–102
 process, 102–103
 role of, 100–101
Cohen, E., 22–23
communication, 145
competence building
 coaching in, 99–111
 feedback workshops, 97–98
 GVFL, 88
 Indian group of hotels, 88–89
 NTPC, 87
 qualities, 85–86
 roles, 84
 RSDQ model, 86–87
 styles, 84–85
 Tata Cummins, 87
 360 Degree Feedback, 93–97
competencies, 185–186
 business, 16
 coach, 101–102
 conceptual, 19
 human relations, 17–18
 leadership, 17
 managerial, 17–18
 model, 198
 technical, 16
 transactional, 17
 transformational, 17
conceptual competence, 19
connectivity, 73–74
corporate competencies, 203
cost, internet applications, 195
cost to company (CTC), 169
Covey, Franklin, 23
critical style, 51

CTC. *See* cost to company (CTC)
culture
   of continuous learning, 76–77
   developing culture, 39
   of dialogue, 183
   functions of, 37–38
   organizational culture and values, 37–39
   problem-solving, 181
   sustaining/maintaining, 38–39
customer feedback, 75–76
customer-oriented survey, 75
customer service, 203
customer–supplier relationship perspective, 201–203

delegation, 85, 86
democratic styles, 46
developmental theory, 186
Dixit, S., 153
Drucker Foundation, 23

Edwards, M.R., 205, 206, 208
effective leaders, xxi–xxiv. *See also* effective person
effective manager
   collaboration, 42–43
   communicating, 34–37
   inspiring employees, 34–37
   teamwork, 42–43
   vision, 34–37
effective person
   drive and passion, 13
   exploratory orientation, 6, 10–11
   goal orientation, 12
   inner core values, 12
   inner directedness, 12
   internality directedness, 12
   interpersonal sensitivity, 7–10
   perceptiveness, 11
   personal effectiveness, 5
   receptivity to feedback, 6–7, 11
   scoring personal effectiveness, 10
   self-awareness, 3–5

   self-confidence, 11–12
   self-disclosure, 6, 11
   trustworthiness, 12
emotional intelligence, 196
empathy, 25
employee-oriented supervisor, 47
empowerment questionnaire, 237–239
Ewen, A.J., 205, 206, 208
exploratory orientation, 6, 10–11

factor analysis, leadership, 20
fairness, 27
feedback, exact source of, 113–114
finance manager, 109–111
First Rate Multi-rater Feedback, 186
Folkman, J., 28, 30, 183
full implementation, 198–199

Gebelian, S.H., 197, 198
Ghoshal, S., 20
goal-oriented person, 12
Goleman, D., 24, 25, 47
Goleman's leadership styles, 47–48
good leader
   definitions of, 20
   observations, 20–25
groundwork, 197
Grow Your Own Leaders (Byham, William), 145
guidance and counselling, 54–55

hard-core networkers, 180
Haworth, S., 190–191
Hesselbein, F., 23
hierarchies, 204
Hoffman, R., 203
honesty, 12
HR interventions, 169
HRIS database, 196
human relations competence, 17–18
human resource development systems (HRDS), 123
human resource manager, 105–107
Hurconomics, 169, 172–176

IIMA. *See* Indian Institute of
  Management Ahmedabad (IIMA)
implementation plans, 198
India, 360 Degree Feedback in
  Indian experience, 143–155
Indian Institute of Management
  Ahmedabad (IIMA), 90
inner core values, 12
inner directedness, 12
inspiring employees, 34–37
inspiring staff, 40–42
institutional manager, 51–52
instrument development, 207
instruments, 187–188
integrating feedback, 188
internal customer orientation, 42–43
internality directedness, 12
Internet-based 360 Degree Feedback, 193
interpersonal sensitivity, 7–10
ispative scoring, 186

job analysis, 185
junior level manager, tasks, 33

key performance area (KPA), 67
key result area (KRA), 67
Khandwalla, P.N., 54, 55

Lala, R.M., 21
LDP. *See* Leadership Development
  Programme (LDP)
leaders, 14–15
  open-minded, 28
leadership, 20. *See also* good leader
  competence, 17
  factors of, 20
  observations, 20–25
  qualities, 27–30
  qualities questionnaire, 236–237
  roles, 14, 21, 43
  skills, 181
  types of, 20
  visionary leadership, 34–37

Leadership Development Programme (LDP), 148
The Leadership Engine (Tichy and Cohen), 22
leadership styles, 17–18, 45–46, 86, 233–235
  impact of, 55–59
  and motivational climate, 52
learning orientation, 18–19
listening behaviour, 27

MAF. *See* Multi-rater Assessment
  Feedback (MAF)
management information systems (MIS), 14
management styles, 233–235
manager, 14–15
  competition, 53
  100 impact-making, 177–184
  independence and interdependence, 52–53
  problem-solving, 53–54
  roles, 14
managerial activities, 14
managerial competence
  human relations competence, 17–18
  leadership styles, 17–18
  transactional competence, 17
  transformational competence, 17
managerial qualities, 86
managerial roles, 44
managerial styles, 45–46
managers effective
  competencies types, 15–16
  conceptual competence, 19
  learning orientation, 18–19
  managerial competence, 16–18
  technical and business competence, 16
Maruti Suzuki India Limited (MSIL), 152
McClelland, David, 91
The McKinsey Quarterly (Bower, Marwin), 26, 27

Meade, J., 201
middle level manager, tasks, 33
MIS. *See* management information systems (MIS)
motivation, 24
motivational climate, 52–54
multi-dimensional feedback, xxi
Multi-rater Assessment Feedback (MAF), xxi, 186
  accepting feedback, 81–82
  advantages of, 67–68
  business-related feedback, 75
  company goals, 74
  connectivity, 73–74
  continuous learning, 76–77
  creative leadership, 72–73
  customer feedback, 75–76
  customer input in, 75
  data, 80–81
  design phase input, 75
  drawbacks, 71
  feedback believable, 78–79
  indicators of, 68–69
  individual goals, 74
  link to strategy, 74
  monitoring change, 74–75
  performance evaluations, 70–71
  performance management system, 71–72
  prerequisites for participation in, 68–69
  score items, 79–80
  translate feedback, 81
  value of, 70
multi-source feedback, 124
myths and realities, 112–130

Nair, N., 154
non-governmental organizations (NGOs), 228–239
normative scoring, 186
Novack, K.M., 185, 186, 196, 199
nurturant task leader, 49–50

open-minded, 28
opportunity cost (O-COT), 169
organizational culture and values, 37–39
organizations, xxvi, 15, 26–31

Paese, Matthew, 145
Pandit, S., 21
Pareek, U., 21
Paul, M.C., 23
peer feedback, for students, 225
peers mistrust, 187
people-centred approach, 25
performance appraisal system, 201
performance evaluations, 70–71
performance management systems (PMSs), 71–72, 99, 138
personality theory, 186
Peters, T., 23, 26
problem-solving culture, 181
production manager, 104–105

Rai, H., 143
Ramnarayan, S., 147
Rao, Raju, 143, 147, 148
Rao, T.V., 144
real cost to company (R-COT), 169
returns on investments (ROI), 99, 169–176
Robins, S.P., 41
Roles, Styles, Delegation and Qualities (RSDQ) model, xxii, 86–87, 144, 177

scoring personal effectiveness, 10
self-awareness, xxi, 3–5, 24, 145
self-confidence, 11–12, 19, 28
self-disclosure, 6, 11
self-dispensing style, 51
self-esteem, 19
self-evaluation, 188
self-motivation, 181
self-regulating mechanisms, 18
self-regulation, 24

self-sustaining mechanisms, 18
self-test, 7
sensitivity to people and situations, 28–30
service provider
  cost, 131–132
  credibility, 132–133
  experience, 134
  KAS, 133–134
  proximity, 133
sincerity, 12
Singh, M., 143
Sinha, J.B.P., 153
Smart, B.D., 24
Smith, Audrey, 145
social skills, 25
Srivastava, M.K., 35
staff, motivation and development, 40–42
strategic planning, 186
supports team initiatives, 203
survey development, 207

task-oriented manager/leader, 46–47
Team Evaluation and Management System (TEAMS), 206
team workers, 179
technical and business competence, 16
360 Degree Feedback. *See also* Multi-rater Assessment Feedback (MAF)
  acceptability of, 201–203
  vs. Assessment Development Centres (ADCs), 158–160
  avoids discrimination and bias, 204
  benefit, 196–199
  chemistry of, 93–94
  competencies, 89–93
  competency model, 198
  conditions for, 131–139
  delegation, 95
  evaluation, 199–200
  exercise, 64

follow-up, 138
groundwork, 197
group work, 95–97
implementation plans, 198
inclusive approach, 161
Indian experience, 143–155
instrument, 136–137
is conclusive, 115–116
leadership styles, 94–95
logistics, 194
mistakes in, 190–193
myths and realities of, 112–130
other countries, experiences from, 185–208
peers mistrust, 187
planning action, 95–97
process, 137–138
process and implementation level, 160–161
purposes, 134–135
qualities, 95
rater overload, 194
rater reliability, 194
readiness, 135–136
returns on investments (ROI), 169–176
roles, 94
stakeholder level, 162–168
strengths, 162
touch points, 162
winning support, 187
360 Degree Feedback Tool
  collect feedback, 220–222
  fellow teachers, 220
  non-governmental organizations (NGOs), 228–239
  for parents, 220, 222–224
  for postgraduate students, 225–227
  principal's assessment, 219–220
  for school principals, 211–217
  self-assessment, 219
  for students, 219, 225–227
  for teachers, 218–219

Tichy, N.M., 22–23
time management, 145
top executives, institution-building role of, 44
Top Grading (Smart), 24
top-level managers
   neglected roles, 33–34
   roles, 32, 43
   tasks, 33–34
total quality management (TQM), 66
transactional competence, 17
transactional roles, 84
transformational competence, 17
transformational roles, 84

trustworthiness, 12, 27
truthfulness, 12
TV Rao Learning System (TVRLS), xxii, xxiii

unassuming, leaders, 27

Vinson, M.N., 188, 189
visual 360 Degree Feedback, 201

Wimer, S., 196
workforce, 204

Zander, Benjamin, 31
Zenger, J.H., 28, 30, 183

About the Authors

T.V. Rao is currently Chairman of TVRLS. He was a Professor at the Indian Institute of Management, Ahmedabad, India, between 1973 and 1994 and subsequently a Visiting or Adjunct Professor at the same institution. Dr Rao also worked as L&T Professor of HRD at XLRI, Jamshedpur, during 1983–85. He is the Founder and First President of the National HRD Network. He was Honorary Director and one of the Founding Members of the Academy of HRD at Ahmedabad, and was President of the Indian Society for Applied Behavioural Science (ISABS). Dr Rao was also a Visiting Faculty at the Indian Business School, Hyderabad, in its early years.

Dr Rao worked as a short-term research associate at Harvard University with David McClelland. Subsequently he worked as a short-term consultant to UNESCO; Ministry of Health, Indonesia; National Entrepreneurial Development Association, Malaysia; FAO, Rome; and the Commonwealth Secretariat, London. Dr Rao also worked as HRD Advisor to the Reserve Bank of India. He assisted the Administrative Reforms Commission in reviewing the personnel management practices for civil services, and also served as a member of the HRM Review Committee of Public Sector Banks set up by the Ministry of Finance in 2009–10. During the mid-1980s, Dr Rao was actively involved with the Ministry of HRD in the New Education Policy and reviewing NIEPA. Dr Rao's consulting experience includes designing and implementing performance management and other HR systems including 360 Degree Feedback in some leading organizations such as SAIL, NTPC, Indian Oil Corporation, HPCL, Bharat Petroleum, NALCO, SBI, Reserve Bank of India, Pfizer, Larsen & Toubro, Aditya Birla Group, Titan Industries, Dr Reddy's, Infosys, to name a few.

A prolific writer, Dr Rao has authored over 50 books in the areas of HRD, performance management, 360 Degree Feedback, education management, organizational behaviour, entrepreneurship, etc. Some of his other publications include *HRD Audit*, *HRD Score Card 2500*,

100 Managers in Action, Managers Who Make a Difference, Performance Management and Appraisal Systems: HR Tools for Global Competitiveness, Organization Development: Accelerating Learning for Transformation, and *The HRD Missionary.*

Raju Rao is a postgraduate in HR from XLRI Jamshedpur (1994) and Ph.D. in Management from M.S. University of Baroda (2008). Raju started his career in 1994 at Torrent where he worked for three years as an Assistant Personnel Manager and subsequently joined TVRLS as a Consultant. He did his certification courses in MBTI with Manasayan, and in Consulting Interventions at NTL, Bethel, USA. He has wide consulting experience in Assessment Centres, 360 Degree Feedback and HRD Audit internationally with Alexandria Carbon Black, Egypt; Kewalram Chanrai Group, Nigeria; Indorama, Indonesia; Nestle, Bangladesh; and Action Aid Asia, Vietnam. He conducted courses for Mauritian Quality Institute, XPertise of Commercial Bank, Sri Lanka. He also conducted seminars for CII Ahmedabad, and Kolkata. The Indian organizations he worked with include AMP India (Tyco); Apollo Tyres; AV Birla Group; Bajaj Auto; BEL, Bangalore; Bosch Rexroth; BPL; Gati Cargo Management Services; GSPC and GSPL; GVFL; HDFC Standard Life; Infosys; Life Insurance Corporation of India; Murugappa Group; Nestle, India; NTPC; ONGC; Taj Group of Hotels; TCI; Transformers and Transmetals; Tyco International, Bangalore; Wyeth; Kochin Refineries Limited (BPCL); BPCL, Mumbai; and Sterlite Industries (Vedanta Group).

He co-edited two books on 360 Degree Feedback and Performance Management Systems. His co-authored book on the Power of 360 Degree Feedback has won two awards by the Delhi Management Association and ISTD. He taught courses in HRD at Nirma Institute of Management and the Academy of HRD, Ahmedabad, as a Guest Faculty. He also worked as a Visiting Faculty at Aurora Business School, Hyderabad, for a short period.